BEYOND BEING

Northwestern University
Studies in Phenomenology
and
Existential Philosophy

BEYOND BEING

Gadamer's Post-Platonic Hermeneutical Ontology

Brice R. Wachterhauser

Northwestern University Press
Evanston, Illinois

Northwestern University Press
Evanston, Illinois 60208-4210

Printed in the United States of America

ISBN 0-8101-1583-2 (cloth)
ISBN 0-8101-1584-0 (paper)

Library of Congress Cataloging-in-Publication Data

Wachterhauser, Brice R., 1953–
Beyond being : Gadamer's post-platonic hermeneutical ontology / Brice R. Wachterhauser.
p. cm.—(Studies in phenomenology and existential philosophy)
Includes bibliographical references and index.
ISBN 0-8101-1583-2 (alk. paper).—ISBN 0-8101-1584-0 (pbk. : alk. paper)
1. Gadamer, Hans Georg, 1900–. 2. Hermeneutics. 3. Plato. I. Title. II. Series.
B3248.G34W33 1999
193—dc21 98-47737
CIP

The paper used in this publication meets the minimum requirements of the American National Standard for Information Sciences—Permanence of Paper for Printed Library Materials, ANSI Z39.48-1984.

Every utterance is by nature just as much
a one as it is a many because reality is
differentiated in itself. It itself is *logos.*

—*Gadamer*

Contents

Acknowledgments

Projects of this sort inevitably generate a great many debts. One cannot, however, let the fear or even the certainty that one is bound to forget to thank someone keep one from thanking those who stand out most in one's mind as having helped make this book a reality.

Thanks are due to Hans-Georg Gadamer for his patience in answering my questions and especially for listening to a paper of mine in 1993 in Heidelberg in which I argued that his hermeneutics was best understood as an instance of the anti-Platonism of our age and for refuting me with one declarative utterance: "I am a Platonist." It was this remark that "turned my soul around" to the Platonism inherent in his work. I hasten to add, however, that Professor Gadamer has not read this work. Whether he would agree with all or even some of it I can only hope. Nevertheless my debt to him is fundamental and I wish to record it.

Saint Joseph's University deserves real thanks for granting me a sabbatical leave during the 1994–95 academic year. Without it, I doubt very much whether this book would have been written.

Robert Dostal has my sincere gratitude for his friendship over the years and for his reading of the entire manuscript. He helped me make many real improvements and I thank him for his care and critical sympathy. He will note, no doubt, that I did not follow all of his advice. For that stubbornness, I will have to bear the responsibility.

Thanks should also go to Heather Kenny, formerly of Northwestern University Press, and Susan Harris, editor-in-chief at Northwestern University Press, for their tireless administrative and editorial care. It's been a real pleasure to work with both of them on this and previous projects.

A word of appreciation is also due to John McCumber, who, as editor of the Northwestern University Press Studies in Phenomenology and Existential Philosophy, reviewed the manuscript and to the unnamed reviewer who did the same. Both of their comments and suggestions were appreciated.

I very much owe a debt to Joanne Devlin who has once again tirelessly typed and retyped various drafts of this manuscript. Her professionalism and good cheer in light of this "infinite task" has made the time I have spent on this book more enjoyable and rewarding.

Lastly, to my wife, Mary, and my children, Kier and Anya, I owe much more than thanks. Their love and commitment have made "solidarity" and "participation in a common reality" everyday occurrences. It is often to them that I have looked to find the courage of my convictions. What I have found in them has not disappointed.

Abbreviations

DNS Hans-Georg Gadamer, "Dialektik ist nicht Sophistik: Theätet lernt das im *Sophistes*," in *Gesammelte Werke* (Tübingen: J.C.B. Mohr, 1991), 338–69.

DSP Hans-Georg Gadamer, "Dialectic and Sophism in Plato's *Seventh Letter*," in *Dialogue and Dialectic*, trans. P. Christopher Smith (New Haven: Yale University Press, 1980), 93–123.

GW Hans-Georg Gadamer, *Gesammelte Werke*, 10 vols. (Tübingen: J.C.B. Mohr [Paul Siebeck]).

HD Hans-Georg Gadamer, *Hegel's Dialectic* (New Haven: Yale University Press, 1976).

HMP Brice R. Wachterhauser, ed. *Hermeneutics and Modern Philosophy* (Albany: SUNY Press, 1985).

HT Brice R. Wachterhauser, ed. *Hermeneutics and Truth* (Evanston: Northwestern University Press, 1994).

HW Hans-Georg Gadamer, *Heidegger's Ways* (Albany: SUNY Press, 1994).

IG Hans-Georg Gadamer, *The Idea of the Good in Platonic-Aristotelian Philosophy*, trans. P. Christopher Smith (New Haven: Yale University Press, 1986).

MD Hans-Georg Gadamer, "Mathematik und Dialektik bei Plato," in *GW* 7, 290–312.

PP Hans-Georg Gadamer, "Plato as Porträtist," in *GW* 7, 228–57.

PUD Hans-Georg Gadamer, "Plato's Unwritten Dialectic," in *Dialogue and Dialectic*, trans. P. Christopher Smith (New Haven: Yale University Press, 1980), 124–55.

RAS Hans-Georg Gadamer, *Reason in the Age of Science* (Cambridge: MIT Press, 1981).

RB Hans-Georg Gadamer, *The Relevance of the Beautiful* (Cambridge: Cambridge University Press, 1986).

SP Hans-Georg Gadamer, "Schleiermacher als Platoniker," in *Kleine Schriften*, vol. III (Tübingen: J.C.B. Mohr, 1972), 141–49.

TM Hans-Georg Gadamer, *Truth and Method* (New York: Crossroad, 1990).

ZPD Hans-Georg Gadamer, "Zwischen Phänomenologie und Dialektik: Versuch einer Selbstkritik," in *GW* 2, 3–23.

ZVM Hans-Georg Gadamer, "Zur Vorgeschichte der Metaphysik," in *Um die Begriffswelt der Vorsokratiker* (Darmstadt, 1968), 364–90.

Works cited above in German are quoted in English translations, which have been done by the author.

Introduction

Hans-Georg Gadamer is best known in the English-speaking world for his major work on philosophical hermeneutics, *Truth and Method.* Specialists in the field also know that he has written a series of very interesting essays on the history of philosophy. Among these essays, studies on Plato far outnumber those on any other single figure in the history of philosophy. Most commentators on Gadamer's work, however, separate his work on Plato from his work on hermeneutics. When they pay attention to his historical studies at all, they tend to separate what Gadamer has said on Plato (or some other figure in the Western philosophical tradition) from his philosophical hermeneutics. As a result of this division of labor there is a tendency to treat Gadamer either as a historian of philosophy or as a philosopher in his own right critically engaged in the philosophical issues of our time. While this division within Gadamer's work can be defended on logical grounds—Gadamer does, after all, write relatively self-contained essays and monographs—and is eminently understandable from the practical need of the commentator to limit her focus, it nevertheless threatens to oversimplify and distort important parts of Gadamer's thought.

The danger of bifurcating Gadamer's thought between his work as a historian and his work as a philosopher can be made clearer in a general way by considering that Gadamer is a philosopher who has consciously developed his thought through a critical reading of the history of philosophy. All of his writings are replete with in-depth references to major figures in Western philosophy, references that go far beyond the usual scholastic trappings of academic discourse. They demonstrate, instead, that Gadamer views the whole of Western philosophy as a living "conversation." This view of Western philosophy as a "living conversation" is not an empty metaphor for Gadamer. Anyone acquainted with Gadamer's hermeneutics knows that "conversation" or "dialogue" (*Gespräch*) is a key technical term for him. Gadamer treats past participants in this discourse as genuine dialogue partners.

To be in a real dialogue with the past implies a complex moral and epistemic relationship with these thinkers. Any dialogue requires that one extend a certain kind of respect to one's conversation partner. Such respect involves taking their viewpoint seriously, which demands that one make every effort to find the truth in it or to put the most plausible interpretation on what has been said. If we consciously look for the truth in the words of the other we can hardly dismiss them outright as irrelevant. On the other hand, however, such respect need not imply that we accept what they say as final and definitive. If we are in a genuine conversation, we are not looking merely to repeat or confirm what our interlocutor has said. Instead, a genuine conversation is marked by a limited solidarity between discussants that manifests itself in a common search for the truth. Such a common search cannot be sidestepped because what drives the need for dialogue itself is a prior recognition that both discussants have an interest in the topic. This interest suggests that both discussants recognize a common good they hope to gain as an outcome of their inquiry. Thus in respecting the demands of a genuine dialogue each partner need not merely confirm what the other has said or treat it as the last word but, instead, an attempt must be made to respond to what is said by trying to go deeper into the very issue that provides the basis for the conversation itself.

In the spirit of entering a true conversation with the past, Gadamer insists that the philosophical tradition is something we can never simply repudiate and transcend, nor should we hope to repeat it exactly as it was. Instead, we must *interpret* it, i.e., we must appropriate it critically and creatively with an eye to the philosophical issues that press in on us and that find significant analogues in the past. Such a conversation with the past that critically and creatively interprets it is not the same as viewing the past as a repository to be arbitrarily drawn on as our needs or whims may lead us. It requires instead that we enter a genuine dialogue with the past, which begins by acknowledging that we do in fact share some concerns with that past, but it also requires that we not forget that there may be differences to be reckoned with as well. Our place in time may make us different in some way from the past. Thus, while we should extend to the past the respect required by any discussion partner, such respect need not lead us to forget that the intent of such a conversation is not to repeat the past verbatim, but to appropriate what is said in a way that advances insight into the issue that provides the focus of the discussion. Such a genuine dialogue with the past demonstrates how the resources of Western philosophy, which coalesce around figures like Plato, Aristotle, Augustine, Aquinas, Descartes, Leibniz, Kant, Hegel, and Heidegger, can be fruitfully applied to the issues of hermeneutics. In doing so, Gadamer demonstrates both a real connection and continuity with that past, as well real differences with it. This enables Gadamer to approach the philosophical past with an openness and generosity of spirit that avoids the pitfalls of either considering the thought of any of the major figures of Western philosophy as null and void or falling into the trap of idolizing any aspect of the past.

Some might find this attitude too generous in its range of reference or too frustrating in its refusal to summarily bury the past. Gadamer would insist, however, that such attempts to simply leave the past behind are futile. Whether we like it or not we are participants in this history. This history, however, is not a straitjacket. It is a fluid source of intellectual possibility that offers both the prospect of continuity and innovation.

One of the most important implications of Gadamer's "dialogical" approach to the past is the claim that historicism represents an oversimplification of our relationship to the past. It is not the case that philosophical history (or any aspect of history) can be divided neatly into logically distinct epochs. History does not consist in a series of separate, discrete, and wholly unique units, each of which is self-contained in its meaning such that we cannot raise questions about its "transepochal" truth, but must instead content ourselves with simply understanding it on its own terms. While historicism represented an unprecedented advance in our critical awareness of history and helped us to see genuine historical difference between different historical periods, and thereby resisted the leveling tendency to see the same things everywhere, nevertheless it represented an attempt to control historical reasoning for research purposes. If history is not divisible into "Cartesian" clear and distinct units of meaning its significance and potential for generating different interpretations is much more unwieldy and difficult to predict. In short, historicism represents the modern subject's tendency to control and dominate reality for its own purposes. Moreover, implicit in historicism's thesis about distinct historical epochs is the self-serving modernist thesis that the present must be viewed as sui generis. For Gadamer, the meaning of the past will not allow us to divide it into clear and distinct epochs with no effective interaction between them, nor will it allow us to view our own time as wholly unique in its meaning. The past lives on in the present, but not in the sense that the present must be viewed as a mirror image of the past or a copy thinly disguised by the superficial contingencies of historical fashion, but in the sense that the past continues to speak and have its effect on the present, even when the present has shown itself to be different in significant ways from the past. Thus, Gadamer says, we find ourselves in a position that allows a genuine "dialogue" with the past, which confronts us with the prospect of both limited continuity and limited novelty.

If we keep these antihistoricist assumptions in mind we can better understand Gadamer's approach to philosophical history in *Truth and Method* and his other writings. Gadamer understands himself to be in dialogue with the past, which he hopes will shed important light on contemporary philosophical concerns. This is nowhere more evident than in his appropriation of materials from ancient philosophy, particularly the later Plato. Anyone who has read *Truth and Method* carefully cannot help but notice how Gadamer's hermeneutics is deeply informed by his awareness of these Platonic sources.[1] Gadamer even goes so far as to claim that "if we are to do justice to the subject, the hermeneutics of the human sciences . . . lead us back into the problems of classical metaphysics" (*TM*, 460). Even more fundamentally, Gadamer confesses that it was "ancient philosophy from which the whole of philosophy and its history disclosed itself to me."[2] Given the importance of ancient philosophy generally for Gadamer's thought, and the predominance of his emphasis on Plato within his study of ancient philosophy, more attention needs to be paid to his work on Plato. Generally speaking, this essay is an attempt to explain how some of the key ideas of Gadamer's philosophical hermeneutics can be best understood by being placed in the context of his Plato studies. A reading of Gadamer's hermeneutical studies in light of his Plato studies not only enables us to avoid certain key misunderstandings of Gadamer, but it also helps us to see more clearly some of the radical implications of Gadamer's thought.

In arguing for the indispensability of Gadamer's understanding of Plato for his understanding of hermeneutics, I will not attempt to argue that Gadamer is necessarily right in his views on Plato. Although I find his standpoint on Plato provocative and inherently plausible, I nevertheless leave this task to trained classicists who specialize in the history of ancient philosophy. For my part, I am interested primarily in the effects of Gadamer's Plato studies on his philosophical hermeneutics. I will attempt to show that Gadamer's hermeneutics discloses itself in its most distinctive contours only in light of his work on Plato.

The burden of this book is to defend this thesis, but readers of this introduction certainly have the right to wonder if my claim that Gadamer's Plato interpretation is indispensable to understanding his philosophical hermeneutics is both interesting and plausible. If not, why read the book?

But before I try to show how certain central Gadamerian concerns presuppose his interpretation of Plato, it is important to say something about the uniqueness of Gadamer's Plato. I have already suggested that Gadamer relies particularly on the later Plato. In fact, Gadamer has an unusual hermeneutical thesis about how the later Plato fits into the

Platonic corpus. Gadamer thinks the later Plato, the Plato present in the dialogues including the *Parmenides* and those usually thought to have been written after the *Parmenides*, such as the *Sophist, Statesmen*, and *Philebus*, provides the decisive clue for interpreting the deepest intent of his work. Unlike some commentators who think the *Parmenides* represents a definitive rejection of the Ideas, Gadamer thinks it reveals a common, mistaken interpretation of the Ideas, an interpretation that Plato himself may have inadvertently contributed to, but one which he never intended when he introduced the theme of the Ideas. According to Gadamer, the *Parmenides* teaches us that we should not think about Ideas as discrete transcendent realities. Instead we should think of the Ideas as internally related to each other and the things they inform. Thus they cannot be defined without various kinds of logically complex relationships to each other and to the things which instantiate them. And instead of thinking of them as occupying a transcendent realm of their own—a kind of repository of discrete ideal types—we should think of them as immanent to the things they inform, without being identical with them. According to Gadamer, Plato begins in these later dialogues to think more explicitly about the nature of participation (*methexis*) and separation (*chorismos*). What these later dialogues reveal is a metaphysical theory that is much more like Aristotle's than even Aristotle himself realized. Thus, for Gadamer, these later dialogues represent the culmination of Plato's metaphysical inquiries and not Plato's self-critical dismantling of his earlier work. Instead these dialogues provide decisive clues for interpreting his earlier works.

Some of the most important insights to emerge from these dialogues are several insights into what later thinkers would call "transcendentals." The transcendentals are those elements of Being common to all beings, regardless of genus or species. Such elements include Being itself, unity (or the one) and difference (the many), "motion," "rest," truth, beauty, and goodness itself. On Gadamer's reading of these later Platonic sources, Plato was always working toward a clearer apprehension of the problematic of this comprehensive ontological vision. According to Gadamer, the upshot of these Platonic efforts to correct a false interpretation of the Ideas—namely, the interpretation that dogmatically asserted the claim that the Ideas represent a second, transcendent reality wholly detached from the realm of ordinary things and logically distinct from each other—shows that such an interpretation is a caricature of Plato's true ontological concerns. According to Gadamer, Plato's true project shows itself more clearly and more suggestively in the later dialogues.[3] It is my thesis that it is precisely Gadamer's understanding of Plato on the transcendentals that decisively influences his own hermeneutics in key ways. If this is so, then understanding Gadamer's ontological reading of the later Plato is essential to grasping many of the key issues in Gadamer's philosophical hermeneutics.

To begin to try to substantiate the importance of Gadamer's reading of the later Plato for his hermeneutical project consider the fact that one of the key issues of *Truth and Method* is the issue of identity and difference in interpretation. On the one hand, we have the supposed identity of a work of art or text; it is reputedly one work of art or one selfsame text and as such it allegedly has one meaning (or one finite set of possible meanings). Consequently, it excludes other meanings. On the other hand, we have both the undeniable fact of many different interpretations of the work and the equally undeniable fact that our only access to the identity of the work is through some interpretation of it. The problem, however, is that the interpretations of any work are often so diverse that it is often difficult to see how they all (or even some subset of them) can be interpretations of one and the same work. In short, the diversity of interpretations threatens to dissolve the identity of the work. Such a loss of identity would leave us without a critical grounding for distinguishing such things as questionable interpolations or invalid extrapolations from legitimate interpretations. Any hermeneutics has to address this question. At the very least the issue of a work's possible identity or lack thereof pertains to the issue of whether one can justify the exclusion of certain erroneous interpretations without falling into an unjustifiable dogmatism that precludes legitimate interpretive diversity. Gadamer is neither a relativist or subjectivist who would say that interpreters may legitimately impute any meaning to the work, nor is he oblivious to the reality of genuinely legitimate but diverse interpretations. Instead, Gadamer always has his eye on clarifying the unique type of identity that characterizes the objects of interpretation. In this vein, he writes, "we ask what this identity is that presents itself so differently in the changing course of ages and circumstances. It does not disintegrate into the changing aspects of itself so that it would lose all identity, but it is there in them all. They all belong to it" (*TM*, 121). His intent is to describe this identity in a plausible way that leaves room for multiple interpretations, without falling into the morass of relativism or the iron cage of dogmatism. This issue is at the very heart of *Truth and Method.* Key to his hermeneutics is the thesis that works like texts always present themselves differently in different historical circumstances, but they do so in such a way that they neither lose their identity nor safeguard it by unduly restricting its possible meaning.

In order to steer between the relativist and the ahistorical dogmatist Gadamer argues that we must rethink the ontology of those things we interpret. His strategy is explicitly ontological. He argues that in order to understand how some interpretations can be wrong without saying that there is one and only one justifiable interpretation of a work one has to understand what kind of being artworks or texts have such that they allow this "identity in difference." To account for this "identity in difference," Gadamer adopts what I call an "ontological perspectivism," which maintains that things like texts are such that they contain within themselves different "faces" or "looks" that present themselves in different historically mediated contexts in such a way that we can say that it is possible for one and the same reality to show itself in many ways. The fact that it is always possible in principle to develop new interpretations based on the similarities between prior interpretations of the work testifies to both the plausibility of an underlying identity as well as the possibility of ever new interpretations.

Gadamer has developed this way of approaching the issue of identity and difference in interpretation in conscious reliance on ontological insights from ancient philosophy. Interpretation, in Gadamer's ontological account of it, turns out to be nothing more than the unending process of discerning "the one in the many and the many in the one." In other words, Gadamer justifies his brand of ontological perspectivism by critically reviving Plato's reflections on "the one and the many." His general strategy is to argue that all Being is such that it is always at one and the same time both "one and many." Thus it is no surprise that interpretation constantly confronts us with the reality of "identity in difference." In fact, wherever we turn, "identity in difference" or "one and many" is the mark of Being itself.

Gadamer appeals to the later Plato's reflections on the nature of number to substantiate his ontology.[4] The upshot of these historical inquiries is an ontology that defines Being by its internal relationships. Just as any number in the number series can be described only by its logical or intelligible relationships to other numbers, so any reality is what it is only by being situated in its logical or intelligible relationships to other realities. With regard to number, the "hermeneutical" implication of this relational ontology is that any number is always both "one and many," i.e., it is what it is in its distinct logical contours but those contours can be described from an infinite number of perspectives generated by the fact that it can be defined only in its relationships to all the other numbers in the infinite series, including its relations of negation. For example, the prime number 3 can be defined in multiple ways, such as being divisible without remainder by only itself and the number 1, or as being the sum of 1 + 2 or the difference between 27 and 30. But 3 is also what it is because of its negative properties; 3 has this characteristic of a prime number only because it is *not* divisible without remainder by any other whole number than itself and 1. Thus both its positive and negative logical properties make 3 the number that it is.

With regard to non-numerical realities, Gadamer thinks the same general ontological pattern obtains. All things are what they are only in their infinite relationships to other things, including both positive and negative logical relationships. Thus all things are always both "one and many," i.e., they can always be identified in principle as one but such identification is only possible by discerning this identity through the many, "infinite" ways any one reality is related logically and semantically to other realities, including the infinite ways any one reality can be set apart from other realities by not sharing this or that common characteristic. Thus various interpretations are inevitable. Nevertheless such variety is not ontologically vicious, i.e., it does not necessarily threaten the identity of things, nor does it preclude a critical rejection of some interpretations in favor of others. Gadamer's ontological perspectivism allows for a "critical pluralism" that steers between a subjectivistic relativism and a one-sided dogmatism.

To understand how the ontology of "the one and the many" is presupposed by Gadamer's hermeneutics one really does have to carefully consider Gadamer's work on Plato. It's in light of Gadamer's Plato work that one of the most important insights of his hermeneutics finds its necessary ontological support and clarification. Failure to consider this ontological presupposition of Gadamer's hermeneutics drives many interpreters of Gadamer's hermeneutics either toward relativism of a historicist sort or a dogmatism which imputes an unbending essentialism to Gadamer. Both of these tendencies have surfaced in students of Gadamer, but both fly in the face of Gadamer's explicit rejection of each. Such mistakes are based in my opinion on a failure to really read Gadamer in light of his deep and ongoing conversation with Plato and the Platonic tradition. Once one realizes that these Platonic sources are Gadamer's starting points and guiding presuppositions, his approach to such fundamental issues as identity and difference in interpretation becomes much clearer and its plausibility more readily apparent.

Failure to consider the deep ties between Gadamer's reading of Plato and his philosophical hermeneutics have also lead, in my opinion, to misunderstandings of his views on language and the intelligibility of reality. On the one hand, Gadamer has been described as a linguistic constructivist whereby language is the means by which we construct or impute meaning to reality.[5] On the other hand, however, he has also been accused of a tendency toward alinguistic essentialism, whereby the intelligibility of reality consists in its ideal, alinguistic structure which the mind can supposedly intuit without any necessary reliance on language.[6]

Both of these perspectives on Gadamer's views on language are mistakes in my opinion that fail to grasp what Gadamer has in mind when he claims that language is a necessary "medium" of all thought. At the risk of oversimplication, we can say that by a "medium" Gadamer means that language is an indispensable place where the intelligibility of the real makes itself manifest for us. To begin to unpack the meaning of such a statement it is important to point out, first of all, that such a view implies neither that language imputes an intelligible meaning to an otherwise unintelligible reality nor that it represents in conventional signs an otherwise alinguistic reality. Instead language can function as an indispensable place where intelligible meaning becomes manifest because Gadamer begins with the assumption that the ideal meaning in language is the same in principle as the ideal intelligibility of reality. In Platonic terms we have a relationship of "participation" between language and reality. Intelligibility participates in both things and words such that words potentially clarify and enhance the inherent intelligibility of things. Moreover, things themselves are inherently intelligible such that we must always look to them as the beginning and end of all inquiry. The intelligibility of language is not to supplant the intelligibility of things but to complement and complete that intelligibility in such a way that the things themselves become more manifest and provide the final warrant for any justifiable articulation.

This is what it means to say that the intelligibility of reality becomes manifest in language itself. Prior to such a linguistic manifestation intelligibility is neither nonexistent nor given with as much clarity as possible. By manifesting intelligibility language neither creates this intelligibility nor does it simply reflect it. Rather language "participates" in intelligibility and the intelligibility of reality "participates" in the intelligibility of language. Thus we can neither speak of a "pure" alinguistic intuition of intelligibility nor of a linguistic idealism which assigns to language the role of imposing rational meaning on a rationally indifferent world. Instead what we have is a manifestation of reality *through language.* It is "through language" because it is relative and limited to the linguistic context of disclosure, and at the same time it is in principle a genuine disclosure of the rationally real in this context because the linguistically mediated context is not in principle foreign to the rational but a potential complement to it. Thus it can be said that language enhances and complements intelligibility without creating it or merely functioning as a sign.

This is Gadamer's way, via ancient ontology, of expressing the Heideggerian insight that all disclosure of reality is both a making manifest and a covering over, both an unconcealment and concealment of the real.

Gadamer grounds this dialectic of unconcealment and concealment of the real in the tendency of language to reveal reality in a limited set of semantic and logical relationships, which simultaneously covers over other possible sets of relationships from which the same reality could be disclosed. Thus language can reveal, but it also simultaneously conceals, how any one thing stands to the whole of all things in which it is what it is.

In speaking of word and thing participating in a common intelligible being Gadamer is neither simply trying to repeat ancient ontology nor leave it behind as an outdated model for the philosophical problems of our age. Instead he sees it as a legitimate conversation partner that still has something to say to us, even though our own insights will require us to amend these insights in certain key ways. As Gadamer puts it: "we cannot simply follow the Greeks or the identity philosophy of German idealism: we are thinking out the consequences of language as medium" (*TM*, 461). Nevertheless he also insists that he is "simply following the internal necessity of the thing itself if we go beyond the idea of the object and the objectivity of understanding toward the idea that subject and object belong together" (*TM*, 461). Such "belonging together" is not the mere correlation of subject and object or the relativity of object to subject as we find it in various modernist philosophies of the subject as the source of all meaning and value. It is, instead, the "belonging together" of subject and object that takes place in our linguistically mediated experience of the world. In such experience what we find is the one-sidedness of trying to think either subject or object alone as the source of meaning. Rather we are driven back by "an internal necessity of the thing itself" to discover a participation of thing and word in a common intelligibility. What this experience is (the "thing itself" that demonstrates this "internal necessity"), is the experience that words neither create meaning nor merely reflect it. Rather words have the capacity to "enhance" and in a sense "complete" an already given meaning. In this sense, language is the medium where thought and reality discover their prior accord. Language is the place where intelligibility can manifest itself in a way that was not completely manifest before.

Although Gadamer does not think that Plato can be attributed explicitly with this view of language, he does claim that Plato himself implicitly struggled with this dialectic in his own dialogues. What we find in the Platonic dialogues is linguistically mediated truth. In other words, the Platonic dialogues demonstrate that every insight is inseparable from a linguistically constituted context of inquiry. The upshot of this Platonic struggle is not timeless insight into the Ideas but a series of "finite" insights whose truth is always relative to the context of conversation in which they were born. In Gadamer's account, the Platonic dialogues are nothing less than Plato's artful accounts of these limited, linguistically mediated insights into what is genuinely real and rational. For Gadamer, Socrates's "flight into the *logoi*" is Plato's testimony to the indispensability of linguistically mediated inquiry to the Platonic project. According to Gadamer, Plato's reliance on the Ideas is not an attempt to escape from the various *logoi* or discourses but a way to illuminate the fact that although our thought is always "in language," or in some discourse with its own way of presenting issues and insights, such discourses inevitably point beyond themselves in their confrontation with other discourses to a truth which transcends them both. This truth, however, is not finally grasped, once and for all, outside of language, but is itself another linguistically mediated truth whose meaning and limits can only begin to show themselves in dialogue with other *logoi.* It is in his reflection on Platonic dialogue that Gadamer most clearly works out what it means to say that all truth is relative to a language of inquiry or a dialectic of question and answer in which we are confronted with a truth that is always limited to the linguistically mediated questions we ask. In other words, we cannot understand these truths without grasping the questions to which they are answers. Such a limitation, however, does not preclude fruitful interaction with other dialogue partners, who may ask different questions. When such dialogical mediation occurs new questions may be asked and new answers or new finite truths may be generated. Such a "finite truth" is neither a linguistic construct nor is it an alinguistic intuition; it is a truth that develops in time *in conversation* between historically situated conversation partners. Moreover it is a truth whose genuine possibility we can understand on the assumption that language participates in the intelligibility of reality such that finding the "right words" enhances and complements intelligible insight without bringing it to final historical closure. In sum, one might say that for Gadamer reason finds its voice through language but it is a voice with many valences that register themselves through the many discourses we engage in with each other.

Some readers may object to these ontological assumptions as being "mere" assumptions. Where, they might ask, does Gadamer provide an indubitable justification for this ontology and its epistemic implications? Isn't this just another reactionary, question-begging appeal to "metaphysics," which in reality is just more intellectual smoke and mirrors? Gadamer would question the assumptions that inform such a criticism. For Gadamer, "metaphysics" is not a historical option that has exhausted itself. In fact, Gadamer argues that metaphysical issues are always implicit in the discourses we engage in. Language itself is implicitly metaphysical. Moreover, the demand for indubitable justification is itself problematic. Such demands are rooted in a conception of knowledge known as foundationalism. Foundationalists draw their motivation from a confrontation with skepticism. The skeptic claims that knowledge must evince an indubitable certainty to count as knowledge at all. Thus foundationalists like Descartes hope to refute the skeptics by showing that all knowledge can be traced back to an indubitable starting point. Not only does Descartes fail to deduce all knowledge from his own unshakable truth, *cogito ergo sum*, but even the certainty he attributes to it is doubtful. As many philosophers have pointed out, Descartes's *cogito* leaves the nature of the "I" that thinks unclarified. One can wonder with Bertrand Russell whether one can deduce an "I" from the fact that thinking occurs. From the fact of thinking one can only deduce that thinking itself exists. Or in a similar vein, one can wonder with Heidegger if Descartes has really shed any significant light on the nature of the existence of the "I" who thinks and says "I am." In light of such questions we can say that it is not clear on Descartes's account whether such an "I" exists or what it means to say that such an "I" "exists." Both the "I" and its "being" remain doubtful. The history of foundationalism shows a similar pattern of failure. Each attempt to trace knowledge back to some indubitable foundation either fails to discover the ultimate foundation, or it fails to show what it would mean for such a foundation to exist. In short, all such foundationalist attempts to ground knowledge fail to show that its claims are intrinsically indubitable.

It is in light of these failures that Gadamer explicitly rejects the possibility of a reflexive self-grounding of any philosophical position.[7] For him philosophy depends on grasping the truth of what is said from the context of the dialogue in which we participate. Gadamer argues that there is a kind of self-validating truth that is available to those who are willing to participate in the dialogue of question and answer which we find in the philosophical tradition. This implies a rejection of the equation of knowledge with certainty, an equation which itself generates the skeptic's unanswerable doubt. Instead, Gadamer insists on a self-validating truth which does not pretend to deliver certainty but which nevertheless argues that many things that are not certain can be known and are true. This pertains especially to those truths we confront in the human sciences. Either we accept such truths as valid on their own terms or not. We cannot find an ultimate foundation or final justification for such truths. They are simply part of our experience, an experience we cannot finally step outside of in order to justify from a standpoint outside of it. What we can do is offer a holistic explanation of that experience that attempts to understand it by thinking through the question of how mind and reality must be related to each other in order to make this experience possible. This is an explicitly circular procedure that avowedly accepts its circularity but does not concede that such circularity is logically vicious. Even logic itself rests on experiences of self-evidence that it cannot deduce.

What this understanding of truth entails for Gadamer is a new openness to our experiences of truth in the human sciences that assumes that such experiences are true (or have their truth) until proven false (or until the limits of such truths are shown). One might say that unlike much of modern epistemology, which suspects our experiences, assuming they are false until proven true, Gadamer assumes that our experiences have their truth until their limitations are dialogically demonstrated. Such a "hermeneutics of trust" may not satisfy the advocates of the "hermeneutics of suspicion" but Gadamer's position is one fully informed by the problems that modern epistemology has generated. His preference for an ontological approach with more ancient roots is neither uncritical nor naive.

The ancient roots of Gadamer's account of a self-validating truth can be found in his reflection on Plato's insight into beauty and its connection to truth. Gadamer writes that

> Plato describes the beautiful as that which shines forth most clearly and draws us to itself, as the very visibility of the ideal. In the beautiful presented in nature and art, we experience the convincing illumination of truth and harmony, which compels the admission: "This is true." . . . The beautiful . . . gives us an assurance that the truth does not lie far off and inaccessible to us, but can be encountered in the disorder of reality with all its imperfections, evils, errors, extremes and fateful confusions. The ontological function of the beautiful is to bridge the chasm between the ideal and the real. (*RB*, 14–15)

Thus one can say that the truth is beautiful in the sense that it presents itself with the self-evidentness of beauty. Such self-evidentness or self-validation is not the same thing as certainty. Any truth-claim can be doubted, but the true shows itself in the beautiful in that the true has a kind of luminosity to it which Gadamer refers to as the "radiance" of the true.[8] By doing so, Gadamer is consciously relying on the so-called metaphysics of light which Plato appropriated from Parmenides. Gadamer thinks this tradition of light metaphysics still has something to say to us today. In fact, he argues that "the close relationship that exists between the shining forth [*Vorscheinen*] of the beautiful and the evidentness [*das Einleuchtende*] of the understandable is based on the metaphysics of light. This was precisely the relation that guided our hermeneutical inquiry" (*TM*, 483). Gadamer thinks that a renewed, critical appropriation of this tradition can point the way beyond the impasses of skepticism and foundationalism by giving us the resources to rethink the concept of a self-validating or self-illuminating truth that does not make the fateful mistake of equating such "light" with certainty. The implications of this revival of Plato's fundamental insight into beauty and its connection to truth is a new way to think about the type of truth offered to us in the human sciences. Such truth has never evinced the kind of certainty sought for by the natural sciences. When measured by this yardstick the truths of the human sciences fall miserably short. If, however, we remember that truth itself is not synonymous with certainty and instead turn to the more ancient insight that truth often presents itself as beauty, as a self-illuminating radiance, we are in a better position to accept such truth and to appreciate its value and limits.

The examples of identity and difference in interpretation, the relationship between language and intelligibility, and the connections between beauty and truth are meant to be merely suggestive of the scope and depth of Gadamer's appropriation of Platonic sources in developing his own philosophy. They are by no means exhaustive of the ways it might be said that Gadamer has learned fundamental lessons from Plato. But rather than continuing to list other ways in which Gadamer has generated a genuine dialogue with Plato I think it's important to point to one of the more radical implications of Gadamer's "post-Platonic" hermeneutics.

Most commentators have noticed that Gadamer owes a fundamental intellectual debt to Heidegger. In fact, many excellent studies on Gadamer take this debt as the starting point for their analysis. Many such commentators, however, fail to point out that Gadamer also sees himself as a fundamental critic of Heidegger. There is a tendency to ignore statements such as Gadamer's admission in 1961 to Leo Strauss that his "point of departure is not the *complete* forgetfulness of Being, the 'night of Being,' rather, on the contrary—I say this against Heidegger and Buber—the unreality of such an assertion."[9] Or consider the even more far-reaching claim that *Truth and Method* represents, despite its real indebtedness to Heidegger, Gadamer's "efforts to withstand this challenge (of metaphysical thoughts' obliviousness to Being) theoretically."[10]

What worries Gadamer about Heidegger can be summed up in two interrelated issues. The first involves the connected Heideggerian claims that all philosophy in the West is "metaphysics" and that "metaphysics" leads inevitably to the nihilism of contemporary civilization. This is what Heidegger refers to as *Seinsvergessenheit,* "the forgetfulness of Being" or, in Gadamer's words, "metaphysical thought's obliviousness to Being." Gadamer thinks that metaphysics is not necessarily driven by its own inherent logic toward such a nihilistic end. The second concern is related to the first but has even more profound ramifications. Simply put,

Gadamer is also worried about nihilistic tendencies in Heidegger's own thought, tendencies, for example, that manifest themselves in a failure to consider how real questions about the human good are integrally related to questions about Being. These tendencies show up, for example, in Heidegger's *Letter on Humanism.*

To address these concerns Gadamer adopts a two-pronged strategy. The first part of this strategy is historical. It consists in challenging Heidegger's reading of the Platonic corpus. By showing that "one could find in Platonic philosophy one possible way to get behind the question as formulated in Aristotelian and the post-Aristotelian metaphysics" Gadamer hopes to show "that the dimension of self-manifesting Being, the Being of *aletheia* that articulates itself in the *logos,* could be recognized in the dialectic of Ideas" (*HW,* 160). In other words, Plato is not clearly the author of the so-called metaphysics of presence. If Gadamer's case is convincing in this regard (and I think it is), then it shows that "metaphysics" is not a univocal phenomenon destined for the nihilism that dominates many parts of our culture. Instead this leaves the door open to the possibility that "metaphysics" contains possibilities or resources for development that have not been adequately explored. This points us to the second prong of Gadamer's response to Heidegger. If metaphysics is not as one-sided as Heidegger has made it out to be, then we can look to the metaphysical tradition for other ways of raising the question of Being. This is precisely what Gadamer does. Not only does Gadamer's hermeneutics rely on Heidegger's insights into "self-manifesting Being, the Being of *aletheia*" but it attempts to expand these insights into a more fundamental ontological inquiry by reintroducing the fundamentally Platonic concern with transcendentals like the one and the many, "motion" and "rest," as well as the beautiful, the true, and the Good.

What this implies, in my opinion, is a demand to rethink the ontological question "beyond Being." Gadamer's hermeneutics implies, in my view, moving beyond Heidegger's near-exclusive fixation on Being by expanding both the scope and specificity of the issue to include a renewed interest in the transcendentals. Simply put, I would say that Gadamer's work implies that one cannot really raise the issue of Being, as Heidegger repeatedly does, in isolation from its internal relationships to such issues as the Good, the true, and the beautiful. These issues are, so to speak, "cut from the same cloth." Although Heidegger might respond that his *Seinsfrage* certainly included the issue of motion or change as well as issues like the one and the many and certainly the issue of truth (*aletheia*), it nevertheless remained precariously one-sided in its refusal to place issues like the Good and the Beautiful at the center of his thought (it is even questionable whether the later Heidegger continued to acknowledge the connections between the Being and truth).[11] Gadamer's thought points beyond this dangerous shortcoming in Heidegger's thought without repudiating its epoch-making profundity. Gadamer knows that it is all too easy to underestimate Heidegger's achievements—to treat him like a "dead dog," reminiscent of the way Marx complained that many thinkers in his generation were treating Hegel—but he is also concerned that we not overestimate what Heidegger has done. Heidegger's ontology is missing a real place for ethical concerns. In his unyielding efforts to resist a pervasive "subjectivism" or "humanism" which projects its own concerns onto Being and thereby reduces Being to a human, controllable project, Heidegger distances Being from these concerns. The result, simply put, is that Being becomes increasingly inaccessible and hidden, to the point where one may wonder if one can say anything at all about it. This sharp division in Heidegger's work between Being and human beings is a ramification of a more general difference which Heidegger always insisted on, the ontological difference between Being and beings. I would say that Gadamer's work on the transcendentals, those elements of Being common to all beings, implies a relativization of the ontological difference itself. By suggesting that the difference between Being and beings is relative Gadamer's thought reopens the possibility of finding a place for ethics within ontology.

Some of the ethical implications of Gadamer's move "beyond Heidegger" or "beyond Being" show themselves in his reflections on the connection between truth and human solidarity. Solidarity, for Gadamer, is made possible by a shared concern for the Good. We cannot avoid such a shared concern because all attempts of the ego to isolate a private good run aground on the fact that the good for the individual is never wholly separable from its relation to others. In short, we cannot seek "the Good" in complete isolation from others but must attempt to identify and work toward common goals. This is very true, Gadamer thinks, for understanding the goods involved in the human pursuit of truth. I have already suggested that Gadamer thinks that truth is always "finite" truth or a truth relative to context of questioning. Such questions are always worked out in "dialogue" with others. This needn't imply a face-to-face conversation, but what "dialogue" does imply is the fact that our thought is always "intersubjective," i.e., worked out in a common language about a shared set of concerns. What this implies is that the quest for truth, for Gadamer, presupposes solidarity. If solidarity exists as a common concern for the Good, then questions about the truth are inseparable from questions about the Good. We cannot have a meaningful dialogue (even with inquirers of the past) and thus generate meaningful questions in terms of which truth can show itself to us in a certain distinctive but limited light unless there is always already a common set of concerns shared by participants in the dialogue. For Gadamer, even disagreements that are real, meaningful disagreements, presuppose prior agreements of a far-reaching sort. There is never sufficient reason to think that solidarity of some sort cannot be found.[12] Thus all debate and inquiry presuppose a limited but real solidarity between inquirers. Questions about truth cannot be raised without also raising issues about the common good that inquirers presuppose and unconsciously rely on as the basis of both their disagreements and agreements. The ultimate horizon of our search for truth is found in our prior search for what is really good.

Of course, not everyone will accept these Gadamerian insights. The arguments are far from complete in the way that I have sketched them here. But I offer this brief sampling of the Platonic roots of Gadamer's thought to suggest that his debt to Plato and the Greeks is both profound and provocative. In going back to Plato, Gadamer has sought neither simply to repeat nor refute him. Instead Gadamer's work attempts to critically appropriate aspects of Plato's thought for the problems of hermeneutics. Students of continental philosophy need to look at this dialogue between Gadamer and Plato more closely. The result, in my opinion, of this dialogue is a direction in philosophical thought that points beyond the nihilism and skepticism of Nietzsche's heirs. While this text can only claim to be a beginning in its exploration of the direction that Gadamer's thought takes "beyond Being," it is a journey that more of us need to take.

It might be said that Gadamer's thought is missing both the pathos of heroic resignation that the writings of other thinkers struggling with the quest for meaning in contemporary civilization evince, as well as the self-serving and self-congratulatory air of those who think they have discovered the one moment when the West fell from intellectual grace. One might ask why this is. Could it be because Gadamer's thought shows that the metaphysical tradition is not dead or exhausted? Could it be because Gadamer does not underestimate the complexity of the intellectual problems involved or the richness of the resources for dealing with them? Gadamer's challenge goes against the tenor of times but it is a challenge that sounds the notes of both hope and reason. He deserves to be heard. Perhaps if we do so we will discover that we are listening to notes that have always resounded from the philosophical past and perhaps we will realize that we are listening to a conversation in which we can participate but never ground or control. For Gadamer this is a "conversation that we are," it is a conversation in which our identities are at stake. There is no "philosopher's stone" that might unlock these identities once and for all. There is, however, the ever-pressing need to participate in the dialogue that has always formed us. Gadamer's hermeneutics is an invitation to participate in that dialogue, an invitation offered with the knowledge that the scope of this dialogue goes back to the very beginnings of our history and to the very heart of the human condition. If we participate well in this conversation we may just find that it has the power, like any true conversation, to change us irrevocably.

1

Situating Gadamer

Beyond "Skepticism" and "Epistemology"

It is a striking feature of Hans-Georg Gadamer's philosophical hermeneutics that it claims for itself a universal scope. All human understanding, according to Gadamer, involves interpretation; all understanding has certain common features which make it appropriate to see any and all understanding as "interpretation." Interpretation is, in Gadamer's view, the most fundamental and defining feature of human cognition. What he means by "interpretation" is something we will address below, but for now it suffices to point out that interpretation, for Gadamer, has to do primarily with the way in which reality discloses itself to us, and secondarily with the role that we play in this process. Thus we might say that interpretation for Gadamer is rooted in the way things are. Gadamer understands interpretation to presuppose certain ontological commitments. Although interpretation is something humans do Gadamer argues that we cannot understand this activity apart from the way things are that makes interpretation possible and even unavoidable. Gadamer's hermeneutics is dedicated to elucidating these two features of interpretation and arguing for its universal scope.

The universal nature of interpretation is often obscured in *Wahrheit und Methode*[1] by the fact that Gadamer spends a great deal of time discussing the nature of "understanding" and "interpretation" in the human sciences. This fact has lead some commentators to see Gadamer's work as just one more attempt to safeguard the autonomy of the humanities. In reality, Gadamer's thought is more ambitious. Gadamer's analysis and defense of the theoretical autonomy of the human sciences is only his point of departure for the more encompassing claim that these same disciplines contain important clues to our general experience of the world. This experience is, however, often overshadowed by the natural sciences' concern with methodological justification and even fundamentally distorted by a philosophical climate which pursues a theory of knowledge that is modeled on the natural sciences and driven by the dream of refuting skepticism. Beyond the natural sciences and beyond the epistemologist's dream of a definitive argument against skepticism there is a universal way of understanding ourselves and the world that is genuinely "hermeneutical." This is Gadamer's principal concern. Thus his hermeneutics "is not . . . a methodology of human sciences, but an attempt to understand what the human sciences truly are, beyond their methodological self-consciousness, and what connects them with the totality of our experience of the world" (*TM,* xxii). In this regard, Gadamer examines the nature of the human sciences as a prism through which to view the "totality of our experience of the world." Of course it is not accidental that Gadamer chooses the human sciences as a model for a more pervasive human experience of reality. Such "experience" or "understanding" often evinces itself in a particularly compelling way in our encounter with great art, history, literature, or philosophy. Gadamer insists that such experiences give us important clues to our situation as knowers. He argues, moreover, that this type of understanding is universal and always possible for human beings, even though the canons of justification in the natural sciences and the specter of skepticism in epistemology have made it difficult for us to grasp the true nature of this kind of understanding and appreciate its own type of rationality. Gadamer believes, however, that our hermeneutical understanding is fully "rational" and defensible, but its rationality can only be seen if we first clear away certain models of reason that distort our vision.

The most radical of these models of human rationality can be found in the Cartesian demand that all knowledge-claims justify themselves before the bar of certainty. Descartes dreamed of absolute certainty in human knowledge; he insisted that genuine knowledge must rest upon indubitable foundations. Any knowledge-claim that failed to rest on such a truly undubitable starting point must be rejected. This foundationalist dream has informed and haunted much of modern philosophy. Philosophers like Richard Rorty have traced in great detail the many variations of this dream and he has argued cogently that this dream has failed.[2] In pointing to this Cartesian demand, I do not intend to rehearse the history of this tradition or to agree with Rorty that pragmatism as he understands it is what must follow in the wake of this Cartesian tradition. But Rorty is right in situating Gadamer as someone who is trying to rethink the nature of human understanding from the perspective of a "post-Cartesian," "post-epistemological" standpoint. As Rorty himself has contended, "hermeneutics" is what you get when philosophy ceases to be "epistemological."[3]

We can understand this claim better by looking to the fact that hermeneutics challenges the claim that human understanding must be measured by the yardstick of certainty. Gadamer flatly rejects the claim that certainty is necessary for truth.[4] To think that it is is to rule out from the start all kinds of knowledge and truth—particularly "self-knowledge" and "practical knowledge," i.e., the kind of knowledge so central to the human sciences—and it threatens our awareness that such knowledge is the most basic knowledge we have. In other words, to accept Descartes's model of knowledge as certainty is to obscure from the outset the real nature of much human knowledge and perhaps even contribute to undermining its validity in the minds of many people. Even Descartes himself found it impossible to rebuild a substantive ethics on the basis of his own method. He counseled "prudence" and fell back on a conventional appeal to traditional normative claims.

But not only does "self-knowledge" of the type we find in the humanities, as well as "practical knowledge" of the type we rely on every day in guiding our lives, fail to evince truly certain starting points, but all human knowledge claims do.[5] The demand for certainty is the demand that any valid knowledge claim must be able to "answer for itself." This implies that any knowledge-claim can only be justified if it can justify all its presuppositions. If, however, this examination of presuppositions is not to go on forever, there must be some presuppositions that are truly presuppositionless or "self-justifying." But are there any such knowledge-claims? Gadamer denies that there are. No knowledge-claim is truly presuppositionless because there are always more questions that can be raised about it. This truth about our knowledge-claims stems from the "holistic" fact that all knowledge-claims, even fundamental claims like the laws of logic, are embedded in a fabric of linguistic, semantic, logical, metaphysical, and historical relationships which makes it impossible to discover any truly self-justifying origins for our knowledge. This makes the skeptic's demand for an ultimate justification truly impossible. There are no indubitable starting points for knowledge; there are no self-evident, self-justifying "bits" of knowledge on which all other human knowledge rests.

This denial of self-evident starting points for knowledge implies more than the claim that no such justification can be found. It implies that even to demand such starting points is to misconstrue the nature and conditions of knowledge itself. From a Gadamerian standpoint, the skeptic's questions, as well as the traditional epistemologist's attempted answers, have framed the issues in a fundamentally misleading way. Gadamer refuses to play by the rules of this game. Thus he never asks "Is knowledge possible at all?" To do so would be to enter the skeptic's frame of reference and tacitly agree to her terms of debate. Rather, Gadamer argues that even to raise the skeptic's question, the validity of some human knowledge-claims must be presupposed. Thus Gadamer wishes to shift the burden of proof away from the nonskeptic to the skeptic herself. In his view, it is never possible to consistently conceive of ourselves as having no claim to legitimate knowledge. This fact is not sufficient to show the skeptic that we do in fact have certainty, but it is sufficient to justify a refusal to accept the skeptic's demand that we measure all knowledge by the yardstick of certainty. Thus Gadamer's point of entry into questions about the nature and scope of human understanding is not the skeptic's question "Is knowledge possible at all?" Rather, he prefers to point out that we are knowers and actually know and understand a great deal about ourselves and the world we live in. Given this fact we cannot so extract ourselves from our condition so as to gain a perspective outside of it from which we could grasp the self-evident starting points of any knowledge whatsoever. Instead, we always find ourselves already knowing a great deal. We always presuppose this knowledge whenever any question is raised. This means that at most we can only consistently ask "*How* is knowledge possible?" How, in fact, do we arrive at the state we call knowledge or understanding? In other words, what makes it possible for us to know ourselves and our world as we actually do?

This may sound as if Gadamer is simply another "transcendental" philosopher seeking the definitive conditions of knowledge in some principle or set of principles which can withstand the skeptic's scrutiny. But unlike transcendental philosophers like Husserl,[6] who seeks a final refutation of skepticism, Gadamer's question does not seek ultimate justification (*letzte Begründung*) for knowledge but proceeds "phenomenologically"[7] to describe what it is that actually happens when we know and understand. We can only describe what it is we experience when we feel compelled to say "now I understand" but we cannot look, as it were, underneath those actual experiences to their nonexperienced foundations on which these experiences supposedly rest. Hermeneutics claims to be "a theory of the real experience that thinking is" (*TM,* xxxvi) and no more. As such it accepts the claim that in our experience of thinking we do in fact come to know ourselves and the world. Of course, the skeptic and the traditional epistemologist may find this dissatisfying, but Gadamer asks them to look clearly at the source of their dissatisfaction. One cannot begin to know the conditions of knowledge unless there is real knowledge. We must be knowers before we can inquire into its conditions. To think otherwise is to fall victim to the ridiculous demand to "know before we know," which as Hegel pointed out, is tantamount to wanting to know how to swim before entering the water.

But if the Cartesian dream of presuppositionless certainty is a philosophical dead-end, a profound mistake from which we are just beginning to recover, how would Gadamer advise us to seek a better approach to our questions about our understanding of ourselves and the world? Gadamer thinks the answer lies in the nature of interpretation. But, what does Gadamer mean by "interpretation"? To answer this question we must situate Gadamer in terms of other models of interpretation current today as well as say something about how Gadamer's notion of interpretation squares with certain commonsense intuitions about interpretation.

Interpretation, Interest, and Truth

One possible answer to the question "What does Gadamer mean by interpretation?", which is widespread today, identifies Gadamer's hermeneutics with a historicized version of Kant's epistemology. When Kant argued that the necessity which seemingly attends many of our knowledge-claims can only be explained as a "formal" necessity imposed on reality by the categories of understanding, he assumed that these categories were themselves changeless and timeless forms of understanding, which the understanding unconsciously and inevitably employed to render its judgments intelligible and binding. However, one of the problems that plagued Kant's thought almost from the outset was how to justify the timeless and changeless character of the categories of thought. The actual categories that Kant outlined in the *Critique of Pure Reason* have a specific and varied history that can be traced back at least as far as Aristotle. This lead some philosophers like Hegel to attempt to show how both truth and necessity are compatible with historical change, and it lead others like Nietzsche to deny the reality of truth and necessity altogether.

The claim that all understanding is interpretation is usually understood today in this latter, Nietzschean sense. In this vein, what we mean by "truth" and "reality" is an interpretation, because all truth and even all reality is in some sense a human construct. Not only the logical "form" of our understanding is contributed by the human subject but in some sense the "empirical content" is as well. Today this claim is often made by reference to what is called "the myth of the given." There are no given truths about reality simply waiting to be discovered; there is no pretheoretical or prelinguistic apprehension of reality. All understanding of the world is "theory-laden" or "linguistically constituted," and never simply "given," awaiting our discovery and "objective" description. Moreover such theory-laden apprehensions of reality always are embedded in a broader sociohistorical context that contains a set of contingent interests and values which inquirers never suspend in their search for "objective" understanding but actually always employ, either more or less self-consciously, as a strategy to advance these same interests. Thus the rejection of the myth of the given is also often taken to imply a rejection of the "myth" of objectivity and truth. Thus, in this tradition, Richard Rorty has recently argued, following Quine, that the distinctions between form and content, logical and empirical content, a priori and a posteriori, necessary and contingent should all be relativized and replaced by a more "pragmatic" view of the human quest for understanding.[8] Moreover, Rorty has insisted that truth is precisely what hermeneutics is *not* about. He has even attempted to enlist Gadamer in his narrative of the triumph of "pragmatism."[9]

There is, however, at least one feature of Gadamer's thought that is incompatible with either a Nietzschean or Rortyean understanding of "interpretation." Unlike Nietzsche and Rorty, Gadamer insists that interpretation is about reality and its ultimate concern is with what is "true." For Gadamer, "interpretation" is not the means by which we construct a reality. It is rather the means by which we come into contact with reality itself and genuinely know it. For Gadamer, interpretations can be "true" or "false" and not simply "useful" for satisfying our purposes. What we rub up against in "true" interpretations is not simply a reality "for us," a reality made in our image to satisfy our own needs, but in principle it is reality itself, reality as it is apart from our purposes and needs. Of course, Gadamer knows that all interpretations are embedded in a particular language that have a "history." Moreover, he knows that these histories can always be construed, in part, as indices of the human interests that always animate our quest for knowledge. Nevertheless, he insists on a "realist" grasp of interpretation.[10] Gadamer makes the provocative claim that there is no fundamental incompatibility between the "interested" nature of our interpretation and its claim to disclose reality to us. This bold claim to combine an acknowledgment of the "interested" nature of human knowledge with a defensible concern for truth has, in my opinion, mislead many commentators to see in Gadamer another neo-Nietzschean account of human thought. Nevertheless, they do this by simply bypassing Gadamer's concern with truth. It is this realist side of Gadamer's hermeneutics that makes it impossible to assimilate him to either Nietzsche's or Rorty's historicized Kantianism. Thinkers like Rorty can only enlist Gadamer in their cause by ignoring or dismissing the fundamental Gadamerian concern with truth.

Of course, we still have not really said what Gadamer means by "interpretation," nor have we answered the question concerning the grounds on which Gadamer bases both the universality and potential truth of interpretation. One way to begin to approach Gadamer's provocative claim that interpretations can be "true," even though they are also always "interested," is to reconsider why we find it natural to call some forms of human understanding instances of "interpretation."

Certainly it's not hard to see why our approach to difficult texts or rich and complex works of art involve interpretation or even why our understanding of another's action requires interpretation. If we take our cue from our own use of language, we immediately see that we tend to speak of "interpretation" in situations where we are dealing with inherently complex phenomena, phenomena whose many possible meanings can never quite be contained in any one account. In contexts where we are trying to understand unwieldy, many-layered phenomena it is natural to talk of "interpretation" as a way to remind ourselves of both the limits of what we say, as well as the inherent "otherness" and inexhaustibility of the phenomena we seek to understand. Given this intrinsically rich and highly variegated nature of the phenomena we single out for interpretation, we can readily see why any interpretation is necessarily a schematic rendering of the object of its focus. Even when interpretations are themselves very complex, they remain outlines or sketches of inherently inexhaustible material. In some respects one might say that interpretations are like maps. Just as maps are designed relative to a set of concerns and are accordingly selective in what they represent about any geographical space, so are all interpretations relative to the interpreter's interests and point of view. Thus no map offers exhaustive or presuppositionless information about the topography it renders accessible. Nevertheless maps can give us genuine knowledge of a place. So, too, interpretations offer selective insights into the phenomena, which, of course, fail to say everything about the phenomena. Nevertheless these same interpretations can give us true understanding of these realities.

These insights into the inherent richness or inexhaustibility of the phenomena we seek to interpret, as well as the schematic nature of interpretation, have consequences. One such consequence is that interpretations are always offered with the tacit admission that other valid interpretations of the phenomena are possible in principle. This admission goes beyond the awareness of fallibility. Of course, interpretations can be wrong and must be open to correction. But the intrinsic openness of interpretation includes an awareness that an interpretation's validity is not dependent on its being the one and only correct interpretation. Many "correct" interpretations can and do exist side by side each other. To recognize this fundamental fact in no way commits us to an uncritical, "anything goes" relativism. It is true to say both that some interpretations are just wrong and that a plurality of valid interpretations can exist alongside each other. Gadamer supports both these claims by a more fundamental ontological claim about the phenomena of interpretation that acknowledges that the things themselves are both complex or rich enough to support multiple viewpoints and well-defined enough to warrant a critical notion of validity in interpretation. Some interpretations are just too superficial, too one-sided, too arbitrary (or what have you) to be taken seriously. Nevertheless, when such invalid interpretations are dismissed as possible models of interpretation, we still cannot escape the fact that the phenomena we seek to interpret, whether it is a text, another's action, or a natural event, is always complex enough to allow multiple interpretations.

However, there is more implicit in the term "interpretation" than a notion of the inexhaustibility of the phenomena. When we say that someone offers an "interpretation" we are usually implying that there is something "occasional" and even "subjective" about what is offered. Just as maps are always relative in some ways to the purposes of the cartographer, interpretations always show signs of the interpreter's goals and interests. Interpretations always seem motivated by conditions of time and place; something of the interests of the interpreter is involved in every interpretation, even where the interpretation strives for and achieves very high standards of faithfulness to the things which form the focus of our interpretative efforts.

Of course, this raises the issue of whether the "occasional" and "subjective" element in interpretation precludes the possibility of validity and truth in interpretation. Even if we rightly dismiss those interpretations that are obviously willful, incompetent, distorted, etc., the "interested" nature of interpretation cannot be circumvented. So integral, in fact, is the interest of every skilled interpreter to the work or phenomenon itself that when we talk of "interpretation" we often mean to imply that the interpreter contributes something positive to the work. In truth, some kind of "change" to the work is often being signaled when we speak of interpretation. Of course, the nature of this change is a key issue. For example, if we compare Olivier's *Henry V* to Branaugh's we see how the subjective and occasional element of interpretation implies that each actor and director is doing something to Shakespeare's work that is more than mere repetition. However faithful each may have tried to be to the original text, something emerges in their respective interpretations that goes beyond the strict limits of the text itself. This does not imply that their respective interpretations are arbitrary or could not be justified. In fact, each interpretation serves the text and enhances its meaning. But this is only possible because *Henry V* is not simply repeated, parrotlike.

Rather, it is *interpreted*—i.e., certain patterns of meaning and their possible relationships to each other and our concerns are emphasized and in this process and only in this process does the true richness of the text emerge. Of course, various interpreters emphasize various things in the text and its relationships to itself and us but this does not change the fact that what we are exploring is one text, one and the same complex configuration of meaning.

If we appeal to the metaphor of a map once again, interpretations, like maps, are relative to the purpose of the cartographers and those for whom they are drawn, but they need not be arbitrary in a vicious sense at all. In fact, such "subjective" and "occasional" interests often function to keep such "maps" as true to the things themselves as possible. An inaccurate map, filled with errors, can hardly be expected to be accepted by its intended users. Like all interpreters, cartographers must strive to be faithful to the things themselves even though their representation of these things is hardly disinterested or divorceable from its intended context of use. Yet if truth must always be a guiding concern in cartography we can begin to see how the "subjective" and occasional elements in any interpretation can in principle complement the phenomena themselves. From such examples we see how the selectivity of the interpreter, which is always interested and committed in historically conditioned ways, can nevertheless enhance the subject matter by highlighting certain important features that might otherwise have remained obscure. We know this very well from any insightful interpretation. The interpreter's interests are not necessarily a stumbling block to "true" interpretations but a foil against which any fruitful and engaging encounter with the phenomena occurs. As such a foil, Gadamer thinks they are necessary to all interpretations. The important question is not whether the interpretation is disinterested but whether the interests of the interpreter are compatible with and complement the thing itself. Just as a map that depicts a certain topography with an eye to, say, its mineral resources, must be true to the landscape itself, even when it selectively represents that landscape for purposes of its readers, so an interpretation of a text must be true to what is really in the text, even when it chooses to explore that textual landscape with an eye to certain features in it and not others. For example, an interpretation of *Hamlet* that emphasizes the connections between power, sex, and madness is just as much about *Hamlet* as an interpretation which emphasizes the relationships between ethical responsibility, self-knowledge, and the unique, complex, and contingent nature of the circumstances in which that responsibility is carried out. All of these "things" are in the text and it is a mistake to think that interpretations, which inevitably emphasize some things in the text and not others, are necessarily substituting their own concerns for the things themselves. If our interests are compatible with what is in the text itself such selectivity is not necessarily arbitrary, but a means of access to the reality of which the text speaks.

But if "interpretation" implies a certain way of coming into contact with reality, is it the case, as Gadamer argues, that all understanding involves a form of interpretation? Aren't there situations where one is not exploring inherently ambiguous and inexhaustible terrain, situations where one can simply say what one means unequivocally and without the nagging sense that something has still remained unsaid? Don't we sometimes experience in everyday life communication with others that is straightforward, final, and unproblematically clear? Isn't it also the case, particularly in science, that modes of speech are developed and finely honed through years of critical scrutiny to such a point that this speech is capable of limning the essential truth about some reality without lingering doubts about its definitive truth or other possible meanings? Isn't it possible to remove all traces of the subjective interests of the inquirer, especially in cases of scientific discovery where more often than not the analytical acumen of many researchers can winnow out the true content from the incidental form in which the research is presented? And what exactly does the researcher *contribute* to the subject matter? In fact, aren't the terms "research" and "interpretation" fundamentally at odds with each other? When we talk of "doing research" don't we imply that the subject matter is fully determinate, waiting only to be discovered, whereas in talk of "interpretation" we are tacitly admitting that the interpreter's interests are involved at some level in the very constitution of the subject matter itself? In other words, shouldn't we admit that any talk of contribution to the subject matter itself via interpretation must signal an arbitrary manipulation and possible distortion of the subject matter's own intelligibility? If every researcher is an interpreter and as such "contributes" something to the meaning of her subject matter, doesn't such a "contribution" imply a necessary distortion of the truth of the subject matter, a distortion, moreover that must serve the subjective or prejudiced interests of the researcher, rather than serving the subject matter itself? How can truth be of paramount importance to such an inquirer if the inquirer plays an inevitable role in "constituting" the very subject matter itself?

Even in the face of such questions Gadamer argues for the universality and potential truth of interpretation. Gadamer bases these claims on his "holistic" account of meaning.[11] He denies, first of all, that there are any phenomena that cannot be approached from an indefinite number of perspectives. One reason that Gadamer thinks this is so is because any individual phenomena or reality always stands in a "web" of intelligible relationships to other phenomena. These relationships include linguistic, semantic, logical, analogical, metaphysical, practical, and historical ties that exist between the realities we seek to understand. Such ties bind them together in a web of innumerable, overlapping, and intersecting strands of meaning. Moreover, Gadamer argues that these relationships constitute the very intelligible being of these phenomena. There simply is no intelligibility of these phenomena outside this ideal web of meaning. As discrete, isolated particulars such realities are mute. There is something to be said for the old dictum that the *individuum est ineffable.* In their interrelatedness, however, such realities speak in many varying ways. In fact, in their interrelatedness their very particularity is highlighted in terms of their various connections to other meaningful realities which act to differentiate particulars as particulars. Given the ontologically constitutive function of these holistic relationships, as well as the fact that this "web" of relationships is inordinately complex, Gadamer argues that there will always be a multiplicity of viewpoints from which any one phenomenon can be elucidated. Thus multiple interpretations are always possible. The truth of the phenomena cannot be exhausted in any one line of inquiry, regardless of how doggedly and conscientiously the research program may be pursued. The inexhaustibility of the phenomena is rooted in this web of intelligible relationships. In this regard, Gadamer's view of interpretation assumes that the possibility of multiple "true" interpretations is rooted in the things themselves and is not simply a function of the different subjective interests of the interpreters.

However, Gadamer does not deny that the historically mediated subjectivity of the interpreter contributes, in a sense, to the many interpretations that arise. As we have already seen, Gadamer thinks of such historicity as a potentially positive source of true insight. Far from dismissing our historicity as inimical to truth in interpretation, Gadamer sees it as a potentially powerful source for new truth. Of course, our historically generated interests and concerns can threaten our access to the way things really are. There is such a thing as unjustifiable prejudice. Such illegitimate "prejudices" or prejudgments (*Vorurteile* as Gadamer calls them)[12] inevitably lead to internal contradictions in the accounts of the things they seek to understand. But inasmuch as Gadamer sees the interpreter's interests as able in principle to bring out hidden possibilities of intelligibility in the things themselves, he creates a space for assessing historicity's relation to truth in a potentially positive light.

In this regard, Gadamer is like Hegel. Like Hegel, Gadamer argues that there is no insurmountable incompatibility between truth and history. But it is also helpful in order to better understand what Gadamer means by "interpretation" to underline certain differences between Gadamer and Hegel. Unlike Hegel, Gadamer rejects the attempt to discover a historically progressive logic of human understanding, which culminates in a presuppositionless and exhaustive account of the structural features of all human knowledge. Gadamer chooses "interpretation" over "absolute knowledge" because, for one reason, the necessary schematic nature of interpretation tacitly allows the particulars or the things themselves to show themselves in new ways in different historically mediated contexts. This points us to a key theme in Gadamer's work, namely, the insurmountable tension between the historically unique nature of the particulars we encounter in our experience and the universal claims of theoretical understanding. Unlike Hegel's vision of theoretical closure, which imposes a halt to the history of inquiry in the name of a final, universal, and unchanging theoretical perspective under which all particulars are subsumed, Gadamer's account of "interpretation" implies the inexhaustibility of the particulars, i.e., their ability to present themselves in new ways in new circumstances. In the final analysis, Gadamer thinks that Hegel's vision of the end point of human inquiry does not serve the real, multifaceted nature of truth but sells it short by prescribing its necessary course and destination. Of course, Hegel does not claim that "absolute knowledge" implies that humanity has reached a point of omniscience, but he does mean to imply that we can know both the formal features of our own knowledge well enough (as well as the possible paths of their historical evolutions) that all its possible forms and their relationships to each other can be made transparent. Gadamer's concern with truth in interpretation is meant to block just such presumptuous claims to give an exhaustive account of all the ways things can show themselves and be comprehended, even one as sensitive to history as Hegel's.

Gadamer has, however, another deeper reservation about Hegel's dialectical logic. Hegel's search for a transparent, presuppositionless account of the "whole" not only ends up doing violence to the particulars that show themselves within any general account of "the whole," but it also fails to do justice to the way in which historically mediated human interests enter into our cognition of any reality. Ultimately, it is Hegel's "scientism" or his Cartesianism that makes him unable to adequately account for the role of human interest in cognition, as well as the way in which this same interest is in no small part responsible for the different ways different phenomena show themselves over time. In this regard, Gadamer seems to be more closely aligned with Nietzsche and Rorty, both of whom move away from modern science, with its disinterested subject, as a model for human thought.

But we should be careful that such a real coincidence of concerns does not obscure crucial differences. Unlike Nietzsche, Gadamer doesn't substitute "interest" (in the form of the will to power) for truth, but he insists instead that "interest" is often the ground of a "finite" grasp of the things themselves. One way to say what this means is to say, contrary to Hegel and other Cartesians like Husserl, that there is no possible presuppositionless approach to the things themselves because the things themselves always show themselves from a historically mediated standpoint that is grounded in the various interests of the interpreters. Far from precluding "truth," however, such a "finite" grasp of the particulars actually serves to reveal ever new aspects of reality and thus creates ever new possibilities of interpretation. The motor of intellectual change and development for Gadamer is not the immanent telos of a final account of the "whole," but our ever-changing entanglement in time which forces on us ever new needs as well as ever new opportunities for understanding the world.

Generally speaking, Gadamer would criticize both Hegel and Nietzsche for running aground on this problem of the relation between truth and interest or what may be seen as a version of what the Anglo-American tradition has called "the fact-value problem." In acknowledging the role interest plays in human knowledge, Nietzsche's account of interpretation ends up sacrificing truth in order to accommodate interest in the form of the will to power. While Nietzsche's account of human thought does more justice to the particulars and the limits of theory than Hegel, he does so only at the price of surrendering a strong account of truth and making his own truth-claims ultimately unintelligible. Hegel, on the other hand, fails in the final analysis to take history seriously as the ground of the way in which different interests emerge and serve as the standpoint from which reality shows itself in new ways. His account of human inquiry thus fails, according to Gadamer, because it introduces a false sense of closure to the history of human inquiry, which history itself does not bear out. In the final analysis, Gadamer cannot identify his position with either Nietzsche or Hegel.[13]

Between Plato and Heidegger

In light of these problems that plagued both Nietzsche and Hegel it is not surprising that Gadamer looks elsewhere for help in developing his own position. Gadamer, in fact, turned to both Plato and Heidegger for key suggestions about how to develop an account of human understanding that would not run aground on the problems that beset Nietzsche and Hegel. Speaking generally, what Gadamer finds in Plato is a thinker whose thought does not suffer from these false divisions and oversimplications. Plato not only had a robust sense of truth, but his emphasis on the Good as the ultimate Form, the Idea of all Ideas, suggests he was very much aware of how "value" and the human interests through which it is expressed is at some level constitutive of our knowledge. Moreover, Gadamer sees Plato's various approaches to different issues in the dialogues as indicative of an ongoing struggle with the limits of philosophical theory and as evidence for the irrepressible particularity of both the knower's situation in which she comes to understand the world in a certain "interested" light and the unique multifaceted nature of the particular things which form the focus of her thought. This dialectical tension between the claims of universal theory and the particularity of both the knower and the objects of knowledge shows itself in the different dramatic setting of the dialogues. Far from being merely incidental to the "real" philosophical content of Plato's thought, Gadamer thinks that the various contingent settings of Plato's work actually show his sensitivity to the contingent particularities of human knowledge. Such a perspective leads Gadamer to a radical proposal for reshifting our understanding of the focal point of Plato's philosophy. Unlike many interpreters of Plato who emphasize Plato's account of universals, the so-called theory of Ideas, as the definitive core of Plato's philosophy, Gadamer understands him as a thinker who has no *one* "theory of Ideas." Instead, Gadamer understands Plato to have worked out several *different* hypotheses regarding universals and as a thinker who, moreover, also always kept his eye on the limits of each of those hypotheses. Instead of the "theory of Ideas" Gadamer identifies the real focus of Plato's philosophy as "the one and the many." This concern is not simply synonymous with Plato's various inquiries into the Ideas, but presupposes the existence of Ideas, leaves their exact nature open, and focuses instead on the irrepressible dialectical relationship between particulars and universals. More specifically, it deals with the irrepressible fact about human knowledge that the objects of knowledge never show themselves in a single, unequivocal way, but instead one and the same thing will show itself differently in different contexts.

Heidegger is also exemplary for Gadamer because his philosophy will countenance no easy reduction of truth to "power," "usefulness," or "interest," nor does it ignore the role that "practical" concerns play in our knowledge. Heidegger's emphasis on "care," as the basic nature of our entire comportment toward the world, is indicative of his sensitivity to this issue. Moreover, Heidegger's general concern with the ground of our grasp of individuality, both our own individuality, as well as that of the unique historically formed particulars generally,[14] is very congenial to Gadamer. Heidegger is very aware of the limits of theory in our apprehension of the world. Both Heidegger's earlier attempt to discover the origin of all meaning in the historically mediated facticity of Dasein with its contextualized "worldly" acts of self-projection and self-comprehension as well as his later concern to ground meaning in Being itself finds its echo in Gadamer's hermeneutics.

At the risk of considerable oversimplification, it can be said by way of summary that what attracts Gadamer to both Plato and Heidegger is that each thinks ontology contains resources for thinking more deeply about the connection between truth and human interest. Plato works as a philosopher whose philosophy is not subject to a simplistic and distorting fact-value diremption, and there are aspects of Heidegger as well that suggest that he wants to rethink the grounds of meaning in such a way that the nihilistic consequences of modern philosophy can be overcome. Moreover, each of these thinkers is very sensitive to the particular-universal relationship in its many guises. For these fundamental reasons, Gadamer's hermeneutics is motivated by the claim that there is a deep continuity between these philosophers, a continuity which Heidegger resisted but which Gadamer seeks to bring out and, as we shall see, even turn back in a critical way on aspects of Heidegger himself.

If this continuity is there and forms the basis of Gadamer's thought we have to pay more attention to Gadamer's understanding of these two thinkers. While it has often occurred that Gadamer's intellectual relationship to Heidegger has been acknowledged and used as a fruitful point of departure for understanding his work, Gadamer's debt to the Greeks, particularly Plato, has generally not been seen as central.[15] I think this is a fundamental mistake. In *Truth and Method,* Gadamer writes, "if we wish to do justice to the subject, the hermeneutics of the human sciences . . . lead us back into the problems of classical metaphysics" (*TM,* 460). Unfortunately, many of Gadamer's interpreters, pro and con, do not take sufficient cognizance of the fact that Gadamer is a lifelong student of the Greeks, particularly Plato. They ignore his own statement that it was "ancient philosophy from which the whole of philosophy and its history disclosed itself to me."[16] Such a fundamental influence should not be ignored or played down. Nevertheless, there is a marked tendency in Gadamer studies to separate his theory of interpretation from its context of a lifetime of interaction with the issues of Greek philosophy. The result is often a reading of Gadamer that either assimilates him too quickly to certain modern preoccupations and commitments or criticizes him for failing to identity himself unequivocally with these tendencies. Moreover, it seems to me that such central Gadamerian themes like "dialogue," "historicity," "truth," and "practical reason" can only be understood properly in the context of Gadamer's Greek studies.

What I propose is that Gadamer's thought be placed in a broader context of Gadamer's Greek studies, particularly his work on Plato. Failure to do so leads, in my opinion, to misunderstandings and distortions of Gadamer.

For example, Gadamer is often accused of being a skeptical relativist because he points out how our truth-claims are always conditioned by history.[17] Such a criticism not only fails to consider Gadamer's denial of such skeptical relativism, but it also makes the far-reaching assumption that the influences of history on the inquirer's mind must be inimical to truth. This criticism assumes that unless the mind can somehow operate outside of history it cannot grasp the truth about reality. Such a criticism fails to question its own assumptions about the nature of time, truth, mind, and reality in general, assumptions which Gadamer explicitly attempts to rethink within his hermeneutics. More specifically, Gadamer wants to challenge the relativist's assumption that the mind must be a morally neutral and timeless observer if it hopes to know. Instead, Gadamer's Greek studies lead him to the view that the mind is never ethically neutral but always concerned with matters of "the Good." Moreover, Gadamer challenges the view that the mind stands over against reality as a merely passive observer and tries to reanimate and reinterpret the view that Plato once held that the mind is both an active "participant" in reality (a view which Gadamer also sees in Hegel's notion of *Geist*) and capable of discovering its essential nature. If these critics had taken the time to place Gadamer's thought in the proper historical context, particularly his work on Plato, such a facile criticism would be impossible.

Similarly, Gadamer is sometimes mistaken as a kind of linguistic constructivist or linguistic idealist (Habermas)[18] because he stresses that the intelligibility of reality can only be found in language. However, this central and important Gadamerian thesis is easy to misinterpret. To say that the intelligibility of reality can only be found in language is not to say that the intelligibility of reality is somehow a *product* of language. Language does not cast its own cloak of intelligibility over a reality that otherwise is unintelligible or unknowable, like the Kantian categories are supposed to project onto the thing-in-itself. Rather, Gadamer argues, as we shall see, that language and reality "belong together" such that the former is "akin" to the latter and as such well-suited to reflect the inexhaustibly rich intelligibility of reality itself. For Gadamer, there is a "parallelism" between the linguistically mediated intelligibility of thought and the very intelligibility of reality itself. Language is the medium in which we discover the ideal in the real. In other words, despite the emphasis on the linguisticality of our thought, Gadamer remains a metaphysical realist. A better understanding of Gadamer's Platonism would have made his realism more apparent and avoided this mistaken attribution of a linguistic constructivism to Gadamer.

It is true, however, that one cannot confront Gadamer's work on Plato without running up against his debt to Heidegger. So close, in fact, is the connection between Gadamer's reading of Plato and his understanding of Heidegger that one can scarcely invoke Gadamer's Platonism without stumbling over his Heideggerianism. It's not an exaggeration to say that Gadamer's work on Plato is largely due to the provocation he received as a young student from Heidegger. Again and again, Gadamer's writing on Plato bears both direct and indirect testimony to this fact.

> The philosophical stimuli I received from Heidegger lead me more and more into the realm of a dialectic, Plato's as well as Hegel's. Decades of teaching were devoted to elaborating what I have called here the Platonic-Aristotelian unitary effect. But in the background was the continuous challenge posed for me by the path Heidegger's own thought took, and especially by his interpretation of Being [*Sein*]. My elaboration and projection of a philosophical hermeneutics in *Wahrheit und Methode* bear witness to my efforts to withstand this challenge theoretically. (*IG*, 5)

But as this quote reveals, Gadamer's debt to Heidegger is both profound and ambiguous. Not only did Heidegger inspire Gadamer to grapple with the nature of philosophical thought in Plato and Hegel, but it also lead Gadamer to follow his teacher's provocations to a critique of Heidegger himself. It needs to be reiterated that Gadamer understands *Truth and Method* as an effort to "withstand [Heidegger's] challenge theoretically." Thus Gadamer's understanding of Plato must be described as "Heidegger-inspired," but, as we shall see, it is not "Heideggerian" in the way in which it understands Plato's role in the history of philosophy. Similarly, Gadamer's understanding of Heidegger, which leads to something of a Heidegger critique, is "Plato-inspired," if not "Platonic" in the conventional sense of the term. In consciously seeking the compatibility of some of the key impulses of Plato's thought with those of Heidegger, Gadamer is consciously challenging our understanding of the meaning of Heidegger's philosophy.

Most commentators on Gadamer acknowledge his debt to Heidegger but they fail to see him as a serious critic of Heidegger. This is a challenge of fundamental importance and I think one that should be taken very seriously. In linking "hermeneutics" to "classical metaphysics" Gadamer is looking for points of connection that point beyond the position of thinkers, like Derrida, for whom the real meaning of Heidegger culminates in Nietzsche and Nietzsche's deep anti-Platonism.

Similarly, I could also say that if Gadamer is right about the connection between Plato and hermeneutics, the meaning of Heidegger's legacy for us would also not necessarily be a pragmatism, like that of Richard Rorty, which is equally anti-Platonic in its self-understanding. For these reasons, Gadamer is of seminal importance today. In ignoring him, we ignore another possibility for thinking about the profound connections that exist between interest, truth, and the limits of human knowledge. What is at issue ultimately is whether or not the meaning of philosophy culminates in such Nietzschean claims that "truth" is nothing more than a "life-serving" illusion and whether talk about the "the Good" is merely a veil for the unquenchable "will to power," which is reputedly at the base of all human constructs of reality. At the risk of obvious exaggeration, I think this question about the meaning of the Heideggerian legacy is nothing less than a question about the future direction of European thought. What Gadamer's interpretations of Heidegger and Plato show is that there is a great deal of continuity between Heidegger and the tradition of which Plato is the primary starting point. By emphasizing this continuity Gadamer wants to show that these lines of inquiry are neither exhausted nor irrelevant to understanding our situation. More specifically, Gadamer wants to show that a Heidegger-inspired reading of Plato shows that Plato is not the one-sided advocate of the "metaphysics of presence" and its accompanying *Seinsvergessenheit* that Heidegger makes him out to be. If this is so, Heidegger's account of the history of Western philosophy will require some critical rethinking. Given the closeness of Heidegger's own thought to this particular reading of the philosophical tradition Heidegger's own thought will need to be reassessed. One important implication of this reassessment is found in the fact that Gadamer's Heidegger-inspired reading of Plato can provide a way of thinking about a transcendental ground of human solidarity, something glaringly and painfully missing in Heidegger's ontology. For this reason, among others, Gadamer's Platonic critique of Heidegger is of fundamental importance today.

The starting point for Gadamer's rethinking of the relationship between the thought of Heidegger and Plato is a reassessment of the role which Heidegger ascribes to Plato in Western thought. As is well known, Heidegger attempted to cultivate a type thinking which is not "metaphysical" in a very specific sense of the word. For Heidegger, "metaphysics" implies a suppression of the question of Being as such in favor of questions about the "whatness" of beings, questions oriented toward hierarchical, classificatory schemes, which culminate in talk of a "highest being." Heidegger roots this tendency of all "metaphysical" thought in Plato's account of the Ideas. More specifically, Heidegger accused Plato of a transformation of the concept of truth. Supposedly, Plato initially understood the concept of truth as unconcealedness or *a-letheia*, but he allegedly transformed it, according to Heidegger, to "correctness" or *orthotes.* This transformation occurred through Plato's emphasis on the "seeing" of the Ideas or getting the proper vision or "look" of things. This emphasis on the Ideas lead Plato to stress the changeless character of the Ideas in contrast to the constant "becoming" of the many particular things. This contrast pointed toward the ontological conclusion of a hiatus in Being, between the higher being of the Ideas and the lower being of everything particular that merely participated in them. Heidegger sees this tendency reaching its first mature expression in Aristotle's "onto-theology," a view which asked about Being as such but inevitably suppressed it because its question was oriented by the cosmological concern with a highest being and how to systematically rank other beings relative to this first being. Aristotle thus became the first "metaphysician," despite the fact that he was also the first trenchant critic of Plato's commitment to the Ideas.[19]

Throughout the history of Western philosophy, philosophy has supposedly been stuck in this basic "onto-theological" orientation. According to Heidegger, this orientation places more emphasis on "correctness" than "letting Being be." The logical result of this emphasis on correctness is an emphasis on the control and manipulation of reality. According to Heidegger, "technology" is the logical outcome of this emphasis because only in technology does control really reach its own measure and goal.[20] But "technology," understood as the historical outcome of metaphysical thought, also brings with it nihilism, because any reality that cannot be brought under the standards of technological control is dismissed as essentially "nothing." Instead of embracing this nihilism, Heidegger strives to develop a type of thinking that is more open to different ways of thinking the question of Being, ways that would not issue in the problems of nihilism. Heidegger reached back to the pre-Socratics, to figures like Anaximander, Heraclitus, and Parmenides, to find possibilities for thought that might suggest a new beginning for human thinking.

With this broad historical framework in mind, Gadamer asks if Plato really can be unequivocally assigned the role to which Heidegger's negative trajectory condemns him. While Gadamer sees Heidegger's interpretation of Western thought as tracing *one* possibility latent in its beginnings, he distances himself from the inevitability of the trajectory. To make this point, Gadamer wants to show that there are elements in Plato, particularly the later dialogues, that show other philosophical possibilities, possibilities which in fact cast doubt on Heidegger's insistence that "metaphysics" is inherently "technological" and nihilistic. In other words, Gadamer is arguing that what is needed is not necessarily a new beginning but a more thoughtful appropriation of the past.

This, of course, implies a critique of Heidegger's reading of Western philosophy. But there is more at stake for Gadamer than how to read Western intellectual history. The question of Being itself is on the line. Gadamer is asking nothing less than how we should best approach this issue. It might be said that Gadamer accepts Heidegger's claim that all human beings always have an understanding of Being, i.e., of their own being and that of Being generally, which precedes and informs the methodological reflections of all the sciences. Moreover, he accepts Heidegger's reading of the "ontological difference," i.e., that the question of Being cannot be confused with questions about specific beings. But Gadamer has also learned through Plato that Heidegger himself is insufficiently dialectical in his approach to the *Seinsfrage*. Simply put, Gadamer's Plato studies imply that the question of Being cannot be taken up apart from questions about "the Good," "the true," "the beautiful," and "the One." Although Heidegger links his account of Being with his account of truth and although some of the earlier work of Heidegger begins to explore the relationships between Being and other transcendentals, Heidegger's thought did not develop by more fully and adequately exploring these connections between the *Seinsfrage* and the other Platonic transcendentals. Gadamer both expands the scope and increases the specificity of Heidegger's question by arguing that any account of Being is inseparable from accounts about the nature of beauty, truth, goodness, and unity. Such "realities" are "transcendent" in a way analogous to Heidegger's insight into the nature of Being. What this implies is that an understanding of these transcendentals is present in all human claims to understand, just as Heidegger insisted that an understanding of Being is implicit in all human comportment. Thus beauty, truth, goodness, unity, as well as other "transcendentals" like non-Being, motion, and rest, are not beings and consequently do not have the same type of intelligibility as beings. Nevertheless, an understanding of such transcendentals is no less urgent for understanding just what human understanding itself is. Put somewhat differently, it is these same transcendentals that provide the ultimate framework for all understanding. Behind our quest to comprehend ourselves and our world, what we find is not the disinterested quest for certainty, but our inextricably "interested" involvement in the transcendentals.

In pushing Heidegger back toward the concerns of Platonic metaphysics, Gadamer is challenging Heidegger's view about the so-called end of metaphysics. For Gadamer, metaphysics is not as one-sided and predetermined as Heidegger would have it. And it certainly has not exhausted its possibilities for shedding light on our situation. On the contrary, Gadamer's Heidegger critique implies that Heidegger did not explore the possibilities of understanding in classical metaphysics with sufficient doggedness and determination. Instead, Heidegger's encounter with the speculative poetry of Hölderlin and Nietzsche's critique of metaphysics lead him toward the bold but problematic attempt to develop a new language of thought. Although this development is understandable given the radical and groundbreaking nature of Heidegger's inquiries, it also lead Heidegger to become increasingly less and less historical and less dialectical in his approach to the question of Being. As Heidegger's thought matured, it gradually moved away from different historical approaches to the *Seinsfrage* and increasingly attempted to forge its own path of thought, which repeatedly involved Heidegger in a search for a new language in which to express his questions and insights. While this tendency was understandable, it nevertheless led to what Gadamer calls Heidegger's "linguistic crisis" or "poverty" (*Sprachnot*).[21] In other words, as Heidegger increasingly became engrossed in his own questioning, he moved further away from the plurality of ways in which the question of Being was both directly and indirectly posed throughout the history of philosophy. As a result, his own philosophy found itself increasingly stammering toward a new language of thought. Although this difficulty was not without its own moments of brilliant illumination, Gadamer's own approach to understanding Heidegger shows that the history of philosophy itself was not so ill-equipped to illuminate Heidegger's concerns as Heidegger's own rhetoric suggested. Such impasses lead the later Heidegger increasingly into a willful reading of the history of philosophy—a reading as willful as Hegel's own grand attempts to bend the facts of philosophy's history to fit his own account of dialectic. One might even draw the conclusion from Gadamer's account that Heidegger's self-willed account of philosophy's development was increasingly ahistorical and even eschatological in its mood, a mood which lead him to shun a more dialectical approach to his questions. I think this conclusion follows from the fact that wherever Gadamer discusses Heidegger's relation to the philosophical influences that shaped the early Heidegger, he is almost always at pains to point out continuities between Heidegger and elements of this tradition, as well as the lost opportunities for exploring his own questions that Heidegger simply passed over. Gadamer claims that this is true not only for Heidegger's relation to Plato and Aristotle, but also true for his relationship to Augustine, Aquinas, Kant, Hegel, and Husserl as well.[22] Even when one acknowledges the groundbreaking nature of Heidegger's thought, which Gadamer repeatedly does, he still emphasizes Heidegger's missed opportunities and continuities with the philosophical tradition that formed him.

In my opinion, Gadamer turns to Plato for the beginning of a corrective of this growing Heideggerian alienation from the living history of his own thought. In Plato, Gadamer finds an incessantly dialectical thinker, who, unlike Heidegger, employs a more explicit dialectical mode of inquiry in his dialogues, which is much more suited to the many-sided questions of his metaphysical and practical concerns. In my view, what is most important about Plato for Gadamer is that Plato offers a dialectical ontology that places the issues of the Good, the true, the beautiful, and the one and the many in the forefront of its concerns. I think that Gadamer's most important insights are best understood when they are placed in this context of his work on Plato's dialectical account of the transcendentals. Gadamer claims that the themes of the Good, the true, the beautiful, unity, identity, difference, i.e., the transcendentals, are best approached "dialectically" through a thought-process that not only juxtaposes opposing viewpoints but "separates" and "combines" these viewpoints in ever-changing syntheses or interpretations. Gadamer understands Plato to do just this in the inexhaustible richness of his dialogues.

However, Gadamer finds in these dialogues more than just examples of dialectic. What gives the ever-changing divisions and combinations of themes in the Platonic corpus a unified meaning is an over-reaching questioning about the Good for human beings. Gadamer shares this concern with Plato. If we keep this in mind as we approach Gadamer's hermeneutics certain far-reaching conclusions regarding human understanding in general begin to suggest themselves. If we place Gadamer's insights into interpretation in this Socratic-Platonic context it can be said that both our agreements and our disagreements, which our various interpretations presuppose, are ultimately about the Good. As we inhabit various interpretations and work out our understanding of ourselves and the world in terms of the interrelationships between these interpretations, what we are working out is different historically determinate forms of the Good. This suggests why these debates are serious, high-staked, sometimes tragic confrontations, but it also suggests something positive about our finitude. Through our entanglement in various interpretations we not only experience our own limitations but we also realize concrete determinate forms of the Good. Our real prospects for the actual goods of a good life often come out of the conflict between interpretations.

By assigning central importance to the Good in his account of Plato's dialectical metaphysics, Gadamer is reading Plato as developing the Socratic beginnings of philosophy. Gadamer reads Plato as a Socratic who is concerned first and foremost with the many-sided question of how we should live.[23] The issue of self-knowledge is paramount here because only by recognizing who and what we are can we begin to answer the ethical question of what type of life we should live. This implies, on Gadamer's reading, that Plato does not gradually move away from the Socratic question concerning the good life as he becomes more and more interested in epistemological and metaphysical issues. On the contrary, he pursues epistemological and metaphysical issues primarily for the light they can shed on the Socratic question. Late dialogues like the *Philebus, Sophist,* and *Statesman* show this intimate intertwining of the "ontological" and the "practical" very clearly. Plato never gave up the basic conviction that all philosophical inquiry is ultimately about "the Good." As Socrates relates in the *Phaedo,* his interest in Anaxagoras's question about the role of the Good in the constitution of reality seemed justified to him because he could think of no question that was more important for humans to pursue. Even when Socrates expressed his disappointment with Anaxagoras's answer, he affirms the centrality of the question about the Good itself. Gadamer's work suggests that we keep the centrality of the Socratic question always in view, not only when we interpret Plato, but also especially when we reflect more generally on the nature of human thought as such. All human thought takes place within the horizon of this question concerning the good life. Socrates went around Athens questioning the received wisdom of his day precisely because he wanted to reawaken a sense for this question. Because we are human and not divine we must always deliberate about what to do and how to live. There is no knowledge available either in the arts (*technai*) or the sciences (*episteme*) that can substitute for this need to deliberate about the Good and give a justification of our choices both to ourselves and others. This is one key reason why in Plato the gods do not philosophize, only humans do. Although the gods' relation to the Good may be one of pure contemplation this can only remind us of how our relation to the Good is always one of protracted inquiry, marked by struggle. The gods may dwell in the full light of perfect knowledge, but we always contend in the half-light of limited understanding.

This fundamental fact points us back to the connection which Gadamer wishes to establish between Plato and hermeneutics. This task of seeking self-understanding with an eye to the Good and seeking to justify our choices of specific determinate goods involves us in interpretation. When we come to understand ourselves in certain ways and seek to justify that understanding and the actions which issue from it we inevitably enter into critical conversation with ourselves and others. This is the process of dialectic, which both Plato and Hegel make so much of. It's tempting to think that somehow, someday we will come to know ourselves and our situation so well that we could escape the need to enter this unending conversation or dialectic. Hegel dreamed of just such an overcoming and culmination of dialectic in his notion of absolute knowledge. Instead of working with the implications of his insight that all thought is dialectical, Hegel succumbed, in Gadamer's opinion, to the Cartesian temptation to think that the whole intelligible structure of reality can be made transparent to thought. Such a final, "absolute" truth is not available to human beings, especially about the issues of the Good, the true, the beautiful, and the one. Nevertheless, Hegel was right to think, according to Gadamer, that these realities exist in a web of intelligible relationships that we can explore dialectically. Gadamer claims in fact that Hegel actually first gleaned this insight from Plato's own dialectic.[24] Be that as it may, what the inextricable interrelatedness of these realities implies is that the multiplicity of interpretations, which is generated, in part, by this very complex interrelatedness itself, is not vicious or inherently irreconcilable. Although we can never achieve a final reconciliation of all viewpoints (a definitive account of "the whole" is not to be had), specific, determinate resolutions regarding some aspect of the whole can be had because these different interpretations are grounded in the same ultimate reality. Moreover, each interpretation is driven by an overarching common concern with the Good. Although Gadamer is very aware of the pain and disruption that the conflict of interpretations often causes, his emphasis on the interrelatedness of the web of Ideas, as well as his insistence on the ultimate practical horizon of human thought, i.e., our common concern for the Good, leads him to emphasize the prospects for human solidarity rather than human discord.

Solidarity and Difference

I think this is a key reason why Gadamer's thought is extremely important today. In an intellectual culture that increasingly emphasizes difference and disagreement, Gadamer reminds us that human solidarity is not only possible but essential for our life together. By asking about the ontological foundations of human understanding, Gadamer is probing into the bases of human agreement and disagreement. He wants to know how agreements are generated that enable us to act together for a common good, even though such agreements are never permanent and seem inevitably to fall apart. For Gadamer such agreements are not primarily "political," i.e., they are not necessarily expressions of the "will to power," as Nietzsche and his contemporary followers would have it.

Instead, Gadamer's thought implies that both the possibility of agreement and disagreement are rooted in our characteristic relationship to such Platonic issues as the Good, the true, the beautiful, unity, Being, and non-Being. To be human involves nothing less than deliberating about the Good, attuning ourselves to what is true, appreciating beauty, recognizing grounds of identity and difference, responding to what is and what is not. To refuse to think of these things is a deep refusal of our humanity as well as a refusal to recognize what Gadamer sees as the basis of human solidarity. In Gadamer's terms, solidarity is rekindled only by repeatedly opening questions about our relation to the Good, the true, the beautiful, etc., questions which look for new ways, in ever-changing historical circumstances, to act on our common human involvement in those issues. This process is reflected in the changing dramatic circumstances of the dialogues themselves and is also reflected in the goal to which the life of Plato's Academy was dedicated. What we have is a common need to repeatedly ask these questions, and asking such questions together leads to a common involvement in a life of inquiry. The dialogues seek to make this plain and their constant experimentation with different approaches to the same set of issues makes it clear that there is no definitive discursive account of these issues available to us. Each path of inquiry is relative to the characters involved and their level of insight and quality of life. The way Socrates speaks to Gorgias is very different from how he speaks to Callicles and it is still different from how he speaks to Lysis or for that matter from how he approaches Glaucon or Adeimantus. Even Plato's Academy promoted and tolerated considerable difference of opinion. The fact that Xenocrates, Speusippus, and Aristotle came from this school is testimony to the freedom of thought that was nurtured by Plato, a freedom which in all probability even included trenchant critiques of Plato himself.

Of course, the multiplicity of interpretations is infamous for its potential to generate strife. Gadamer has not lost sight of the fact that differences in theoretical commitments can and do present profound practical problems which threaten human solidarity. The point, however, is that solidarity can only be won by working through our disputes toward what underlies them. Only by moving toward these elemental issues can we discover the commonality that undergirds our often conflict-ridden life. Such a commonality can even go beyond a commonality of need to inquire into these issues; it can go beyond a shared involvement in inquiry and issue in historically mediated agreements about the issues that prompted the inquiry in the first place. Although such agreements are never permanent stopping points in the life of deliberation about the Good, they are nevertheless potentially powerful but provisional points of substantive agreement on which communities can base their decisions. However, we can only discover these temporary stopping points if we confront these conflicts openly, without the presumption that the conflicts themselves are irresolvable because each one represents an irrepressible quest for power that rests on nothing more than itself. It is a moral truism that power is empty and valueless apart from the ends it serves. However, by focusing on these ends we come face to face with the Platonic-Socratic concern for the Good itself and everything this involves. Such a realization does not stop the conversation between protagonists in the way that playing the trump card of "power" tends to do. Instead, discovering a common concern for the Good, even when one disagrees with one's conversation partner about where the Good lies, reanimates the conversation to seek a firmer basis for this common concern.

This common concern for the Good should not, however, be misunderstood as either agreement about the Good as such or agreement about a theoretical standard for deciding where the Good lies in a particular case between disputants. The transcendent character of the Good precludes a definitive theoretical account of the Good as such and it also precludes our more common tendency to want to explain conflict resolution in terms of a common standard shared between conflicting parties. Such a standard or principle is meant to function as a rule or yardstick, independent of the actual situation of the dispute. In reality, such standards or rules only emerge out of these contexts of dispute and their independent applicability to other contexts is often problematic for precisely this reason. Instead, Gadamer's emphasis on the Good might be called a regulative idea for the exercise of practical intelligence in that disputants can find a solution to their disagreement only if they both "look to the Good." What this means is not that they both "look at the Good" and discover definitive, timeless knowledge of its nature or a standard for adjudicating their differences, but that by striving to discover what the Good means for them in the particular circumstances they find themselves in they create the conditions for discovering the best solution for their case. Thus a common involvement or concern for the Good generates neither timeless knowledge of the Good nor an independent standard applicable to any future dispute, but rather by "looking to the Good" we create the situation in which a real solution to the dispute can emerge from the debate. Such solutions recommend themselves as "reasonable" not in the sense of applying a certain rule but in the sense that the parties involved have a shared sense of what is best for them in this particular case. For example, parents and their daughter might come to agree about the best high school for her, not by applying a rule to their daughter's case but by their common knowledge of the child's needs, abilities, and opportunities and a shared concern to figure out what is really best in this contingent tangle of possibilities. In this sense, Gadamer thinks that we can discover what the Good is in the concrete situation that parties share and this knowledge can serve as the basis for a fragile but real human solidarity. In short, if we "look to the Good" we can discover what is best to do here and now. Such a common inquiry into the Good transcends Kant's notion of the "good will," which pertains solely to the quality of the agent's intention. Gadamer would not dispute the need for such a "good will," but "looking to the Good" moves us beyond the character of certain inner states of the agents involved by requiring all of them to seek agreement in the object or common goal of action. Although such solidarity in goals is temporary and relative to the "here and now" it is nevertheless real and necessary for human life together. "Looking to the good" is a regulative ideal that can lead to substantive bases for human action.

But Gadamer has often been taken to task for his concern with human solidarity. When Gadamer speaks of the grounds of solidarity his critics often respond that Gadamer has overlooked how it is that agreement between people, which is necessary for solidarity, inevitably suppresses the differences between them. Thus it is often heard that Gadamer's hermeneutics is inherently repressive because in seeking solidarity or agreement it rides roughshod over the ontologically distinct identity of others and undermines unique individualities because of its emphasis on agreement and on sameness between individuals. In short, it is said that Gadamer fails to recognize sufficiently the importance and value of "difference" and "otherness." Thus, for example, Robert Bernasconi writes that "Gadamer tends to enclose otherness in the circle of self-recognition, according to a gesture that he himself acknowledges owes its inspiration to Hegel. Only rarely is otherness allowed to remain in its otherness."[25] James Risser raises the critical point that "repression enters the system in the form of exclusion and exclusion is precisely what occurs when one seeks unity rather than difference. The community sought must be a "community of difference."[26] And John Caputo warns us with regard to Gadamer's insistence that the pursuit of truth is a necessary condition of fruitful interpretation that "deep truths are purchased by deep violence, by excluding what contaminated the system of truth, by repressing what disturbs its unity, by swatting away those who trouble the guardians of truth with bothersome questions. It has an idea that the tradition maintains itself in no small part by reason of its success in erasing the dangerous memory of those who have questioned it."[27] These criticisms are typical of what is often voiced against Gadamer. He is suspected of a reactionary politics, which is supposedly based on his no less reactionary ontology. The fact that this criticism comes from philosophers knowledgeable of Gadamer and to varying degrees sympathetic with his program has made this criticism into something approaching a new orthodoxy in some quarters. For these reasons it's important to confront this criticism head on.

There are, as I see it, two sides to this critique, an ontological and political side, which are by no means unrelated. As I have already suggested, the alleged political consequences of Gadamer's thought are grounded in his supposedly suspect ontological commitment. Because Gadamer's ontological assumptions are really the primary focus of this book, let me deal here with the political aspects of the criticism.

Everyone in this debate agrees that Gadamer's overtly political statements show him to be a strong advocate of parliamentary democracy. Such a democracy must constantly strive to make room for new and different voices, all of which have a vital stake in the future direction of society. Gadamer is well aware of this need. Gadamer is, however, criticized for being insufficiently cognizant of the way that historical democracies have often silenced voices of protest by refusing to do such things as validating the various "languages of protest." Such a "language" might, for example, be the natural language of an ethnic group like the French of the Quebecoix, or it might be the critical "language" of an ethical position like the languages of various feminisms, for example. What is common to such "languages" is that they have a way of putting the issues that divide a political community in a certain light, a light which is more than a disinterested description of the issues at stake. Such "languages" also simultaneously point to responses to the issues, responses that are usually deeply threatening to the status quo. By refusing to let that light in, by suppressing various modes of discourse in the name of an overriding "agreement," "unity," or "solidarity," such voices have been silenced and repressed.

I would not deny that such cultural politics have been and continue to be part of our political reality. But it also seems to me that it is wrong to shackle Gadamer with a reactionary political position simply because he stresses the fact that some significant level of "agreement" is necessary to political community. Of course, political community does not require agreement on all things—it allows room for "difference"—but community as such cannot exist without some significant agreement about basic and important issues. We need not attempt to elaborate what these issues should be (we might even doubt that such agreement must be in terms of theory rather than agreements about how to act) in order to see that the notion of a "community of difference" is a deeply ambiguous term. If it is a community of "mere" difference it would be no community at all. On the other hand, if a community of "mere" difference is a caricature of what such critics of Gadamer have in mind, then presumably the door is open to consider how both "difference" and "sameness" are necessary for a viable political community. To the extent that certain political factions have used the notion of solidarity as part of a repressive rhetoric they have been able to do so only because a real but limited solidarity is a genuine element in any real political community. In attacking the misuse of such appeals to solidarity—or pseudosolidarity—it's important not to lose sight of the fact that genuine solidarity is an indispensable but elusive goal of all communities that strive to attain a genuinely common good.

I think, however, that there is more behind this critique of Gadamer than a lack of appreciation for the need of a limited solidarity in human communities. In my opinion, there is a "utopian" element in these critiques that should be considered. To some extent, these critiques can be considered "utopian" in the best sense, i.e., the philosophical sense in which Plato offers a utopian critique of society in the *Republic.* The purpose of such a utopian program is not to give a detailed program of social change, but rather to provoke us to a detailed program of thought.[28] In this sense, the fact that these critics put the issue of "difference" before us performs a useful and essential service. On the other hand, however, to the extent that the valorization of difference is "utopian" in a negative sense, a sense that seems to suggest that political communities of pure difference are actually possible and desirable, such critiques are naive and, if not politically dangerous, at least politically ineffectual and irresponsible. I say this for the very basic reason that real human interaction, real intersubjectivity, either in "personal" relationships or in "political" relationships always involve both agreement *and* disagreement, both identity *and* difference. The joy and pain of human interaction is rooted in both the discovery of unsuspected "agreement" or "identity" as well as the painful necessity that we change who we are. Such changes sometimes involve irrevocable losses but they also may form new bonds of solidarity. Real politics, of course, is about just what identities to preserve and cultivate and what "agreements" and prior commitments, spoken and unspoken, must be put to rest or at least be allowed to die. That this process is fraught with pain is doubtlessly true. Something in the individual is always lost or at best suppressed when we resolve to act for the greater good, but it should also be obvious that this process offers new gains for individuals as well as new positive opportunities for any society of "loss" and "gain." Gadamer reminds us that we can never extract ourselves from this constant movement between "agreement" and "disagreement," between "identity" and "difference." Gadamer's critics seem to forget that the individual is constituted as a "dialogue," i.e., that its identity is inextricably tied to a process of give and take, of loss and gain from other persons. The real question is not one of some kind of abstract absolute autonomy for individuals, but of which sacrifices we should make for which gains of the greater good. Gadamer is always aware of this dialectic of individuality, identity, and difference. It is fundamental to Gadamer's limited reflections on politics and it is even more fundamental to his ontological concerns. If we look at this political criticism of Gadamer in light of his ontology the criticism appears highly ironic. Gadamer offers nothing less than an elaborate ontology of *both* identity *and* difference, an ontology that argues for the inherent openness of human experience, as well as the possibility of provisional agreements for shared practical ends.

Gadamer's "Foundationalism"

For some critics, however, it is precisely the fact that Gadamer tries to ground his ethical and political concerns in an ontology that raises basic problems for them. What these critics so object to is that Gadamer offers a version of what has come to be called "foundationalism."[29] For these critics, foundationalism is simply defunct and ought not to be resurrected in any guise.

"Foundationalism" is a very general term for a family of theories all of which claim that human knowledge or understanding rests on some common "foundations" or identifiable structural features, be they "epistemological," "metaphysical," or "ontological." So general, in fact, has the use of this term become that it is not clear that it refers to the same thing in different writers. Some, like Richard Rorty, have argued that the purpose of this search for the common foundations of human understanding is to block skepticism once and for all. Thus, on Rorty's epistemological model of foundationalism the foundationalist is searching for "an overarching permanent neutral matrix"[30] for all human knowing in terms of which all conflicts can be definitively adjudicated. On this model Gadamer is an antifoundationalist, because he does not think that there is any such "overarching permanent neutral matrix" that is sufficient to sort out our differences in a way that would satisfy all reasonable people. For Gadamer all inquiry is historically mediated and thus what we understand truly and how we understand it changes as the historical horizon of inquiry shifts. Doubtlessly these historical shifts in how we understand ourselves and our world cause us innumerable problems which make the dream of a method for adjudicating conflict eminently understandable. Nevertheless, Gadamer insists that such a quest is vain; to pursue it presupposes that a basic fact about human life—our historicity—can be ignored or side-stepped. Gadamer insists that our relation to time is ignored only at the cost of a great distortion in our self-understanding. Nevertheless Gadamer is still interested in the "foundations" of human understanding. Gadamer still thinks it is meaningful to inquire into the basis of human agreement and disagreement but not in order to discover "an overarching, permanent, neutral matrix" that would block skepticism, but in order to show that historicity is not inherently vicious to the human quest for truth and solidarity.

But as I have already argued, Gadamer is very interested in the question of truth and maintains the thesis that historicity is compatible in principle with truth, but as we have also already pointed out, Gadamer is not really interested in "blocking the skeptic." The skeptic can, in fact, almost always raise doubts about any determinate truth-claim. Nevertheless, the question is whether, in light of our historicity, we must concede that the skeptic is right. Gadamer wishes to show that no such concession is necessary. Although the skeptic cannot be definitively refuted on her own terms and thus the Cartesian program of discovering indubitable knowledge is wrongheaded and destined to failure, it does not follow that skepticism has won the day. The appearance of victory for the skeptic is generated only if one accepts the skeptic's identification of truth with certainty. But no such identity need be accepted. Gadamer sets out to examine the foundations of human knowledge in light of our historicity to show that although our historicity may indeed preclude certainty in almost all areas of human thought, it does not preclude truth. If this strategy is valid, Gadamer's hermeneutics does not block skepticism as much as it renders its objections moot because it disagrees with its fundamental assumptions about truth. In this regard, Gadamer is indeed interested in the "foundations" of human thought but he does not approach this issue with the same presuppositions that have informed much of modern epistemology.

It would also be a mistake, however, to see Gadamer as a "metaphysical" foundationalist, i.e., as a thinker who seeks the first principles of all reality in the hopes of then somehow "deducing" the essential structural features of the world from this common origin. One of Gadamer's arguments against this possibility—a possibility we see in a variety of forms in thinkers like Spinoza, Leibniz, Wolff, Hegel, Fichte, and even Husserl (at least as a regulative ideal)—is the straightforward empirical one that all such attempts have simply failed to capture the multitextured, empirical variety of the world. Reality is simply so rich, so complex, and so varied that it slips through the fingers of those who have the audacity to attempt such a conceptual containment. This kind of hubris shows itself in both the claim to have discovered the "first principles" which are sufficient for deriving the essential structural components of reality and in the claim to dialectical completeness. Gadamer rejects the need for such *ultimate* grounding or the presumption of exhaustive analysis.[31] Reality may be without a final justification and it is certainly rich enough to defy complete description even at the formal level of the structural features of all cognition. Gadamer insists that our conceptually mediated understanding is always "finite." The finitude of human understanding is a recurrent Gadamerian theme to which we will turn in upcoming chapters, but for now it suffices to say that Gadamer's claim that our understanding is "finite" means at least a denial of the possibility of deduction from first principles or dialectical completeness. When we understand, we understand from the middle of things, *in media res* as it were. The full height, depth, and breadth of Being is not available to us. However, the search for the foundations of understanding should not be misconstrued as a presumption to find a god's-eye view of things. Talk of "foundations" simply exhorts us to look as far down as we can see and to explore the implications of what we can see. This does not imply that Gadamer denies the value of metaphysics as such. He rejects claims to deduction from first principles and dialectical completeness but not the attempt to understand our place in reality in the most general and illuminating terms possible. Truth can still be found in metaphysics even if such truths are not "first truths" or final truths.

What we see, according to Gadamer, when we look into the order of things is not some first principle from which the essential structure of reality can be deduced but something like the Platonic Ideas and, ultimately, at bottom, i.e., the point beyond which we cannot see, is the concern for the Good. It is concern for the Good and the question of how to live or what Heidegger called "care" that forms, for Gadamer, the foundation of our attempts to know. All attempts to know the world are motivated at bottom by this ultimate ethical concern of how to live or, in other words, to discover the Good. Such a concern does not culminate in a clear and distinct idea but it is an ideal which forms the constant and final framework for our thought. As an ideal, it is neither empty nor intuitively transparent. Rather, knowledge of the Good is only gained indirectly or perspectivally in and through our attempts to understand this or that aspect of our situation. Knowledge of the Good is given only in and with our interpretive efforts. Exactly how it is given along with our hermeneutical awareness of ourselves will occupy us later but it's important to see why Gadamer is sometimes seen as a foundationalist and at other times as an antifoundationalist. In that the Good is the final ontological "foundation" for human thinking according to Gadamer it would seem that Gadamer is indeed a foundationalist of a certain sort. But inasmuch as his foundationalism rests on the transcendental ideal of the Good, his foundationalism offers neither indubitable starting points for reflection, nor the source of a dialectically complete account of reality, nor does it offer a neutral matrix for conflict resolution. Consequently, he is hardly a foundationalist in the usual sense at all.

Gadamer's insight into the Good also leads him to other criticisms of the assumptions shared by both epistemological and metaphysical foundationalism. Both of these philosophical programs assume that the knowing subject can so control the conditions of understanding that it can view reality "absolutely," to borrow Bernard Williams apt phrase.[32] What an "absolute" grasp of reality entails is a view of reality untouched by the historically mediated concerns of the knowers. It is simply a timeless view of reality, in no way relative to the historical context of the knower's situation and as such "disinterested" or free from the human needs and concerns which animate the inquirer's interest in the subject matter. Gadamer doubts that a single instance of such absolute knowledge can be found in either the human or natural sciences, but he also objects more fundamentally to the ideal of an absolute, ahistorical, disinterested knowing because affirmation of such an ideal distorts the *positive* role that history and human interest play in understanding. For Gadamer it is only through our historically mediated interests or "prejudices" or prejudgments (*Vor-urteile*), as he calls them, that reality first becomes intelligible in a determinate way. Reality discloses itself to us in the first place only because we are "needy," "interested" beings who pose specific, focused questions, which can then receive answers. These answers are relative to these "interested" questions, which we pose out of a variety of needs. This is *not* to say that the reality we know is at base an illusion, fabricated by projecting our needs unto the world and then simply receiving back from the world a refracted image of these same needs. On the contrary, what we know, according to Gadamer, is reality itself, but how we came to know it is not a process of creating and fabricating our own world but a "dialogue" with reality in which reality always discloses itself to us "finitely" or "perspectivally," relative to the "interested" questions we pose. Such questions are always "interested" precisely because we can never avoid the question of the Good. To say that we always approach reality through our historically mediated "prejudices" is another way of saying that we are always already involved with historically mediated involvements in the Good. It is precisely in our historically conditioned prejudices that many determinate forms of the Good (and its surrogates) show themselves to human beings. This is as true in the natural sciences as it is in the human sciences.

For example, what we are currently learning about the AIDS virus is as animated by its human urgency as it is conditioned by the specific questions being asked about viruses and their effect on the immune system at this point in the history of the disciplines involved. What we learn is both true of reality and "finite" in that it is limited to the questions asked, which are by no means exhaustive of everything that could be asked. In this situation, we are dealing both with an "interpretation," i.e., an inherently incomplete account of an inherently rich set of phenomena, *and* we are concerned with questions of truth. Of course, these questions are historically conditioned by both the social factors surrounding the AIDS crisis and the state of viral and immunological research at this time, but this is still a *rational* and *critical* process of inquiry. Gadamer would insist that such historicity does not make it less rational than it otherwise might be, but actually gives a point to what it means to be rational. Thus, for Gadamer, the fact that we are historical beings does not imply that we are without critical resources in our historically mediated dialogue with reality, as some like Habermas have at one time accused Gadamer.[33] But more fundamentally it is Gadamer's point that these very critical capacities themselves are not only historically conditioned but they are also grounded in our ultimate concern for the question of how we should live.

Gadamer's "Essentialism"

It's at this juncture in Gadamer's thought that some critics want to pin Gadamer with a more specific contradiction. The charge is that talk of the historically conditioned character of all understanding precludes any talk of *universal* foundations of understanding. The only way we could talk of universal foundations of understanding, according to these critics, is if we could somehow step outside or rise above history itself and grasp what is common to all understanding in all times. The fact that we cannot rise above history, particularly the history of future generations, which in principle we have no way of knowing, supposedly shows that any universalism whatsoever is impossible.

Thus Joseph Margolis and, more recently, John Caputo have taken Gadamer to task for being a "closet essentialist," as someone who has lost his will to carry through his own best insights into the historicity and linguisticality of human thought.[34] Despite the presence of what Caputo calls "much brave talk" about the fluidity of the historical and linguistic contexts that govern all human thought, Caputo insists that Gadamer has "lost his nerve" by virtue of the fact that he, Gadamer, repeatedly points to a "deep truth" behind our many different interpretations of any phenomenon. This "deep truth" accounts for the overlapping but not identical meaning often found in our different points of view on some reality. Such a "deep truth" enables us to talk with plausibility of a continuity of meaning or what Gadamer calls a *Richtungssinn* or direction of meaning that can evolve and change over time without fracturing into a myriad of mutually exclusive positions whose difference is beyond all reconciliation.

While Caputo and Margolis assume that any talk of "essences" and historicity is incompatible, their criticism makes assumptions that are highly questionable in my opinion. Generally speaking, I think these critics fail to see that the implications of historicity are not self-evident. To begin with, these critics ignore self-referential problems in their own position. To say that *all* understanding is historical and that *all* human understanding is subject to conditions that change historically, as these critics themselves insist, is itself a universal claim that is not meaningless and can certainly be understood even though this too is a historically mediated claim. We are warranted in making such self-referential statements and nothing about our historicity prevents us from doing so despite the fact that such statements make a universal claim. It seems to me that these critics do not take this ability seriously enough in part because they seem captive to their own metaphors. Talk of "rising above" history or "stepping outside" our historically mediated understanding in order to grasp its constant conditions does not exhaust the possibilities. It is possible that from "within" history universal features of human understanding can be grasped. In fact we do this all the time. We are capable of grasping general trends in history. Of course, these critics are right that no one can see the future and thus any theory is subject to possible refutation in light of discoveries in an unknown future. But this is just fallibilism and simply one sign of the finitude of our thought. The fact that we might be wrong is a fact that accompanies all claims to understanding. Nevertheless, the fact that we *might* be wrong is never sufficient to show that we *cannot* be right. Awareness of history can indeed check our tendency to superficial generalizations—as indeed it should—but awareness of history does not preclude a grasp of certain general and universal features of our situation, even though our awareness of history will introduce an appropriate consciousness of fallibility when making such claims. Although history does deny us triumphalistic claims to certainty in such matters, it's important to remember that certainty is not necessary for truth. To make this mistake is not only to fall victim to the Cartesianism such critics oppose, it is also to fall victim to a version of the genetic fallacy. The fact that conditions seemingly necessary to the discovery of a truth were contingent and historically relative in no way implies that the truth discovered under these conditions cannot be valid for all time. Doubtlessly Pythagoras was a child of his time, but this in no way undercuts the universal truth of the Pythagorean theorem. History no sooner precludes the possibility of transhistorical truth than having a body with a brain precludes a grasp of nonphysical realities, like numbers. I think it is as naive to say that having a body means we cannot grasp nonphysical realities as it is to maintain that being historical means that nothing transhistorical is accessible to us. What historicity does preclude is dogmatic certainty in our truth-claims, but it does not preclude truth as such. Just as our bodies constitute a deep condition of our understanding, so history is also a deep condition of understanding in which understanding somehow occurs, even when we cannot explain exactly how it occurs. The challenge is not to use history as an excuse for avoiding the hard work of explaining just what it means to say that history "conditions" our understanding. Gadamer's project can be described from one point of view as the sustained attempt to think the condition of history more profoundly and adequately, an attempt that strives to be consistent with the fact that we know that we are capable of truth in history. As such, it refuses to obfuscate something as essential to our condition as the ability to grasp truths whose validity stretches beyond our own time.

Caputo and Margolis are right, however, to point out that historicity implies a rejection of absolute truth-claims. They are also right in pointing out that Gadamer affirms the eidetic identity over time of universals or "essences," like "justice" or "beauty." Such an identity is supposedly an identity that is recognized with a self-evident or a priori certainty or in an ahistorical intuition which presents itself with a timeless, presuppositionless self-evidence, much like what Husserl called "apodicticity." Thus the supposed contradiction in Gadamer's position. Although such a rendering of Gadamer's position is right to point out that Gadamer affirms both the historicity of our understanding and the identity over time of certain universals, it goes astray, in my opinion, in thinking that our grasp of that identity is given in a timeless intuition. Gadamer's affirmation of the identity of certain universals cannot be understood as an achievement of a timeless intellect. Rather, identity can only be affirmed when it is demonstrated in concrete circumstances in historically mediated terms that the questioners of such an identity actually share. There is nothing dogmatic in this general assertion of the identity of universals over time because Gadamer would insist that the de facto identity be demonstrated in time. Such an identity is never given once and for all but can only be maintained when and insofar as it can be shown to obtain. In short, it is a question of interpretation and what can be convincingly demonstrated in real acts of interpretation. The fact that identical elements may be shown to exist in different accounts of a phenomenon like "beauty" makes the claim to an underlying identity plausible and defensible but it does not mean that such claims are "apodictic." One must be careful not to assume that by demonstrating such a limited identity, one has demonstrated the identity of beauty as such once and for all. No certainty or infallible necessity is being attributed to these identity claims. One cannot know a priori that history will not confront us with different accounts of beauty that are so fundamentally at odds with each other that all talk of one and the same beauty would be impossible. Historicity does indeed prevent us from ruling out any such occurrences and from making dogmatic judgments of any sort, but it does not prevent us from pointing out identities whenever and wherever we find them to be empirically or "hermeneutically" available. Gadamer's essentialism is compatible with his emphasis on history and his own thought is careful not to presume a self-certain cognizance of such essences. From an awareness of our own involvement in history, the affirmation of the existence of such essences cannot be dogmatically extended into an unknown future, but it can be provisionally affirmed if it stems from an insight into the things themselves, as far as we can know them.

Such misunderstandings of Gadamer arise not because Gadamer is duplicitous about his essentialism. Gadamer has never been "in the closet" about his Platonic and Husserlian roots. Many of Gadamer's writings acknowledge these sources and some writings even reveal how he understands this Platonic and phenomenological inheritance. But if a misunderstanding has arisen about Gadamer's essentialism, it is due, in my opinion, to insufficient attention to what Gadamer means by "Platonism" or "essentialism." Gadamer's critics jump to conclusions about his supposed inconsistencies because they presume that Gadamer's essentialism could not possibly be compatible with his emphasis on historicity. Thus we have all the more reason for examining the "Platonic" nature of Gadamer's hermeneutics.

In talking about the phenomena which provide the focus of any interpretation Gadamer uses the term *die Sachen* to denote these realities. *Die Sachen* are related to the Latin legal terms "causa" or "case" as well as the Greek term "*ta pragmata*," or things that concern us.[35] In German, *die Sache* is the thing or subject matter that forms the intentional focus of our efforts to understand. In using this term, Gadamer wishes us to keep these connotations always in mind. Moreover, Gadamer is well aware that by using the term "*die Sache*" he is associating his hermeneutics with Husserl's phenomenology. *Die Sachen* are "*die Sachen selbst*" that Husserl called a generation of phenomenologists to attend to before all theory or the claims of common sense. This places Gadamer's hermeneutics in close proximity to the phenomenological tradition with its insistence that the things themselves, which thought attends to, are noetic or essential realities. Gadamer, in fact, explicitly acknowledges this connection. *Die Sachen* of interpretation pertain to the intelligible structure of reality, which is often found in the common eidetic components that unite temporally and spatially distinct particulars in common species and genera. In Husserl's terms, these things are "essences" (*Wesen*) and in Plato's terms they are called "Ideas."

However, unlike some of Plato's texts and unlike the earlier, more conventionally Platonic Husserl of the *Logical Investigations* and *Ideas*, Gadamer sees these essences as subject to "temporal constitutions."[36] Without entering into the technicalities of Husserl's evolving notion of intentionality or the intricacies of Plato's various accounts of the Ideas we can say that Gadamer's appeal to "essences" or "eidetic realities" does not entail a conception of these realities as timeless forms existing apart from the temporal world of change and becoming. Instead, these intelligible structures of reality cannot be known outside of their relation to time. In my opinion, Gadamer understands this to mean that these intelligible realities are what they are in themselves but we only can see changing historical aspects of them. They are nothing less than the sum of their many, varied changing aspects. I think we can only understand Gadamer's claim that when we understand we always understand the *same* realities, but we only understand these *same* things differently at different temporal points[37] if we keep this fundamental fact about our temporal access to these things always in mind. Otherwise Gadamer's claim that interpretation constantly confronts us with *different* understandings or perspectives of the *same* phenomena remains unintelligible and incoherent. We understand the same things in different ways at various junctures in history because these same things remain the same despite the fact that their entanglement in time allows us to see only varying perspectives on them and never the "whole" thing, all at once, once and for all. Without imputing a certain "ontological perspectivism" to Gadamer, his claim that whenever we approach a text from the past "it is enough to say that we understand in a *different* way, *if we understand at all*" (*TM,* 29) threatens to undermine the identity of the text and its subject matter. But in light of the fact that Gadamer affirms these identities as well as the real differences in different historically and linguistically mediated interpretation, "ontological perspectism" is a necessary assumption to understanding Gadamer's claims consistently.

Gadamer makes this crucial point by using an example from Husserl's theory of perception. The perceptual object in itself is, according to Husserl, "nothing but the continuity with which the various perceptual perspectives [*Abschattungen*] on objects shade into one another. . . . In a way similar to perception we can speak of the 'linguistic shadings' that the world undergoes in a different language-worlds" (*TM,* 448). Thus, for Gadamer, history presents us with different "shadings" (*Abschattungen*) of these ideal realities, it continually shows different sides or a different face of one and the same underlying reality. For Gadamer, these realities do not change in themselves. In this respect these noetic realities are like Platonic Ideas. But our grasp of them changes as history gives us access to some different, highly variegated side of them. These realities are what they are apart from our apprehension of them but their "look" varies, their appearances in time are widely varied. Nevertheless a limited, finite grasp of them is possible through interpretation even though that interpretation can never claim to be timeless, eternal, definitive, or exhaustive. "Knowing occurs as the self-presentation of the thing [*Sache*] which is known. Such self-presentation is a process full of movement. The aspects of the existent thing, the views which it offers of itself, shift and at the same time the points of view or opinions which the human soul develops also shift in that they refer to the thing in different respects" (PUD, 146). Both the highly variegated nature of these appearances as well as our changing temporal points of acccss make an exhaustive and timeless account impossible.

Gadamer's emphasis on "*die Sache*" as the object of interpretation not only affiliates his hermeneutics with Husserl's phenomenology but also with Hegel's dialectic. Gadamer's claim that "knowing occurs as the *self-presentation* of the thing" (PUD, 146) is very much indebted to Hegel. In the *Phenomenology*, Hegel claims to trace the path that human thought necessarily traverses of its own accord. The *Phenomenology* is Hegel's account of what Gadamer has labeled as the "self-unfolding thought"[38] of spirit. It is by looking to this "self-presentation of the thing [*die Sache*]" or the "self-unfolding thought" that Hegel develops his dialectic of *Aufhebungen* or *sublations*. Hegel's dialectic claims that his work is not the arbitrary construct of a philosophical system-builder but an accurate and fruitful tracing of the way things unfold themselves in rational thought. The fact that for Hegel this self-unfolding thought implicates both the things of reason and reason itself in history is a consequence that he embraces. This conclusion also finds a strong echo in Gadamer. Thought is temporal and historical because the objects of thought, the things themselves, are temporal and historical. This does not mean that the things themselves have no identity of their own. It implies instead that their identity develops over time. Time is the medium in which the identities of the things of thought are established and worked out.

In this fundamental claim about the necessity of incorporating temporality into ontology Gadamer and Hegel are in agreement. It also obviously affiliates Gadamer with Heidegger. Rather than develop this connection here, however, we will have occasion to return to the themes of historicity and ontology in the last two chapters. For now I want to focus on a point that is not sufficiently appreciated in my opinion by many philosophers writing on interpretation today. Gadamer's emphasis on the noetic nature of *die Sachen* of interpretation sets Gadamer's hermeneutics apart from theories of interpretation like deconstruction that see the object of interpretation as language itself or "the text." By contrast it might be said that Gadamer sees *die Sachen* as "the path and goal of understanding" (*TM*, 180). Far from exalting textuality as the medium of interpretation, this emphasis on the things themselves makes texts secondary to that which they are about.

Die Sachen can be said to be the "path" of understanding in that it is these phenomena that are the subject of our interpretive debates. Interpretation should not be about texts-in-themselves, i.e., texts abstracted from what they say. Rather it is precisely *what* they say, their subject matters, that interest us and form the focus of our debates. We concern ourselves with the linguistic formalities of the text only as a means to *die Sache*. This is not to suggest that textuality is mere linguistic "form" to the pure ideal "content" of *die Sache*. Gadamer is clear about the intersubjective *Sprachlichkeit* or "linguisticality" of *die Sache* and the untenability of any categorical form-content distinction.[39] Nevertheless, texts can be said to "mediate" a subject matter that is extratextual and of deeper significance to us than the formal structures of the texts. If the subject matter had no transtextual identity it would not be possible to interpret at all; we could neither compare our own experience of the phenomena with what the text says, and thus win a purchase on it, nor could we compare two or more texts that all speak of the *same* things.

The irreducibility of thing to word does not, however, imply that we ever have a "pure" nonlinguistically mediated vision of things. For Gadamer there is a constant movement between intuition or nonlinguistic vision and our discursive, linguistically mediated articulation of that vision. Such vision is neither pure in the sense that it is never influenced by language and history, nor is it simply a product of these factors. Similarly, linguistically mediated understanding rests on this vision, not in the sense that it simply mirrors what it sees by ways of conventional signs, which we call language, but in the sense that it looks to that vision and to the language in which that vision finds expression, and tries to adjust its language to what it sees. This can only happen, according to Gadamer, if language is both somehow "akin" to the ideality the mind grasps and somehow different as well. We must be able to account for both the possibility of "agreement" between word and *Sache*, language and intelligible reality, as well as the possibility of distortion by language. Gadamer's hermeneutical account of language and reality is meant to do just this. But these are matters that we will take up in subsequent chapters. For now it is important to emphasize that Gadamer is an "essentialist" of a nonconventional sort in that he insists that real essences are not to be found outside of language but in language. Nevertheless such essences are not mere language. Hermeneutics, for Gadamer, is not a nominalist enterprise. Despite the emphasis on the *Sprachlichkeit der Sachen selbst*, these things have an ideality that is not reducible to words. Consistent with his Platonist roots, Gadamer remains a metaphysical realist.

Gadamer finds this realist commitment necessary in order to give a robust account of truth. The things themselves must not be reducible to language if we are to be able to say why some accounts are more "true" than others. This especially is true if "true" means something more like the way things actually are and not something merely "consistent," "warranted," or "useful in the way of belief." We can easily imagine beliefs that are "useful" in significant ways, but untrue. Much propaganda fits this bill all too nicely, and even much scientific hypothesis that is recognized as *mere* hypothesis by responsible researchers can nevertheless be highly "useful in the way of belief." Nevertheless, its usefulness is heuristic rather than probative. We can also easily imagine beliefs that are warranted in certain epistemic contexts but flatly false. Surely the belief that the earth was created sometime in the last ten thousand years was, at one time, just such a belief that we now know is false. Even consistent beliefs, beliefs that are internally consistent with themselves and with many other beliefs we have, can be false. Self-deception, for example, is all too often consistent or coherent in this way, as are many false interpretations. "Truth" demands, despite all recent attempts to deflate this concept, that we can somehow measure our beliefs and language about ourselves, the natural world, texts, artworks, etc., against a reality that is not a simple construct of these beliefs or our language. If we could not perform such tasks no valid interpretation at all would be possible; we would be caught in the chains of our own beliefs or language, the straitjacket of pure textuality. Gadamer insists that despite the fact we will always articulate our understanding of these same *Sachen* in terms of some linguistic structures and never as unmediated intuitions in "pure" ideal realities, that these *Sachen* have their own ideal reality, which our language can capture in better or worse ways. For Gadamer the connection between *Sache* and word, although extremely intimate, never collapses the distinction between them. In every *Sache* there is an element of ideality never wholly amenable to a given language, but present nevertheless in various linguistic shadings or perspectives which makes it impossible to reduce *die Sache* to some linguistic account of it. Linguistic mediation is not the same thing as linguistic construction.

Gadamer's defense of the "real" character of essences, coupled with his "realist" defense of truth, enables us to further explain the sense in which Gadamer insists that *die Sachen* of any text are the "goal" of understanding. As I have already intimated the things themselves are the goal of understanding in that they are for us the ultimate touchstone of truth. When we come to an understanding with each other we do so in terms of the truth-claims of the texts, even when the understanding we arrive at involves an understanding about how we disagree with either the text and/or each other regarding these truth-claims. Such an understanding is an understanding made possible by a focus on the truth of things, the issues about which we disagree or agree in the name of truth. Ultimately we want to learn something about *die Sache* under consideration, something about ourselves, who we are and how we should live. This means that we take the text's claim to truth seriously (but not uncritically) and we seek to test it against itself, against our prejudices and against other texts, any one of which may come up short. We can claim to understand a text only when we are in a position to assess its truth. Even when we disagree with its truth-claims we cannot be said to understand a text until we can claim to understand what it is about (*die Sache des Textes*) and give an account of where in our judgment it is true or false. This means that we must always start by seeking agreement with the text, i.e., by operating on a principle of charity which assumes that the text is correct until it shows itself to be wrong. In operating with this principle it is *die Sache* and its truth which lead us and which finally provide the *telos* we seek to reach. When we reach agreement at all in our interpretive disputes we reach it in terms of these subject matters, i.e., in terms of a judgment about its truth, even if that judgment is negative. For example, we might study Kant's work because of our interest in "reason" and "duty"; these are, among other things, *die Sachen* of Kant's works. Our preliminary understanding of these *Sachen* serve as a "path" of understanding in that it is our concern with an understanding of these phenomena which guide us into Kant's work and they serve as the ultimate "goal" of our critical inquiries in that we always interpret with an eye to the truth of Kant's claims about these matters. Even when we disagree with Kant and see his texts as advocating positions we cannot defend we understand him vis-à-vis our grasp of these *Sachen.*

Moreover, it can be said from a Gadamerian viewpoint that the things themselves are the "goal" of understanding in that it is these *Sachen* that we ultimately *care* about. It is these *Sachen* that animate our *interests* and form the historically evolving substance of our lives. Our keen interest in *die Sache* stems from the fact that *die Sachen* of a text always pertain to human possibilities. We are defined, at least in part, by how we think, speak, and act in regard to phenomena (*Sachen*) like reason, sexuality, morality, faith, etc. In fact, a key feature of what constitutes our essential difference from other lifeforms is precisely the fact that we understand ourselves in terms of such *Sachen.* Because we are intimately identified with the various issues that the human sciences study and because there are both logical constraints on actualizing all these possibilities as well as very real practical constraints, we cannot help but feel "interested," "concerned," "engaged" by these phenomena. We have an "ontological stake" in these issues; apart from them we have no other way to define ourselves as human beings. *Die Sachen* are "*was uns angeht*"—they are "our business," they are "what we are about," they pertain to who we *are*—we cannot help but be concerned about them. Thus they constitute the very goal of understanding itself. We want to get at the truth of these matters because only with the truth can we pursue our overarching goal of a good life. Nothing less is at stake in these disputes than the Good itself.

Both Gadamer's emphasis on the transhistorical identity of *die Sachen* of interpretation and his insistence that our own self-questioning regarding how we should live is ultimately behind our concern with *die Sachen* of the human sciences point us back to his "Platonism." But Gadamer's Platonism is hardly conventional. The incorporation of historicity and linguisticality into Gadamer's "essentialism" is sufficient to make it plain that Gadamer's Platonism stems from a unique and controversial reading of Plato. It is to a more detailed and in-depth consideration of Gadamer's Plato interpretation that we now turn. In doing so we hope to show just how Gadamer hopes to combine both a certain "essentialism" with an awareness of the "linguistic," "historical," and "ethical" horizon of human understanding.

2

Gadamer's Dialectical Platonism

Platonism, Conventional and Unconventional

We have seen that Gadamer has strong, identifiable Platonic roots, but by now it should be clear that his Platonism is anything but the conventional, textbook variety. Gadamer explicitly distances himself from what he calls "the vulgar concept of Platonism," which he "holds without qualification to be a transformation of Plato's actual intentions" (ZPD, 13, 14). Gadamer's unconventional Platonism is based on a reading of Plato that moves from the later to the earlier dialogues, a hermeneutical procedure that itself is very unusual for current Plato scholars, although in the nineteenth century this type of approach to Plato was more common. Gadamer traces the source of this interpretive strategy to Hegel's rediscovery of the "speculative" content of Plato's later dialogues.[1] Gadamer thinks that the later dialogues like the *Parmenides, Thaeatetus, Sophist, Statesman,* and *Philebus* show us a Plato who has reacted to criticisms and misunderstandings, as well as ambiguities in his earlier dialogues, and has taken steps to make the final direction of his thought known. In Gadamer's opinion, these later dialogues *do not* signal a departure from Plato's earlier agenda—as some commentators have argued that some later dialogues, like the *Parmenides* and *Philebus,* imply a rejection of Plato's commitment to the Ideas[2]—but represent its true culmination. Thus Gadamer treats the evidence from the earlier dialogues in light of evidence from the later ones because he thinks that such a reading lends the greatest amount of coherence and plausibility to Plato's project. The result is a Plato whose overall intent is highly unified throughout his corpus and a Plato that looks significantly different from what the more orthodox interpretations have claimed for him. The surprising consequence of this hermeneutical approach can be identified by pointing out that Gadamer's reading of Plato sees him as committed to the immanence of forms in particulars, a position which brings Plato closer to Aristotle's ontology. It is Gadamer's contention that Plato himself was always closer to Aristotle than either Aristotle himself or most commentators since Aristotle have noted.[3] Whether Gadamer is right about this proximity is a question for scholars of ancient philosophy to debate and need not concern us at present. For our purposes it is important to look at how Gadamer's unconventional interpretation of Plato contributes to his general philosophical insights into the nature of human understanding.

Gadamer arrives at what might be called a reversal of most current Platonisms by reassessing four general, interrelated issues: (1) the place of the Ideas in Plato's philosophy, (2) the nature of Ideas, (3) the place in Plato's thought of the issues grouped under the rubric of "the one and the many," and (4) the nature of "participation" (*methexis*) and "separation" (*chorismos*). These issues are the key, in my opinion, to Gadamer's unconventional Platonism, as well as to both his reflections on the universality of interpretation and his insight into the basis of human solidarity in our common involvement in such transcendentals as Being and non-Being, identity and difference, the Good, the beautiful, the true, and the one.

Today's conventional Platonism places the Ideas in the forefront of Plato's philosophy. They are, in F. M. Cornford's phrase, "the pillars of Platonism."[4] These Ideas are conceived as the nonlinguistic, ideal, and transcendent ontological and logical principles of all reality. As such, each Idea has a perfection and existence in its own right that is "separate" from the many "imperfect" particulars that "participate" in it. As such, these Ideas exist as discrete, ideal, and changeless entities in a transcendent realm of reality that is "pure," "separate," and "distinct" from the world of change and confusion; they exist, as it were, in a second, perfect, static, and intelligible world. Thus in this view the fundamental problem that confronts Plato's philosophy is how these two worlds are related; how the intelligible world of discrete, changeless Ideas is connected to the sensible world of the many, different, particular things that are in a constant process of interaction and change. In this view, it is often said that Plato's philosophy runs aground on just these issues, the issues of "participation" and "separation." The criticism maintains that these metaphors of participation and separation are nothing more than metaphors. In other words, they clarify nothing of the complex ontological issues involved. Moreover, when taken seriously, i.e., "literally," they lead to logical paradoxes of the first order such as those that have come down to us as the "third man argument." These fundamental, insolvable problems—so the story goes—were not only pointed out by Aristotle's far-reaching critique of Plato's Ideas, but Plato himself anticipated them in a powerful way in the *Parmenides*. Thus many commentators think that Plato abandoned the

Ideas in dialogues that postdate the *Parmenides*, dialogues like the *Sophist* and the *Philebus*.

Gadamer takes issue with many aspects of this traditional picture of Plato. Without entering into a discussion of Gadamer's relative merits as a Plato scholar, I want to go over the outlines of his position on certain aspects of Plato's thought in order to explore their relevance for the fundamental issues of his hermeneutics. Whether Gadamer is ultimately right about Plato need not concern us here. Although his position will hardly win universal assent, I think his position is at least plausible and it stems from an intimate study of Plato extending over a remarkable period of almost seventy years.[5] What is more important for our purposes is whether some of the insights which Gadamer ascribes to Plato can help us to understand our activity as interpreters in important ways. It's with this question in mind that we turn to look at Gadamer's Plato.

At the forefront of Gadamer's Plato interpretation is the rejection of the *centrality* of the Ideas in Plato's actual philosophy. Gadamer is well aware that Plato advanced a number of different hypotheses about the Ideas over the course of his career. For example, it has often been pointed out how the account of the Ideas in the *Republic*—the central middle period text that most scholars appeal to when they discuss Plato's so-called theory of Ideas—is different than the account of the Ideas in earlier dialogues like the *Euthyphro* and also different than the notion of Ideas that comes to the fore in such later dialogues as the *Sophist* or *Philebus*. Such differences might even lead us to wonder if there really is one consistent "theory of Ideas" in Plato's corpus. Be that as it may. Suffice it to say that for Gadamer these differences are at least evidence of Plato's self-critique and willingness to explore the notion of the Ideas from a number of different perspectives. Moreover, such differences also suggest that although Plato never repudiated his commitment to the real existence of universals, it is, nevertheless, a much more provisional and critical commitment than is usually acknowledged. Gadamer goes so far as to claim that Plato's commitment to the Ideas is more a presupposition of his thought and not its true epicenter. Gadamer contends that "the assumption that there are Ideas remains for Plato an inescapable conclusion to be drawn from the nature of discussion and the process of reaching an understanding of something. It is not by accident that in the *Phaedo*, i.e., where it is presumably given its first literary circulation, the assumption is characterized as 'old hat' (76d). Far from being Plato's philosophy itself, the assumption occasions his real philosophical endeavor" (DSP, 119). And Gadamer writes that "the acceptance of Ideas as such and in particular the acceptance of individual Ideas is not at all to be regarded as the essence of Plato's philosophy" (SP, 145). Let us look more closely at these claims.

For Gadamer, the hypothesis of Ideas is an assumption that Plato feels compelled to accept because in every act of speech, common usage refers us to meanings which have a different kind of being than the discrete, particular things and actions that make up the world of common sense. For example, when we speak of a phenomena like friendship we assume that friendship *is something;* that it has a relatively determinant meaning which is compatible with some descriptions of it and incompatible with others. Common usage assumes that there is such a thing as true friendship which functions as a kind of standard against which we can measure all particular friendships as more or less true to type. Thus common usage points us toward a unified meaning, even when we are aware, as we often are, that real friendships are often equivocal and never perfectly instantiate the ideal. Even in this situation, our language assumes an underlying meaning that structures our awareness of the differences between individual instances, differences that can be readily discerned. Thus we can make true judgments about friendships like the ones we make when we say things like Jane and June have a better friendship than John and James. What we imply when we say such things is that there is in fact an ideal type of friend and Jane and June come closer to it than John and James. However, Gadamer contends that this assumption that there are such logical and ontological standards or principles is not the primary focus of Plato's thought. Plato certainly believed that such Ideas exist but his primary philosophical interest was not to develop a definitive account of their nature and function in our thinking.

Like Plato, Gadamer too accepts the claim that something like Ideas exist and this claim also functions most often in this thinking like a presupposition of his thought. Consequently, he often fails to treat it as an explicit thesis. However, there is one place I know of where this commitment to the Ideas is made very explicit. It's worth quoting this passage at length because it reveals something crucial to both Gadamer's commitment to Platonic Ideas, as well as his understanding of what Plato had in mind when he spoke of the Ideas. For Gadamer knowledge concerns

> the relationship of Ideas and the complete articulation of what is meant, which is reached at times as an indivisible *Eidos* as the shared goal of all who seek understanding. Such is in truth the final goal [*Grenzziel*], for which we strive in light of the commonality of the interpreted world. This has to do with the essence of language. I am not capable of seeing how

> one can see this basic constituent [*Grundverfassung*] of all speaking other than how Plato described it as a relationship of Ideas. That may sound "idealistic." However, the substitutions of the *Eidos* or the intuitive unity of what is meant with the concept of a rule and its applications—whose validity insists upon itself here in opposition—appears to me as only another way of describing the same eidetic turn that we all perform, even when we only use signs or open our mouths. (DNS, 345, 346)

One thing we learn from this passage is that on Gadamer's reading, the Ideas are ideals or limits that we strive for in our speech (and our action as well). Simply put, we strive to get clear on what the exact nature is of the things that form the focus of our discourse or we seek to act in such a way as to be true to the ideal we aspire to. In this respect, Gadamer is not far removed from a neo-Kantian interpretation of Plato's Ideas like that of his *Doktorvater*, Paul Natorp, who saw the Ideas as regulative in nature.[6] Unlike Natorp, however, Gadamer does not see the Ideas as another way of speaking about the "infinite task" of articulating perfect laws of nature. For Gadamer, Plato's Ideas are more basic than natural laws. Ideas, according to Gadamer, refer to the most basic structures or patterns of intelligible meaning that lend reality whatever intelligibility it has, whether we are speaking of a reality amenable to the methods of the natural sciences or not. We strive for an indivisible unity of fully articulated meaning, whenever we seek to understand any aspect of the meaningful world, on the reasonable assumption that our speech is about the same things. We assume, in other words, that we share a common world governed by common patterns of meaning. This means we seek both a coherent and complete account of whatever reality we have identified as the common focus of our inquiry. Such a common world is articulated in language. Given this common object of meaning, it certainly does not follow that the goal of an indivisible, eidetic grasp of some aspect of it is easy to achieve. Experience tells us otherwise. But given the shared nature of reality it is reasonable to assume that all insights into it are, in principle, consistent and reconcilable with each other. Thus we always seek a unified, consistent account of any phenomena, even when the differences in our understanding of the phenomena force us to see this unified account as something we strive for as our "final goal," i.e., our regulative ideal. This is Gadamer's presupposition and he thinks that he shares this assumption with Plato. As such, it undergirds both thinkers' understanding of the nature of human thought. We presuppose that such unified meanings exist because our pattern of inquiry and debate ineluctably points us to that conclusion.

But if some version of the theory of Ideas is a presupposition and not the central focus of Plato's philosophy what, then, is? In order to answer this question we need to delve into the nature of Ideas, i.e., their manner of being once again.

The Web of Ideas

Gadamer not only rejects the thesis that the existence of Ideas is the center of Plato's thought, he also rejects the claim that Ideas exist as discrete, individual entities. "In my opinion," writes Gadamer, "any theory of the doctrine of Ideas which made the latter look like Eleatic atomism was always inadequate and Plato himself seems to have recognized that at an early state" (PUD, 135). But if Ideas do not exist as discrete, ideal particulars, how do they exist? What is their real mode of being?

Gadamer thinks of Platonic Ideas as a nexus or web of ideal relations, which are internally connected to each other in inseparable ways and at many different levels. The metaphor of a woven fabric, a metaphor Plato avails himself of,[7] is suggestive. Ideas are like strands of thread in a woven cloth. They exist and function like strands, i.e., like Ideas, only in their interconnectedness in the warp and woof of the fabric. If the metaphor of the weave could be extended to include three rather than just two dimensions, the level of complexity that Gadamer has in mind here would be even plainer. The general point, however, is that all discourse requires a kind of "weaving" or "blending" of Ideas. The very subject-attribute structure of predication "blends" or "weaves together" the Ideas of the subject with the those of its attributes. The subject is both distinct from its attributes and as such not its attributes and at the same time it is somehow nothing but its attributes appropriately combined. The subject both is, in a certain sense, its attributes and, in another sense, is not its attributes, but is instead itself. It is a "blend" or "weave" of these Ideas, metaphors Plato often uses in the later dialogues like the *Sophist* and *Statesman.*

But even if we take a less metaphorical approach the same basic point can be made. For example, the Idea of "justice" in the *Republic* represents just such a nondiscrete Idea. Justice or "right living" as we might translate *dikaiusune* cannot be conceived apart from an Idea of the proper goal of human life. For Plato, that implies a proper understanding of such things as "reason," "spirit," and "appetite," each of which points us to a deeper account of eros and its place in human motivation. Moreover, we cannot begin to elaborate on the Idea of "justice" without speaking of such things as "merit" or "just desserts," which in turn thrust upon us more reflection on just what a human being is and what constitutes a virtuous life for human beings. As the *Republic* makes plain, these questions in turn involve us in questions of education and human responsibility, both individual and social responsibility. What is more, none of these issues can be approached apart from an Idea of truth which our analyses must appeal to, as well as some sense of the overall "good" that is at stake when a multifaceted issue like "justice" is raised. As the *Republic* shows, all of these issues are "cut from the same piece of cloth," they are part of the same "fabric" of interrelated issues which are indeed logically distinct but ontologically inseparable from each other. Each "discrete" Idea invoked, be it justice, reason, appetite, spirit, human nature, virtue, education, responsibility, society, truth, goodness, or what have you, is in reality part of the "fabric" of Ideas, the nexus of intelligible relations in which these Ideas take on whatever distinct contours we are able to make out.

On this model, what it means to think, the meaning of thought itself, involves entering this "fabric" of relations—of "unweaving and reweaving" the cloth—in order to discover how these various strands are individually and collectively related to each other. Such thinking involves "interpretation," because it is never a wordless intuition of the whole. The multidimensional nexus of relationships, with which such ideal aspects of reality present us, can only be unraveled a few threads at a time. Thus our understanding of reality is always a selective analysis and explanation, a partial "unweaving and reweaving" of various parts of the fabric. It is, in other words, nothing but "interpretation."

Interpretation or thinking on this model is a human accomplishment that nevertheless takes its cue and finds its justification from the order of ideal reality itself. When we engage in the weavers task, the task Plato called "dialectic" and Gadamer calls "interpretation," we look to these things, these interrelated ideal realities, and we may even discover something about them that another thinker does not see. Hence, there is a real sense in which we can say that interpretation of these terms is about the *same* things but it is also possible for these things to offer themselves with different "visages" or "looks" to different interpreters. Such differences can and do occur without undermining the fundamental identity of the realities under interpretation. The inherent complexity and richness of this "nest" of Ideas allows for a great deal of diversity in interpretation, but it is equally important to remind ourselves that such diversity does not undermine the real identity of the things about which we often differ in our views.

The One and the Many

Given this identity, it always makes sense to seek ways to reconcile conflicting accounts. In fact, Gadamer thinks that this same "identity in difference" marks all valid interpretive efforts. Although Gadamer might be inclined to use the Hegelian terms of "identity in difference" to describe the ontological roots of our interpretive endeavors, he would also argue that Plato knew about the problems of ideal identities that always somehow seem to persist, while at the same time entangling us in various "looks" or self-presentations of themselves. For Plato, these problems gathered themselves under the banner of "the one and the many."

It is, in fact, "the one and the many" that Gadamer regards as the actual center of Plato's thought. Far from advocating the mere acceptance of the existence of Ideas as such and the existence of discrete Ideas as what is essential to Plato's thought, Gadamer sees "the dialectical relationship of unity and multiplicity [*Von Einheit und Vielheit*] that stands under them [the Ideas]" (SP, 145) as the true heart and soul of Platonism. For Gadamer "the one and the many" is the way Plato often talks about the nexus of Ideas, i.e., their fundamental interconnectedness or reciprocal determination. As we said above, Gadamer thinks that "far from being Plato's philosophy itself, the assumption [that there are Ideas] occasions his real philosophical endeavor" (DSP, 119). In other words, the Ideas provide a jumping-off point for Plato's philosophy, but they do not constitute its true focus.

This more basic philosophical enterprise is elaborated primarily in the dialogues after the *Parmenides.* It is the *Parmenides* that shows, according to Gadamer, that "a single Idea by itself is not knowledge at all, and here is the source of the error which the young Socrates makes. In any insight an entire nexus or web of Ideas is involved, and Plato's actual questioning is in regard to the constitutive, organizational, structural principles of this interconnectedness of the Ideas" (DSP, 119). Grasping the interconnectedness of the Ideas is, according to Gadamer, "the felicitous experience of advancing insight, the *euphoria* which the *Philebus* says (15c) happens to a person who proceeds along the proper path to the solution of the problem of the One and the Many" (DSP, 119) or, as Gadamer puts it more plainly in another context, "Someone understands what cognition, knowing, insight is only when he understands how it can be that one and one are two and how 'the two' is one" (PUD, 135).

That the interconnectedness of the Ideas is expressed in the problems of the one and the many can be readily grasped by going back to our previous example of the Idea of "justice." That justice is "one" is not disputed. Even common sense assumes that justice *is something,* something that has its own defining features, features which some acts or situations have and which other acts or states of affairs do not have. This leads Plato to assume that justice has its own, unique ideal contours that distinguish it relative to other Ideas, even if it cannot be absolutely distinguished in itself. This is so, because in addition to being "one," justice is also "two" or "many" in that we can never say what justice itself is without relating it to the many other Ideas which either make it up or of which it itself is a part, e.g., the Good. Thus it is always the case that "the One necessarily transforms into the many and the many into the One" (PUD, 136). This is true not only of justice but of any "aspect" or "part" of justice like reason, spirit, appetite, human nature, virtue, responsibility, etc. Each aspect of justice is itself an Idea that can be seen as both one and many, i.e., what its unity consists in is itself a complex web of Ideas, each of which in turn can be divided into further constituent parts. This process of division is in principle infinite.

Gadamer sees this process of division, which Plato called *dihairesis,* as the heart of Plato's dialectical method. Later dialogues like the *Statesman* and *Sophist* are meant to make just this point. Moreover, Gadamer compares the type of being that is uncovered in such a division to the type of being characteristic of number. It is not just the case that numbers are paradigmatic noetic realities, i.e., "that there is," as Gadamer puts it, "something that we cannot grasp with our hands, something that even the natural scientist cannot comprehend within the means of his own ontological criterion" (PP, 238). Numbers are even more puzzling because "in them we produce something that exercises the force of reality [*Realitätszwang*] on us" (PP, 238). Like language, numbers are a human creation that nevertheless seem to "belong to" reality, i.e., seem to adhere to what is real and be present in what is real in a way that is independent of our will and imagination. The eidetic reality of numbers is an aspect of reality itself just like the eidetic reality in language is not simply in language alone but also in the world.[8] For Gadamer the ideality of numbers and language is real; it is part of the world never just "in our heads." In this commitment, Gadamer shows himself a true Platonist.

It is in light of the common ideality of numbers and language that Gadamer makes another surprising and far-reaching point for grasping the nature of interpretation. Whenever we analyze an Idea, according to Gadamer, it's like counting in that we separate out its constituent parts in a process of "division." The purpose of the "division" is to grasp each part of an Idea in turn in order to be able to see how it is that "in sum" they "add up" to the Idea. Thus thinking or interpretation follows, according to Gadamer's hermeneutical reading of Plato, an arithmetical model, based on the processes of division and addition.

> In Plàto, the definitional *logos* is formed by the addition of definitions run through in a *dihairesis* and then counted up—yielding a collected multiplicity which as such constitutes the unitary essence of a definite thing. Thus precisely insofar as it is arrived at by the procedure of dividing, the definition displays the role of number. The compatibility of all definitions in a genus with one another, or, what is more, the necessity of their coexistence with the final determination common to all of them, is what constitutes the unitary nature of the thing. This means that the statement of the essence, the definitional statement [*logos ousia*], is the collected sum number of all the essential definitions which have been run through, and as such it has the structure of "number." (PUD, 149)

Gadamer believes that the various definitions of the sophist given in the dialogue of the same name, as well as the procedure of "counting" the various definitions of the statesman in that dialogue, demonstrate the point here. On the one hand, such a "sum" of different definitions or accounts of the same human type, like the sophist or statesman, imply that all these perspectives, if true, must be consistent with each other in principle and thereby point to one, indivisible, coherent account of the whole thing. On the other hand, however, the fact that we are almost always striving toward this unified account shows that such "counting" or "summing" of definitions forces us to face the "finitude" of our grasp of these realities.

Such definitions reveal the "finite" nature of our understanding because they confront us with the fact that the various plausible perspectives we find on the things under consideration is incomplete. They are "incomplete" not only because the coherence of the different perspectives needs to be worked out and is often not self-evident, but such accounts are "incomplete" or "finite" because it is not clear how these definitions are related to the rest of the intelligible realities, whose meaning they either presuppose or imply. In this regard, Gadamer argues that such definitions involve, like counting, the imposing of a limit on an inherently unlimited reality. In this case the unlimited reality is the web of Ideas, each of which can be infinitely divided into its many constituent parts. Thus offering an essential definition (*logos ousia*) involves the imposition of a relative limit where essentially no absolute limit can be found.

> Human knowing, which, as human, is incapable of comprehending the entire order of being and ideas *uno intuito*. Instead it is capable of

> uncovering only limited ordered sequences as it goes through the Ideas one by one and must then relinquish these sequences again to a whole without internal differentiation (cf. *Philebus*: *ean eis to apeiron* [let fall into the unlimited-indefinite]). It is exactly like that in counting. (PUD, 151)

This thinking, which is like counting, this *dihairesis*, which is modeled on the arithmetic functions of division and addition, is itself a model of interpretation, i.e., our "forever finite" grasp of reality. Plato's understanding of philosophical dialectic shows how all understanding is relative to its limited access to the web of Ideas. When we think or interpret we analyze relations between Ideas, but that analysis is never exhaustive of the entire nexus of Ideas; it always breaks off somewhere in the middle of things. Thus all interpretation is finite.

However, there is more in the basic fact that numbers can be seen as "sums" that sheds light on the general nature of interpretation. What is key here is that a "sum," or a number generated by addition, can have characteristics not shared by the units that make it up. Thus, for example, a sum can be "even," even when the numbers by which the sum was arrived at through addition are "odd." Yet these odd numbers are there in the even sum. Somehow the sum contains them. This basic arithmetic fact leads Gadamer to make an ontological point about the different type of unity of which any hermeneutical ontology must be cognizant. On the one hand, we have the typical unity of a genus where there is something in common between the genus and its exemplars. All fish, for example, are cold-blooded vertebrae with fins and gills. Such is the essence of what a "fish" is. All fish are what they are because they exemplify this principle. There is something "in common" between all fish and this defining principle. On the other hand, the unity of the genus itself, the eidetic unity of the principle of "fishness" itself, seems to have a unity like that of a sum in that it has characteristics beyond what is common to its exemplars.[9] In our day, Russell's Paradox makes a similar point, but Gadamer argues that Plato was well aware of this issue. Gadamer argues that the identity of the beautiful in itself, as set out in Diotima's account of eros, shows that the beautiful as such, beauty in itself, is not the same in all respects as what one finds in the beauty of bodies, or the beauty of character, or the beauty of institutions and laws, etc. And yet beauty as such, beauty in itself, contains these other beauties.[10] Beauty itself is somehow present in them. Because this is supposedly so, one may "rise"—to use Plato's metaphor—from them to glimpse beauty itself.

The ontological problem behind the puzzling fact that a sum may not share all the characteristics of the numbers which are in it and from which it is constituted as a sum finds expression in Anglo-American

Plato scholarship in the issue sometimes called "self-predication." In this context eminent Platonists have puzzled over the strange possibility that beauty as such may not be beautiful or justice itself may not be just or triangularity as such may not be three-cornered, etc.[11] The possibility that "beauty as such may not be beautiful" or that "justice itself may not be just" is another way of saying that as "sums" beauty and justice may not share all the characteristics of the "units" that make them up.

Unlike the majority of his Anglo-American counterparts, however, Gadamer does not see the problem of self-predication as a mere logical puzzle. Instead, Gadamer sees in these puzzling facts about the nature of sums a prototype for what interpretation is all about.

Gadamer's point can be generalized in the following analogy. Interpretation is like addition in that it is a process which combines eidetic units, each of which has a distinct meaning, the combination of which nevertheless creates a new meaning, not reducible to the individual units involved. Thus, for example, in the arithmetic function symbolized as 3 + 5 the units 3 and 5 each have a distinct unitary meaning, which can be combined, or thought together by a distinct intellectual act of addition to yield 8, which itself has a unitary meaning that transcends the meanings of the numbers of which it is a product. Similarly, when we arrive at an interpretation, we offer a unified discourse compounded of many distinct meanings, i.e., the words and ideas combined in the discourse. This unified discourse, or the meaning of the interpretation, goes beyond the meaning of its constituent units. What's puzzling in the process of addition is how both 3 and 5 can be odd and yet yield an even 8. More generally, the very nature of number itself involves this puzzle of addition in that by adding 1 + 1 + 1 and yet another 1 new eidetic realities are generated in an infinitely extendable series. Each new number is a new and distinct eidetic reality, which is nevertheless intelligibly related in discoverable ways to other numbers. Like addition, interpretation, according to Gadamer, is an unending process that produces countless new syntheses, which are both as distinct from each other as 3 is from 5 or both 3 and 5 are from 8 *and* as integrally related to each other as the members of the number series itself. This gives Gadamer some grounds for maintaining that even interpretations that come to very different conclusions about some phenomenon can, nevertheless, be about one and the same phenomenon. Gadamer hopes to show how Plato's reflections on number shed light on the dialectical relationship between identity and difference that undergirds all interpretive disputes.

This same dynamic between identity and difference leads Gadamer to another analogy between addition and interpretation that is important for our purposes. Just as each number is a distinct eidetic unit, it is "one" in itself, but inasmuch as it is seen as a product or a sum it consists of "many" such units. It is both "one" and "many" at the same time. This puzzle about the nature of number was well-known to Plato. It is significant that the Greeks did not think of one itself as a number but as the principle of all number. As a principle, "one" is present in all number but does not itself share in all the characteristics of number. Unlike any other number, "one" is not both one and many, i.e., it is not a sum (at least not of any two whole numbers), but the condition for the being of sums or numbers. Interpretations, like numbers, are both "one" and "many"; they offer a distinct unified view of some subject matter, a view which is generated by relating that subject matter dialectically to "many" other issues. Thus each interpretation is eidetically distinct in itself and as such distinct from other interpretations of the same issue, yet also integrally related to the things which form the focus of such interpretive disputes.

This implies for Gadamer that interpretation has something of the same clarity and ambiguity of meaning as number. Just as each number can be, in one sense, clearly grasped in its eidetic unity, this same eidetic unity is also ambiguous in another sense and genuinely puzzling in being "many," in its being a product whose meaning is more than a mere grouping or concatenation of units. Thus Gadamer writes "it is this very dialectic of the One and the Many which establishes the finite limits of human discourse and insight—our fruitful situation halfway between single and multiple meaning, clarity, and ambiguity" (DSP, 119, 120).[12] Interpretations can be clear in their basic contours, yet deeply ambiguous in that the eidetic relationships involved in the interpretations harbor puzzles the solutions to which are never transparent. That eidetic unities can be combined or synthesized into interpretations is well known but what happens to such unities in the process, the transformations they undergo without losing their real identities is a puzzle of the first rank. Gadamer would insist that this puzzle is tremendously fruitful in that the constant challenge it provides generates a great deal of genuine insight in the process of reflection and illumination, even if the puzzle itself is never definitively solved. He would also insist, however, that failure to solve this puzzle should not undermine our belief in the unity of the things we interpret. Such things present themselves as a "unity in difference," as both "one and many," and as such they draw us into their own inherent dialectical nature.

This dialectic between clarity and ambiguity, which Gadamer sees as characteristic of all interpretation, is modeled in the number series in yet another way. As any schoolchild can tell you, the number series is infinite. When we conceptualize any particular number in the series as a sum of at least two other particular numbers in the series we are doing something arbitrary in a sense, despite the fact that we do so according to prescribed rules. It is arbitrary because each act of addition focuses on some particular relations, which even though they genuinely obtain between some finite set of numbers (say, 4 + 5 = 9), they can nevertheless be seen to do so only in abstraction from all other possible relations to which these particular numbers may stand to all the other numbers in the number series. The fact that there is a rationally defensible relation of addition between 4, 5, and 9, say, does not change the fact that in focusing on this relationship something arbitrary is going on. It would be wrong to think that the meaning of 4, 5, and 9, for example, is exhausted in their eidetic relations to each other for, in reality, they cannot be exhausted at all. They are what they are as numbers only in all their individual and collective relationships to all the members of the number series, relationships that are in principle infinite. One could say that these numbers are "parts" of a "whole" and only as part of the whole can we completely grasp their meaning. Of course, if the whole is "open" or infinite, so is the process of explicating the relationship of the parts to the whole. This is a fundamental point that Gadamer wants to make about interpretation. Even though interpretation involves eidetic realities analogous to numbers, these eidetic realities belong to an infinite whole as its constituent parts. As such, we can know them in sufficient clarity just as we can know numbers, but as is the case even with numbers we cannot know them exhaustively or definitively. Instead, we know them in "interpretations," which are in principle "open," i.e., endless and inconclusive. "Inconclusiveness and endlessness is obviously characteristic not only of our finite, discursive penetration of Ideas in knowing, but also of the generation of a series of numbers in counting. Both 'generations' depend on the principles of the One and the indeterminate Two. . . . For Plato the decisive point to be made clear in the doctrine of the generation of numbers is that *they can be continued indefinitely*" (PUD, 151). The hermeneutical analogue is that interpretation is inconclusive and endless because we can never reach the whole in which these beings are what they are. Moreover, such interpretation is "arbitrary" in a special sense in that it constantly abstracts from the whole in a selective way. Such arbitrariness is not overcome when we realize that we have no other choice but to be selective or arbitrary in some way. Rather, the necessity of such arbitrary determination reminds us of the inherent possibility of multiple interpretations. Thus Gadamer writes that

> the very procedure of conceptual definition itself contains something arbitrary and uncertain, for the genus under which a thing is to be subsumed obviously lacks singleness of meaning. The variations in the

> conceptual determination of the sophist with which the dialogue of the same name begins, as well as the corresponding considerations in the *Statesman*, make that fact completely clear. Viewed logically, the ideal might be to portray the arbitrariness of such possible definitions against the background of the system of Ideas which supposedly lies behind Plato's doctrine of ideal numbers and thereby to eliminate this arbitrariness. But it seems highly questionable to me whether the principles of the One and the Many, upon which this system rests, are really meant by Plato to guarantee that we can attain unequivocal meaning in classificatory structure. . . . The interweaving of the highest genre in the *Sophist* and even more, the dialectical exercise which the young Socrates is put through by the elder Parmenides, lead only to the *negative* insight that it is not possible to define an isolated Idea purely by itself and that very interweaving of Ideas militates against the positive conception of a precise and unequivocal pyramid of Ideas. . . . Is it not always the case, as Plato so effectively teaches us here, that as human beings we can perceive the order of good and bad, the order of reality as a whole only in finite limited attempts? Perhaps in the final analysis the indeterminacy of the Two is meant precisely to imply that for us there exists no ideal unambiguous structure of Being. (DSP, 110)

It is this very structure of Being itself that Gadamer sees at stake in Plato's reflections on the one and the many. Plato's choice of number as a paradigm for thought is not incidental. The nature of reality itself is schematized in number. By focusing on it we learn about Being itself. Thus Gadamer writes:

> In Plato, the "principles" of the One and the Many are not advanced as the foundation for genealogical tales such as those told by earlier thinkers. Rather his concern is with the meaning of Being [*der Sinn von Sein*] as that meaning displays itself in its unity and multiplicity in the *logos*. And it is this question of the meaning of Being which leads him to the One and the Two, an entirety of the *logoi* in which reality, according to its ordering principle, both unifies and unfolds itself. The entirety of the *logoi* is a true entirety but one which is given to finite human knowing only in its basic structure and only in concretizations of it in specific contexts. What is, is as the whole of the infinite interrelationships of things, from which at any given time in discourse and insight a determinate, partial aspect is "raised up" and placed in the light of disconcealment. (DSP, 120)

In all the passages cited in this section what is suggested is that our mode of access to reality is inherently interpretive because the inexhaustibly rich, interrelated nature of reality frustrates any other approach. Gadamer goes so far as to say that "Plato's doctrine of Ideas turns out to be a general theory of relationship from which it can be convincingly deduced that dialectic is unending and infinite" (PUD, 152). The most fundamental insight is that thought is unending because in it we can never completely explicate the infinite relations in which any given reality stands to all other things. The dream of "having the last word" is the dream of transcending our finitude and exchanging our hermeneutical mode of thought for the eternal vision of omniscience or *nous.* Perhaps for this reason Plato reminds us that the gods do not philosophize; only humans do.

The *arithmos* model of reality does more, however, than shed light on the limits of human understanding. It is also an excellent point of departure for considering Gadamer's grasp of two other important issues in Plato interpretation, i.e., participation (*methexis*) and separation (*chorismos*). We will begin by looking at Gadamer's insights into *methexis* or participation for what they might tell us about his idea of interpretation.

Methexis

As we pointed out earlier, the issue of how Ideas "participate" in each other (as well as in concrete particulars) and how, despite the fact that as "participants," these Ideas are seen as "parts" of other Ideas (and particulars) they can nevertheless be said to be "separate" from them, has often been the focus of speculation and debate. Gadamer points out how Plato himself was not really concerned to use exact terms when characterizing the ontological relation he sometimes called "participation" (*methexis*). As many scholars have complained, Plato used a great variety of metaphorical terms to characterize this relationship. This is so, Gadamer thinks, not because Plato was a sloppy thinker. Instead, he sees in these Platonic vagaries more evidence for the thesis that Plato's focus was always elsewhere on the logical problem of unity and multiplicity:

> It is obviously of no concern to Plato which concept one uses to envision the relationship of the appearances to an Idea—participation, *synousia, parousia, mixis, symploke* or whatever. For him the problem does not lie here at all. Instead it lies in the logical question of how it is possible in the first place that one can be many and many one. What is said of a thing is supposed to be different from the thing and nevertheless it is supposed to be attributed to it. What a thing is supposed to be in truth is supposed to hold for each of its appearances and yet the appearances are supposed

> to be different from the thing itself. Plato uses the [nature of] number to illustrate what he finds puzzling here. Number consists of units each of which by itself is one and nevertheless the number itself, according to the number of units it includes, is not many but a definite "so-many," the unity of multiplicity bound together. Every *logos* has this formal structure, however puzzling that structure may be. (PUD, 147)

So, for example, 1 and 2 are logically implicit in 3; one might even say they "participate" in 3 or are "part" of 3 but 3 is also itself—3—and, as such, *not* 1 or 2, i.e., it is "separate" from 1 and 2. How it is that 1 and 2 can be "in 3" or that 3 is "nothing more" than the sum of 1 and 2 and yet 3 is logically distinct from 1 and 2 is a real conceptual puzzle about the inherent interconnectedness of noetic realities such as 1, 2, and 3. Moreover, 3 as a single number is not many but it is a single number; it is one and not just many. How can this relation between one and many be better understood?

If we take the analysis one step further and look at the relation between numbers and the things to which numbers are attributed, other aspects of the participation problem arise. For example, any three things, like three coins, raise interesting puzzles that Plato himself pondered. Each coin is itself "one"; one is attributed to each coin; one is somehow present in each coin. Yet as present in each distinct and separate coin, one is not in each coin distinct and separate from itself, as each coin in fact is distinct and separate from any other coin or for that matter from any other discrete thing. Rather, the same one is equally present in all three coins or anything unified at all. In being present, or in participating in a range of particulars, one is not parceled out, or cut up into tiny pieces and distributed either equally or unequally to each particular coin. Rather, one is somehow wholly present in each coin; it is itself present along with the other attributes which make the coin what it is. Yet together these coins are not one but three and three is present in them jointly. What happened then to the oneness? Did it disappear? How is each coin's oneness compatible with their joint threeness?

In Gadamer's opinion, these puzzles do not arise from the mistake of thinking essentially logical relations like "attribution" and "predication" in physical terms like "part" and "whole," "presence" or "participation." They arise, Gadamer thinks, from the undeniable nature of the things themselves; "oneness" is an ontological attribute. "Oneness" really is present, as itself, undivided and whole in each of the coins (and for that matter in all the infinite things of which one can be predicated). That its presence is not physical is clear from the fact that its presence is not diminished by being present in many particular things; it is wholly present in each separate coin without loss or substraction from what it is. To say that it is "part" of each coin is not to say that it is *a* part like "heads" and "tails" might be called "parts" of the coin or, in another sense, nickel and steel are "parts" of the coin. Unlike physical realities that cannot be wholly present in more than one space at any one time, oneness is itself wholly present in infinitely many spaces and across infinite expanses of time.

Gadamer thinks that this puzzling phenomenon of "participation" or "presence" is paradigmatic for thinking and it was Plato's contribution to bring it to our attention. It's important to remember that when Gadamer, in the passage just cited, was describing the problems of the one and the many in terms of number, he was insistent upon generalizing this relationship to every rational account. "*Every logos* has this formal structure, however puzzling that structure may be" (PUD, 147, emphasis added). Participation, according to Gadamer, is nothing other than "presence" in the puzzling sense that a reality like oneness is wholly and immediately present in each and every determinate thing but unlike these determinate things, each of which is distinct and separate from each other, oneness is not distinct and separate from itself but wholly present in each thing. In order to grasp how things participate in realities like oneness, it is important to keep in mind that this kind of participation "does not mean to have a part of something particular, rather it means that they are there with [things]. As every being is one (but also identical with itself and from all others different) so that being one [*Einsein*] is immediately 'there' (*parousia*), so also is everything that is two immediately 'there' " (MD, 292). And in another context he writes that

> *methexis* refers to coexistence with something. Of course, like the Latin *participation* and the German *Teilhabe,* the word *methexis* evokes the images of parts. That it does is shown by the early usage of *metechein* (to take part in something). That the part belongs to the whole is precisely what the new word underscores. Even in what is perhaps the earliest allusion to the Ideas, in the *Euthyphro,* the question is formulated in such a way that *to hosion* (what is pious), for instance, could be a *morion* (part) of *to dikaion* (what is just). In the first place that means that where one of them is, the other is too: the part is present "in the whole." However, Plato is fully aware of the paradox in a participation or taking part (*Teilhabe*) that does not take *a* part, but participates in the whole—as the day participates in the light of the sun. (*IG,* 11)

This type of "presence" or "participation" is admittedly somewhat mysterious but it is not impossible to understand and it is not a "mere" metaphor. Rather, it denotes a real ontological relationship that is key to our self-understanding as beings who think. Gadamer is very clear that "every *logos* has this formal structure" (PUD, 147). It was, according to Gadamer, precisely this difficulty that caused the "young Socrates" in the *Parmenides* to become entangled in logical conundrums of considerable difficulty. Gadamer sees it as significant that Plato describes Socrates as young and inexperienced in philosophy in this dialogue. This is, according to Gadamer, Plato's way of signaling the reader that the refutation of the Ideas offered in this dialogue is not definitive. In fact, Gadamer thinks that the theory of Ideas represented in the *Parmenides* shows us how not to interpret Plato's views on this subject and was intended by Plato precisely to show how such a caricature of what his statements about the Ideas amounted to would indeed lead to irresolvable problems. The mistake of the young Socrates, Gadamer holds, is to hold fast to an uncritical eleatic account of Being. It is "uncritical" because "Socrates" (unlike the mature Plato) had not yet realized that Being can only be conceived in a dialectical fashion.[13] What Socrates had to realize was that it was as impossible for the historical Parmenides to think Being, only Being, without any reference to non-Being (or what is other than Being) as it was for him to hold onto the concept of a single, unified Idea in itself that could be thought in isolation from its relation to the many other Ideas. This implies, Gadamer argues, that "the Platonic *Parmenides* is therefore not the expression of a crisis phase in the development of the Platonic theory of Ideas but rather the central formulation of its problem. The unity of the Ideas in themselves is a youthful assumption that just as much needs to be overcome as the unity of the eleatic thought of being" (ZVM, 388). Only by overcoming this assumption could "Socrates" mature to the point where he could think "presence" in another way (along the lines of the light of day which is itself supposedly one and present everywhere in many different spaces without being separate from itself), and thus avoid the logical problems associated with the claim that Ideas are *a* discrete, separate part of reality. Instead, he needed to see their presence more along the lines of the way in which numbers are present as a part of things to which they are rightly attributed. In being present in a discrete thing, number does not become separate from itself, from what it is as a whole. A piece of number is not divided off from it and added to the thing as one of its parts. Rather, number is such that it can be wholly present in things without losing anything of itself. Each coin, to go back to a previous example, can be wholly one, without either being more or less one and without any loss to what one itself is. In an analogous way any Idea may participate or be present in a particular, or for that matter, another Idea.

So it is that Gadamer thinks the issue of the one and the many or the "participation" of one Idea in many particulars and in many other Ideas is paradigmatic for Plato's thought and human thinking generally. Gadamer argues that Plato had this issue of identity and difference always in mind. Plato first points out the puzzle in the *Hippias Major*, but he draws no consequences from it in this dialogue. And in another early dialogue, the *Protagoras*, the issue is whether the virtues like justice, self-control, holiness, and wisdom are one or many (*Protagoras*, 329ff.). In an early middle dialogue, the *Phaedo*, Plato uses perceptual problems having to do with the issue of the one and the many. How is it that one and the same man can be both large and small, large relative to one person but small when compared to another? It is this example, Socrates says, that should cause us to think about the relation of the Ideas to each other and Plato explicitly ties this problem of perception and relative predicates to the elementary problems of number, like adding one plus one (*Phaedo*, 96de). Similarly, in the *Republic* Plato raises the issue of the relative size differences between the last three fingers on our hand. How is it that the ring finger between the little and middle finger can be both large and small, depending on whether one compares it to the little finger or the middle finger? Such seemingly trivial puzzles are meant to summon us to think in radical ways. And he also reopens the issue of the unity of the virtues when he describes the good soul as one which has unified its parts and the good state as one which has become one despite the various differences between the many citizens that threaten to divide it. Gadamer sees all these examples as pointing to the coherent interconnectedness of the Ideas, a theme which Plato deals with explicitly in the *Parmenides* and takes up again in such later dialogues as the *Sophist* and *Philebus*. In these dialogues the issues of how Ideas are "present" as "one" identical Idea in "many" different realities moves from the background to the foreground of Plato's thought.[14]

Chorismos

Of course, the contention that "participation" is presence of a paradoxical but not unintelligible sort raises another issue that is central to conventional Platonism—separation (*chorismos*). "Separation" involves the ontological chasm that supposedly yawns between sensory appearances and ideal realities, as well as the separation between Ideas themselves. On the one hand, "separation" raises issues about Plato's reputed two-world metaphysics, and on the other hand it points us back to what

Gadamer takes as the primary Platonic concern—the interconnectedness of Ideas.

With regard to the view that Plato held a two-world ontology, the world of physical appearances in their constantly changing variety and the utterly different world of ideal realities—constant, invariable, eternal, and perfect in themselves—Gadamer is skeptical. "The complete separation of a world of the Ideas from the world of appearances would be a crass absurdity. If Parmenides, in the dialogue of the same name, pushes us in the direction of that complete separation, he does so, it seems to me, precisely in order to reduce such an understanding of the *chorismos* to absurdity" (*IG,* 16). Gadamer even goes so far as to claim that "it is not really Plato, but Aristotle who is the originator of the theory of two worlds" (*GW* 7, 380). It was Aristotle's polemic against Plato that led him to exaggerate the differences rather than stress the similarities between himself and his teacher. But if the *chorismos* in Plato does not refer to an *absolute* ontological hiatus, Plato does speak of such a chasm, according to Gadamer, in order to insist upon a *relative* difference in the things themselves.

Gadamer thinks that Plato posited a *chorismos* for two significant reasons. On the one hand, there is an important difference between the sensory and the noetic or ideal side of things; for example, there is a difference between the physical aspects of many things of one type, which are constantly changing, and the ideal component of things which offers itself to thought as that which is common between sensory particulars and to which we sometimes refer in terms of genus and species. Such a distinction is particularly essential to mathematics if mathematicians are to understand their own thought by its own inherent standards and not mistake it for a type of empirical research, a temptation to which apparently even a gifted mathematician like Thaetetus was susceptible. Numbers are not discrete particulars, subject to constant change, but ideal types that enjoy a kind of permanence that enables eidetic analysis. Gadamer contends that one key motivation that Plato had for positing the *chorismos* was to delineate in an adequate fashion for the first time the basic elements of an ontology of mathematics.[15] This was necessary for the advancement of the flourishing mathematical enlightenment in Greece at the time, which Plato experienced, supported, and to which he perhaps even contributed.

But such a distinction or separation was no less necessary to another fundamental concern of Plato's, i.e., the foundations of morality.[16] According to Gadamer, this points us to the second reason that Plato had for talking about a *chorismos.* By insisting on a relative separation between the sensory and noetic, Plato laid the groundwork for a distinction between inexact experience and experience tested by reason. This distinction is fundamental to ethics. Plato knew that in pursuing ethical matters of the utmost importance one could no sooner dispense with popular opinion and common sense than one could look to these sources of moral insight for an adequate response to difficult moral issues. The point is to reflect on popular moral experience and test it for its accuracy, completeness, and internal consistency. Only moral opinions that pass these tests can be justified and it is often by applying these tests that one transcends these conventional norms to a firmer grasp of what is good and right. Socrates did just that, as does Plato in such dialogues as the *Gorgias, Republic,* and the *Philebus,* and Aristotle was simply following good Socratic and Platonic precedent when he sets out in a more systematic fashion in his various ethical treatises to test and probe the moral wisdom of his day. This points, in Gadamer's opinion, to a key reason for Plato's talk of a *chorismos.* In moral thinking, there is an essential distinction between what is merely right by convention and that which lends itself to a more rigorous justification. There is a "separation," as it were, between these ways of approaching the moral facts of the matter, and Plato has nothing less than this basic and indispensable distinction in mind when he talks of a *chorismos.* The *chorismos* in this case, as well as the case of mathematics, characterizes a relative difference in things between what is more intelligible and less intelligible. In ethics this is not a distinction between uncertainty or inexactitude and certainty or exactness, as it is in mathematics, but it is still a distinction between confused experience and experience raised to a higher level of rational rigor. In ethics this level of reflection cannot give an account of itself that yields logical necessity—a fact of which both Plato and Aristotle were well aware—but it can offer a justification of its claims that is both clearer and more coherently reasoned than popular opinion.

In a way similar to mathematical thinking, moral reflection depends on there being a side of things that reveals a clearer and more rigorous understanding, when attended to properly. This side of things Plato called *Idea.* Gadamer hastens to remind us, however, that this side of things is itself a part of this world. If Plato often called this world a world of appearances, these appearances themselves have a noetic or ideal side which thought can learn to grasp. Gadamer makes the fundamental point that the Ideas that thought aspires to grasp are nothing less than the Ideas of appearances.[17] Thus there is a fundamental connection between appearance and Ideas that enables Gadamer to speak of them as two sides of the same reality. If this is so, then there is no two-world ontology that must be attributed to Plato. All such talk of "separation" presupposes a prior unity or connection between these aspects of our world. If such a connection did not obtain, if the separation were absolute and not relative, any talk of a noetic reality in itself would be irrelevant and unintelligible nonsense as Aristotle indeed contended. As it stands, however, Plato's *chorismos* is essential for understanding what thinking is about. "The actual meaning of *chorismos* is the separation of knowing from the accidental character of uncertain experiences" (DNS, 345). Without this distinction there is no way to set real knowing off from mere opining. Even today, this "separation" of knowing from merely asserting one's beliefs is fundamental to any responsible intellectual endeavor.

But if talk of a "separation" between Ideas and their appearances implies a prior unity because Ideas are precisely Ideas *of* appearances, what about a separation between the Ideas themselves? Here, too, Gadamer sees only a relative difference. We have already seen how according to Gadamer Ideas do not exist as discrete, isolated eidetic realities, but in a nexus or fabric of intelligible relations. With regard to the issue of separation, this implies that Ideas are no more "separate" from each other than the parts of any whole are "separate" from it. One might say that Ideas are about as "separate" from each other as the various "parts" of the face, nose, mouth, eyes, etc., are separate from each other. This is a metaphor used by Plato in the *Protagoras* to speak suggestively about the unity of the virtues. One can say that these "parts" of the face are logically distinct from each other but they are ontologically inseparable. We put the word "parts" in scare quotes when talking about the "parts" of the face because these "parts" are so integrally related that they hardly seem like "parts" at all. They are in fact so integrally related that if they were physically separated from each other they would scarcely be recognizable for what each is. Nose, mouth, eyes, chin, forehead, etc., is each what it is only in connection with the other parts from which a whole face is constituted. Torturers and batterers know this truth only too well. A disfigured or dismembered human face is one of the most shocking atrocities imaginable; it is an egregious violation of the whole being of a person's identity to which their face is essential. But just as parts of the face must be properly related to each other in order to function as parts of a single whole face, so it is with Ideas. They are not ontologically separable from each other, although we can and must draw logical distinctions between them if we are to talk about them at all.

Platonic Transcendentals

It would be misleading, however, to leave the matter of the "separation" of Ideas here. Despite the fact that the Ideas exist in a nexus of ideal relations as integrated (or more so) as a human face, there is still a sense in which a "separation," even an ontological separation of sorts, must be recognized between some of them. As we pointed out earlier, Gadamer recognizes a difference between Ideas that, on the one hand, function like genus and species and, on the other hand, Ideas that transcend this relation and function differently in the web of Ideas. The fact that we can recognize generic commonalities between certain groups of things and further specify these commonalities into subgroups or species by adding a differentia to the generic description is a fundamental achievement of human reason and language. Such an achievement is necessary to communication, which is based on the recognition of a shared world of innumerable things grouped in common patterns of intelligibility. But all such differentiation by genera and species presupposes a grasp of categories which are not really that of genera or species at all. Gadamer, following Plato, would say that categories such as Being and non-Being, identity and difference, one and many, finite and infinite, good, beautiful, true, and even motion and rest are such categories. They can be called "transcendentals" because they function across all distinctions of genera and species, universal and particular, and, in fact, make it possible for us to communicate in these terms in the first place. Moreover, they make it possible for that communication to go beyond a mere recognition of the taxonomy of the world. "These 'greatest' classes are 'transcendental,' which means that they may not be thought according to the order of genera and species. They should be much more [thought of] as what makes all differentiation, specification, identification and therewith, all knowledge and recognition possible at all, as the vowels make articulated speech possible—and even 'kinesis' and 'stasis' (motion and rest) belong here" (DNS, 363). Such transcendentals function like the "vowels of discourse" that always "accompany" or are "present with" all speech. They are the formal elements that are present and undergird our speech.[18] Just like vowels make the combination of various letters recognizable as distinct words, so the transcendental "elements" of discourse make it possible for us to both group together things in terms of various unities and differentiate them by recognition of difference. In this sense, Gadamer says, they make all speech possible; they make it possible to say what something is and how exactly it is different and similar to other things.

In this regard, these Ideas might be called "syncategorematic" Ideas. They are always "there with" other Ideas and make their combination possible. Wherever we grasp a determinate something we have an understanding of its being, of what and how it is, as well as what it is not: we grasp it as a unity of properties and a "true" instance of its kind; we see its "beauty" in its rational structure and we even grasp it in terms of "motion" and "rest," i.e., as being located somewhere on a continuum of change either toward or away from its true kind. In short, these transcendentals are always "there with" our apprehension of anything whatsoever.

Such transcendentals are not, however, known like Ideas that we can analyze in terms of genera and species. There are no genera or species of Being (of *beings*, there are genera and species, but not of Being) or non-Being, of identity and difference, and for that matter of goodness, truth, and beauty. Moreover, these Ideas do not present themselves in direct visions or insight but, rather, they are always already there whenever we become aware of our own thinking. One might even say they are "recollected" out of our thought. In any event, we seem to have a prior understanding of these terms, which enables them to function in their syncategorematical role but which we can never transform into a direct intuition. This is another respect in which these transcendentals or elements of reality are like vowels. Just as vowels can be grasped for what they are only in their function of combining other letters and never in isolation by themselves, so it is with the elements of reality, like Being, the Good, the true, etc. "The point of the theory is that the elements of a complex are inexplicable (aloga) as such and can only be specified and named. By contrast an explication (logos) of a complex is possible as the syllable can be explained by offering its letters, but the individual letters cannot. Only so is the syllable knowable, i.e., explicable" (MD, 305). In this sense, an intuitive grasp of these transcendentals is presupposed by all intellectual intuition of common types. Such a grasp is "primitive" in that we must always presuppose them and can never break such intuitions down into more basic units of meaning.

The fact that we always function with an understanding of the transcendentals which is not the same as a transparent knowledge of them is suggested very clearly by the role of non-Being or negation in human thought. Platonism, for Gadamer, includes an understanding of non-Being, of "nothing," which, according to him, Plato incorporates into his thinking in his later dialogues like the *Parmenides*, the *Sophist*, and the *Philebus*. This understanding of non-Being moves conventional Platonism beyond its orthodox Parmenidean and Pythagorean roots and gives it resources to present a much more complicated account of reality and human understanding. In essence, this move amounts to an insight into how it is possible to account for our awareness of difference, i.e., of one thing being different from another, either accidentally or essentially different. The general insight that Gadamer picks up on in Plato is that non-Being must be included in our account of Being or that the reality of something can only be demarcated by a combination of its positive as well as its negative predicates; i.e., by what it is and by what it is not.[19] Thus, for example, it is just as essential to a human being that she "is" a rational being as it is that she is *not* divine and as such *not* immortal. The "not" in these predicates is just as constitutive of her being as is the "is." Or the sophist is characterized variously by Plato as *not* practicing a craft (*techne*) but a "knack," as not understanding the proper relation between knowledge and power, or as not understanding the relation between reason and pleasure.[20] And by Aristotle, the sophist is characterized by his *lack* of certain disposition to seek the truth, the lack or "not-being" of which defines who he "is." Or another example would be Plato's portrait of Socrates which characterized Socrates as much or more so by what Socrates is not as by what he is. Socrates is *not* like other Athenians, he is *not* like them in not knowing the answers to the questions he poses, *not* like Euthyphro in his impiety, *not* like Callicles in his violent pursuit of power, *not* like Thrasymachus in his brazen contempt of justice, *not* like Alcibiades in his self-deception, etc. Only by thinking the many things that Socrates is *not* does it begin to dawn on us what Socrates *is* and why his existence itself is such a provocative puzzle. Gadamer sees in this Platonic insight the key to understanding reality as a self-differentiating whole, a whole that is what it is only in these positive and negative relationships.

A great deal of the concrete richness of reality, the richness that makes our access to it interpretive or hermeneutical, resides in the fact of this kind of ontological interrelatedness. The fact that every individual stands in a nexus of relations and can be described from a number of nearly inexhaustible viewpoints is a key part of what makes understanding a form of interpretation. This inexhaustibility resides in part in the fact that this nexus of intelligible relationships that makes us what we are not only includes an unlimited list of positive predicates but also an innumerable list of negative relationships. Thus anything can be approached not only by saying what it is but also by saying what it is not. Moreover this "choice" of approaches is not up to us in the sense that no thing can be described exclusively in either its positive or negative terms but must always be approached by a finite combination of both. Thus the transcendental element of non-Being is present in all attempts to understand and say what anything is.

The "transcendence" of these elements is further suggested by the special role that Plato assigns in the *Republic* to the Good in the economy of Ideas. Here Plato makes the famous claim that the Good is "beyond all being" (*epekeina tés ousias*) (509b). Its unique role is further suggested, Gadamer thinks, by the fact "that Plato uses only the word '*idea*' and never '*eidos*' for the *agathon* (the good)" (*IG,* 27). Although these words are nearly synonymous in the Greek of Plato's day, there is a subtle difference that Gadamer points out.

> *Eidos* always refers only to the object, as accords with its being neuter. In following the natural tendency of our thinking to objectify, the feminine form, *idea*, can certainly designate an object too, as do *doxa* and *episteme*. But in *idea*, taken as a "view of something" the viewing or looking is more pronounced than in *eidos*, taken as "how something looks." Consequently, *idea tou agathon* (idea of the good) implies not so much the "view of the good" as a "looking to the good," as numerous turns of speech such as "*apoblepein pros*" show. (*IG*, 28)

What the turn of phrase "*apoblepein pros*" implies is a kind of looking which is directed to something by looking past all else. In short, it is a kind of indirect vision. This is seen in the *Republic*, for example, in the way that

> Socrates treats the Idea of the Good as something that is difficult to grasp and that can be observed only in its effects. Like the sun, which by granting warmth and light, gives everything visible to being and perceptibility, the good is present for us only in the gifts that it bestows, *gnósis kai aletheia*, insight and truth. It would seem futile to want to grasp the good directly and know it like some *mathémata* (learned insight), for the very nature of it appears to preclude this possibility. (*IG*, 28)

We can readily see that this indirectness of vision is not total blindness, but it does bespeak a limit in our grasp of such Ideas as the Good. That our grasp of other Ideas can be similarly limited is indicated by Plato when he says that the philosopher who has made the journey out of the cave may still be dealing with images of true reality reflected in smooth surfaces like water and not a direct and completely clear vision of the things themselves, but it applies all the more to the Good and the other transcendentals. There is no pure vision of such categories as Being and non-Being, identity and difference, etc., and yet these Ideas are indispensable to understanding and are themselves somehow understood sufficiently to perform their functions.

What Plato says about the Good is paradigmatic in Gadamer's mind for all thinking about the highest principles of Being as such. This is the implication of Gadamer's point that "the Good is the being of the Ideas generally and not an Idea itself" (*IG*, 124). When we grasp it we do so "alongside" or in connection with other Ideas. Another way to say this is that we can only say what it is like (e.g., the sun), but we can never say exactly what it is. Its "what" is not that of an Idea or a genus but of a syncategorematic principle that is presupposed in all speech about reality and as a fundamental metaphysical reality that is present and determinative of all that is. We grasp the Good as it is "dispersed" in its various functions in our discourse with each other, which in turn reflects the rich variety of the ways the Good constitutes the interrelatedness of the real.

This "transcendental" function of the Good points us to what Gadamer sees as a fundamental connection between Plato and Aristotle's ontology. Gadamer holds that the "problem that Plato's mythical question about the Good contains is the same one that Aristotle later singles out as the problem of analogy or the *analogia entis*" (*IG,* 124). That the issue of the Good is an ontological issue is both indirectly and directly attested to by Aristotle. Indirectly, in his critique of Plato's concept of the Good in all three of his ethical treatises, Aristotle makes the same point repeatedly: the Good is not of practical relevance in ethical matters. However, this leaves the door open for its ontological relevance to emerge.[21] Moreover, the fact that he treats both the question of the Good and the question of Being by referring us to the problem of analogy is significant in Gadamer's mind. Of course, in the ethical treatises Aristotle suppresses this parallelism in his approach to the question of Being and the question of the Good because he is primarily concerned with practical matters and not with how we can predicate "good" in analogous ways of different things and events. Nevertheless this parallel comes out again more directly in Aristotle's *Physics* and *Metaphysics* when Aristotle argues that all things seek their own proper perfection (*entelecheia*) and how all things are each named according to their own immanent *telos* which is determined by each thing's respective emulation of the highest perfection of Aristotle's God. Aristotle's God is, like the Good, "beyond being, in a sense that prohibits being called an existent thing" (*IG,* 132). Plato knew this was true of the Good and thus he never intended for the Good (or any of the Ideas) to fall victim to the Aristotelian critiques of false concretion, i.e., he never posited the Good or the Ideas as existing in a separate space (*chora*). Instead he sees the Good and the other Ideas as logically distinct principles which commonly inform things in various ways. This no more implies a two-world ontology than Aristotle's distinction between what a thing is (*ti estin*) and its changing accidents (*symbebekota*) postulates two realities.

But it is precisely in Aristotle's doctrine of God as the highest being that Gadamer sees the connection between Being and the Good.[22] When Plato refers to the Good as what is common in all things, he suggests that the Good is the principle of Being of all things, although it itself is not a being. Similarly, Aristotle's God, as the highest being, becomes the one principle uniting all beings as the one principle to which all Being must be referred if we are ultimately to understand how all beings "move" for the sake of a *telos* which is not synonymous with their mere existence. Thus we can only speak of their being in light of this *telos*, which in turn can only be comprehended in light of the highest being, of the unmoved mover. Thus all Being is spoken of analogously in that Being is predicated of things "to one end" or what Aristotle called "*pros hen*" predication. All beings have this one being in common in that what they are can only be comprehended in analogy with this highest being. The relative perfection of each thing is a matter of degree of approximation to the highest being. The fact that both Aristotle's God and Plato's Good are different ways of talking about this principle of perfection shows the connection that Gadamer thinks obtains between Aristotle and Plato here.

In showing, however, that Aristotle continues in his *Physics, Metaphysics,* and *Ethics,* the quest for the teleological order of reality that Plato tells us in the *Phaedo* first prompted Socrates to begin investigating *logoi,* Gadamer has more in mind than a point of scholarship of interest only to scholars of ancient philosophy. What is important here is that this connection between Aristotle and Plato allows Gadamer to stress the importance of motion and change for comprehending reality. It is precisely in Aristotle's distinction between a thing's *dunamis* (potential) and its *energeia* (actuality) that this teleological movement most clearly emerges in Aristotle's ontology. Things "move" or strive toward their completion, or that for the sake of which (*hou heneka*) they exist. Gadamer thinks that Plato anticipated this fundamental idea in a mythical way in the *Timaeus.* Moreover, Plato includes motion (*kinesis*) and rest (*stasis*) in the highest classes of Being in the *Sophist.* But what Plato only anticipated mythologically and schematically, Aristotle "transferred to the cautious and tentative language of philosophical concepts" (*IG,* 178).

Despite this Aristotelian accomplishment and advance over Plato, Gadamer's thought is still predominately indebted to Plato. For this reason, the details of Aristotle's ontology can be put to one side while we return to Gadamer's grasp of Plato and its significance for his hermeneutics. In this context, the notions of "motion" and "rest" as transcendentals provide a fundamental clue that allows Gadamer to introduce the key concepts of historicity and linguisticality into his ontology of human understanding. Just how Gadamer connects Plato's account of the transcendentals to his own principal concerns of historicity and linguisticality is the concern of our next chapter. We will begin by focusing on the relation between linguistic discursivity and intellectual intuition. According to Gadamer, there is a dialectical movement that characterizes all human thought between the changeless, timeless vision which the mind grasps as its ideal goal and the discursive or time-bound articulation of that vision in language. On Gadamer's reading of Plato, Plato himself saw this tension as the heart of dialectic, and his own writings bear testimony to his efforts to comprehend this movement. In the next chapter we will focus on language as the site of this movement, and in Chapter 4 we will focus on the nature of movement itself as an ontological principle.

3

Into the *Logoi*

Contemplation and Dialectic

In the *Republic* Plato considers the close connection between contemplation and dialectic, particularly in the passages following the Allegory of the Cave. After having described the arduous journey out of the cave into the true light of reality one would expect Plato to describe the experience of the philosopher in triumphalistic terms. Instead he emphasizes the difficulties which attend the philosopher even outside of the cave. Even the enlightened thinker who has stepped outside the ever-shifting shadows and implacable half-light of the cave often has to settle for contemplating "the phantasms created by God in water and shadows of objects that are real" (532c). What this suggests is that although the philosopher seeks a changeless contemplation of the Good and the other Ideas, he finds no such life possible. This claim is born out by the fact that in the rest of the *Republic* (and, for that matter, in *all* the dialogues) Plato never gives what he purports to be a definitive account of any of the Ideas, knowledge of which the philosopher outside the cave has supposedly reached. Instead Socrates speaks in images and analogies and with a tentativeness which repeatedly suggests his awareness of the limitations of what he is saying. If we keep in mind the fact that most of this account is in "images," as well as the fact that, according to the "divided line," images give us the least exact account of reality we can begin to see the tentative nature of Plato's insights. In fact, what we see is that there is a continuity between the philosopher's journey out of the cave and her experience in the true light of the Good. Even Plato's account of justice, which rests on his tripartite account of the soul and which represents the central focus of the *Republic*, is marked by repeated references to the tentativeness and provisional way in which Socrates offers these insights. More significant still is that after the Allegory of the Cave the nature of this tentativeness is attributed to the very nature of dialectic itself, which Socrates sees as the difficult but only possible path to truth, *even for those outside the cave.*

Although Glaucon seems very optimistic about the power of dialectic, Socrates is not so sanguine. He backs away from Glaucon's demand to give a complete account of dialectic (532d) and, instead, affirms dialectic more tentatively as a somewhat problematic procedure he must adopt because he knows of none better. He laments the fact that he cannot simply give a statement of the truth itself that is "no image or symbol of [his] meaning." Instead, dialectic proceeds indirectly to the things themselves by availing itself of the existing learning which, Socrates says, "we called sciences often from habit, though they really need some other designation, connoting more clearness than opinion and more obscurity than science" (533d). The purpose of this route is to gently turn the eye of the soul that is "sunk in the Barbaric slough" to the true essences of reality, the ability to give an account of which is the only sign of "full reason and intelligence" (534b).

But who, indeed, ever possesses this full reason and intelligence? Despite the dramatic rhetoric of conversion and full enlightenment we are forced to conclude that such a change is not only difficult and rare, but at best a matter of degree. Even the Platonic philosopher must remain "on the way," on the journey toward truth, a journey that does not culminate all at once in the timeless, unquestionable contemplation of the Good, but remains on the difficult path of dialectic. Contemplation may remain the goal of the philosopher's search but dialectic is the path she must tread. Even the philosopher kings, whose existence is extremely tenuous, if not impossible, only reach a level of wisdom sufficient for ruling very late in life. Even then, Plato does not exempt them from the need for deliberation with each other. And deliberation itself is always fraught with disagreement and tentativeness. As Aristotle reminds us, we cannot deliberate about that which we have necessary knowledge. Plato makes this connection between dialectic and tentativeness in that he describes the philosopher's task as beginning with the received wisdom on any given topic, against which she develops her own thought. In this sense, the philosopher strives to test the learning of her day and, if necessary, to move beyond it. But she also remains dependent on this learning, even when she challenges it and extends it in various ways. This dependency show itself not only in the fact that she remains influenced in what she can see by this set of knowledge-claims but also because any correction or extension of this received learning only makes sense as a correction or extension *of* this prior learning. Thus dialectic places the philosopher in a line of continuity and dependence on her starting points even as she seeks to change that tradition of learning. Even though she seeks a timeless vision of her subject matter, the philosopher always finds herself in the unending movement between what she sees and what she and others have said about the subject matter.

In Gadamer's vocabulary this dialectical movement of probing, questioning, and reformulating received truths is nothing other than interpretation. I would say that interpretation, for Gadamer, is nothing other than the *constant movement* between "seeing and saying" that every interpreter engages in. When we interpret, what is logically prior is an intellectual vision of the intelligible structure of the thing we are trying to understand. This "seeing" need not be a "simple" or "pure" vision. Quite often such intuition is very complex, so complex that what we see is almost always more than we can say. Linguistic discursiveness, "saying what we see," is logically secondary in that it is clearly dependent on what is seen. The ultimate point of such speech is to disclose the reality we have seen; its intent is to be true to the things themselves.

Gadamer knows, however, that the moments of "seeing" and "saying," although logically distinct, are factually inseparable from each other. This is so in the expected sense that seeing affects what we can and should say. What we see is normative for our speech and it is perfectly justifiable that speech should try to conform itself to what is there in both the perceptual and intellectual realms. Yet, despite the fact that language tries to take its bearings from the things themselves, what we say also affects what we are able to see. Language opens up or closes off possibilities of discovery. Language enables us to see from this or that perspective. Nevertheless, the fact that we always see from some linguistic perspective does not absolve us of having to take our bearings from the things themselves. Interpretation still arises from the effort to "get it right." Getting it right involves moving between an intuition, which is often so complex that it almost always frustrates speech (at least to some extent), and a speech whose own complexity not only is capable of mirroring what is seen, but which can also sometimes either enhance or, as the case may be, distort what is seen. When we understand something there is a selection (often implicit) going on not only between which aspect of the reality seen we should focus on and which we should overlook or ignore but also between which speech we should employ to bring that vision to fuller focus and which ways of speaking we should avoid lest we distort what is there. This complex process of selection is integral to the very act of interpretation itself. Interpretation occurs in the movement between intellectual intuition and linguistic discursivity.

This process, however, is never solely governed by a norm of adequation or correspondence between speech and reality. Although speech must seek to conform and submit itself to what is there, this is not its sole function. If one were to stress the function of speech alone it would obscure another function that is just as important. *Speech not only mirrors reality but it also has the power to disclose and enhance the intelligibility of the real.* The key to understanding Gadamer correctly is, in my opinion, to be found in understanding this dual function of language to both *reflect* and *enhance* the intelligible world.

This theory of understanding immediately aligns Gadamer with elements of both ancient and modern accounts of thought, elements that make it impossible for him to be fully at home in either world and which can make him susceptible to several misunderstandings. With the ancients, Gadamer assigns logical priority to intellectual intuition or "contemplation," because it is nothing other than the very things themselves that are the ultimate standard for our thinking. What we say must always be measured by what is there to be seen. In this sense, the *truth* of what we say, understood as "correspondence" and "adequation," is always a valid issue to raise for or against any interpretation. In the final analysis, such truth is measured by what is there and what, consequently, we can see to be the case. In this sense, Gadamer does not join those advocates of interpretation who insist that the world is a text and thought is about "mere words." Thought is about reality, the very things themselves, and it's possible to get it right or to get it wrong.[1]

On the other hand, Gadamer resists inferring from the relative priority of intuition the conclusion that language is a "mere sign," a thesis that Plato seems to have been the first to explore in the *Cratylus,* and that finds its modern proponents in advocates of formal languages.[2] The ultimate priority of the things themselves and our intuition of these things is always conditioned by language even if it is never simply determined by speech. Language often gives our seeing a "bent" or "direction" even though it need not prescribe what we are in principle capable of seeing. Gadamer resists the notion that the intelligibility of the world, which we grasp in intuition, points us toward the ideal of a wordless knowing, a pure vision of the whole, like Aristotle's *nous* or, in a different sense, Hegel's absolute. The intelligibility of reality remains for Gadamer inseparable from language, even when it is never simply dictated by language. We proceed from language toward a better understanding of reality in the sense that we proceed from the received teaching of a body of learning. This body of learning that Socrates hesitates to call "science," but hesitates even more to call "mere opinion," Gadamer calls a tradition.[3] This linguistic heritage always influences what we can see. Nevertheless, dialectic or interpretation is the process of testing this way of speaking against the things themselves. We are to seek the very things themselves by first learning what others have said about them and then by testing that received learning by what we ourselves can see. In this process, questions arise and the tradition we began with is both appropriated and transformed in the process. In this sense Gadamer can be understood as exploring the inherently dialectical relation between "seeing" and "saying." The two belong together by virtue of the fact that each constantly tests the other. Plato calls this testing "dialectic"; Gadamer calls it "interpretation."

One way to understand this relationship between "seeing" and "saying" more profoundly is to point out that Gadamer argues that language contains the Ideas. This formulation is suggested by Gadamer's claim that "the ideality of meaning lies much more in the word itself" (*TM*, 417). What he means by such claims must, however, be carefully considered. I would say that language is not a transparent medium of Ideas but it carries the Ideas with it in the sense that in any linguistic formulation language is able to point beyond itself by means of itself to something that is not merely language. This admittedly awkward formulation can be illustrated by the following example: in talking about a triangle as a "plane, three-sided figure" the words themselves point us to the principle or essence of triangularity, which itself is not language or the product of language. Nevertheless, language enables us here to grasp this basic truth. Our speech about triangles carries with it the Idea of triangularity. We have no adequate access to this Idea without this speech. Nevertheless, what triangles are is not a function of this speech. We neither stipulate this essence by fiat nor linguistic convention. What a triangle is is something different in kind from the speech we find necessary to apprehend this reality.

Thus Gadamer's texts imply that we find ourselves in a situation vis-à-vis language which is neither one of entrapment in a web of linguistic conventions nor that of a wordless intellect that can adequately function without language. The languages we speak, the linguistic traditions that provide the framework for all inquiry, both limit what we see but also contain within themselves the means for transcending those limits in a real but relative way. This transcendence is a relative transcendence because we never arrive at a stage where we grasp the Ideas, the things themselves, without words. Every such advance is a limited advance, an advance subject to critique as the thing itself shows itself differently in different linguistic contexts. Thus "seeing" and "saying," although logically distinct moments in our intellectual lives, remain inseparably entwined. Language has the capacity to point to something that is not a product of language, but which is nevertheless always grasped by linguistic means. In this way the languages we use are always in principle self-transcending. By this I mean that any particular linguistic formulation may point to a reality beyond itself in light of which that first linguistic account is superseded by another.

In this way, Socrates repeatedly follows the language of his interlocutors and shows them how their words open up meanings they had not yet considered. For example, in following Euthyphro's language in the dialogue of the same name, Socrates does not simply focus on the definitions of the words that Euthyphro uses, but he shows Euthyphro how his own words point to realities of which Euthyphro was not sufficiently aware. As a result, Euthyphro must change his speech and, perhaps, his actions as well. He is driven on the path of dialectic, from which he may certainly flee (which is precisely what he seems to do at the end of dialogue), but it is a path which can bring him both to a more adequate account of holiness and a better assessment of his own motives and actions. In this way, Euthyphro's various linguistic formulations each point beyond themselves to something which is not a mere construct of language, but they do so in a way that never leaves his dependence on language as such behind. All of us, like Euthyphro, can begin to explore the meaning of our experience only through the language that articulates that meaning. Oftentimes we reach for the linguistic conventions that are at hand and in terms of which we have implicitly understood ourselves, however confused that understanding may have been. In looking to the conventions and cliches of our natural language we begin with some linguistic account of that experience which inevitability seems to point beyond itself to something extralinguistic in light of which we may be forced to repeatedly change our language and then "explore" further. In other words, we look again, and what we see may suggest yet another different linguistic account. Although our language may become more and more refined and sophisticated by virtue of our submission to the dialectical process, we never leave the sphere of language behind. By engaging in this interpretive process, we experience how any particular linguistic account may transcend itself without enabling us ever to transcend our dependence on language as such. For us, seeing and saying always remain connected.

Language and Being

If we keep this notion of the inseparability of "seeing" and "saying" in mind or what I referred to as the complex ability of language to limit, reflect, and enhance intelligible relationships, we are in a position to better understand Gadamer's rather strange claim that "Being that can be understood is language" (*TM*, 474). Gadamer is not saying here that everything is a text or a linguistic construct, but what he is saying is that the intelligibility of language and intelligibility of reality are, in principle, compatible. There is no inherent conflict between the claims that human understanding is always linguistic and that it is possible for that same understanding to mirror and even enhance the very intelligibility of Being itself. Like Plato's claim that the soul is "akin" to nature (*Meno,* 81cd), and that the soul belongs to the same sphere of being as the Ideas (*Phaedo,* 80b), or Aristotle's assertion that *nous* is, in a sense, all things (*De Anima,* III, 8, 431b21), or Hegel's fundamental thesis that reality is *Geist,* Gadamer is saying that the intelligibility of the world is reflected in language. What can be intelligibly said in words parallels what is intelligible in the world. In this regard, Gadamer's hermeneutics belongs in the "idealistic" tradition, but where "idealists" like Hegel argue that *spirit* or *Geist* reflects the very structure of reality itself, Gadamer assigns this function to language. Once again, this does *not* imply that reality as we know it is a linguistic construct. Much more, it implies that language is the place where intelligible reality shows itself and realizes its inherent potential for meaning. Language is not an insurmountable obstacle placed between us and reality but the very medium in which human cognition takes place; it is the place where thought and reality meet. Thus Gadamer writes that "the verbal world in which we live, is not a barrier that prevents knowledge of being-in-itself, but fundamentally embraces everything in which our insight can be enlarged and deepened" (*TM,* 417). Far from separating the intelligibility of the world from us, or substituting its own intelligibility, the thesis that "Being that can be understood is language" roots language in the world and points instead to its integral connection with the things themselves. "Reality does not happen 'behind the back' of language, it happens rather behind the backs of those who live in the subjective opinion that they have understood the world or can no longer understand it, that is, reality happens precisely within language" (*HMP,* 292).

Although Gadamer's formulation of this thesis seems to some to suggest a kind of linguistic constructivism and has been mistaken for this viewpoint, this is not his intent. When taken in the context of *Truth and Method* where it appears, and in light of Gadamer's other writings as well, what it suggests is the compatibility and, even "belongingness" (*Zugehörigkeit*) of the intelligibility of language and the intelligibility of the world.[4] Just as the ideality of number can be found in reality, the ideality implicit in language can be found in reality as well. Number is a "part" of things and, for Gadamer, so is language. "Being that can be understood is language" is the thesis of someone who sees that human reason's linguistic nature is not in principle an impediment to truth but its very condition. Gadamer knows as well as anyone that language can distort our grasp of reality; it can encourage us to focus our attention on it rather than on the realities it contains. We know this very well from the fact that a technical vocabulary can just as well facilitate an understanding of things as it can obfuscate them and put in its place a pseudo-understanding. But when language functions properly it is self-effacing; it does not point to itself but allows the things themselves to become present in their inherent intelligibility; it acts in part like a perfect mirror that shows only the things it reflects without any distortion from the reflecting medium.[5] To go back to a previous example, the language of triangularity enables us to grasp the nature of triangles as "plane, three-sided figures." Such language brings the nature of triangles as such to light. In principle, any linguistic utterance has the capacity to bring reality to light. In this fundamental sense, Gadamer argues language is like light itself in that it makes things visible without necessarily drawing attention to itself.[6]

If we keep in mind Gadamer's insistence that language is capable of bringing out the inherent intelligibility of things, we are then in a position to consider another respect in which all understanding is interpretation. Because all understanding has an integral, linguistic aspect to it, this linguistic component, this understanding in words, actually makes a *contribution* to the intelligibility of the things themselves. Of course, this contribution may be negative. I have already conceded that language can distort or obfuscate the intelligibility of reality. But in principle, language is capable of making the intelligibility of things fuller, more complete, more accessible than it would otherwise be. Any speaker, even when she speaks only to herself, makes a potential contribution to the things themselves. In this sense, language is more than a mere mirror because it does more than merely reflect an intelligible structure of reality. Language also has the capacity to enhance that intelligibility. If interpretation always implies adding something to the original, this contribution of the interpreter can be seen in a positive way in terms of the function of language in enhancing understanding.

> The thought seeking expression refers not to the mind but to the thing. Thus the word is not the expression of the mind but is concerned with the *simultudo rei.* The subject matter that is thought (the species) and the world belong as closely together as possible. Their unity is so close that the word does not occupy a second place in the mind beside the "species"; rather the word is that in which knowledge is consummated, i.e., that in which the species is fully thought. Thomas points out that in this respect the word resembles light, which is what makes color visible. (*TM*, 426)

Language is not an ontological substitute for the things themselves, but it is not a mere sign either. In its discursive and disclosive function, language can manifest and enhance the truth. Like light, language makes it possible for the truth of things to be more fully and adequately grasped. Gadamer tries to explicate this point by claiming that language "belongs" to reality like a "symbol."[7]

What Gadamer has in mind here is the ancient Greek sense of *symbolon.* A "symbol" was originally given as a gesture of friendship and hospitality between households that were able to visit each other only rarely. This symbol, this *tessera hospitalis,* was created by taking a simple object, like a piece of pottery, and breaking it in two. One piece was given to the guest and the other held by the host household. If on some date, far in the future, a descendant of the original recipient presented this token of friendship, it was acknowledged as a symbol of the accord and bond of hospitality linking both families over generations. The key idea is that such a "symbol" represents a prior accord and the presentation of the symbol functions not only as a sign of that accord but it actually functions to make that accord palpable and real. In this sense, the symbol is not a *mere* symbol or a sign that has no essential effect on the reality it stands for. In this case, the "symbol" *completes* the pledge; it plays an integral role in fulfilling the promise once given. What was not manifest—the bond of hospitality between households—becomes manifest with the presentation of the *symbolon.* The "symbol" actually has an effect on making the bond between households real. It is not a "mere symbol" that the friendship could just as well do without. Without the "symbol" the friendship between households is weakened and perhaps would be lost forever, but with the "symbol" the prior accord is recognized and thus serves as the basis for a renewed relationship, even across the span of years.

As it is with this symbol of friendship so it is with language also. Language is a "symbol" in that it has the power to make a prior accord between human reason and the intelligibility of the world manifest. As a "symbol" it actually has an effect in manifesting this accord. Without language's "symbolic" function the intelligibility of world is weakened and depleted. With language, the world's intelligibility is enhanced.

Even more suggestive here is Plato's use of the term "*symbolon*" in the *Symposium.* In this dialogue, "Aristophanes" tells the resonant myth of a race of originally spherical human beings who needed no erotic partners for their happiness because they were complete and whole in themselves. Such self-sufficiency lead to an irrepressible hubris. To punish them for their arrogance, the gods divided them down the middle and turned their sexual organs outward toward each other thus making each a half and in the process condemned each to yearn for its necessary other part, without which it was doomed forever to be incomplete and never whole. This "*symbolon tou anthropou*" (*Symposium*, 191d), this other half, is what each longs and searches for incessantly.

The relevance of this myth for language is that in Gadamer's terms language stands to reality like these two lovers stand to each other. Language belongs so closely to intelligible reality that although it is never synonymous with intelligible reality it is capable of "completing" it in a sense by enhancing its intelligibility. Understanding is never merely a receptive act in which the intelligible form is, as it were, poured into us from without, but also always an achievement of language. Reality and language "belong together," like two lovers each of whom is essential to the other. This "belonging together" that lovers experience is never simply experienced as "fate," as if it were preordained that they find each other and "complete" each other. Such a "belonging together" of lovers is *also* an achievement and a work of the lovers themselves. I say "*also* an achievement" because it is never *solely* their achievement. Love between two people cannot be forced; it depends on a prior disposition of each person, which allows them to "fit together." But love also does not succeed automatically; such "elective affinities" require work and always remain, in part, a genuine achievement of the persons involved with each other.

These observations have important consequences for the analogous relation that exists between language and reality. The claim that language and reality "belong together" is meant to imply that language and reality share in principle a common intelligible structure. This common structure or bond between language and reality allows language, when it functions properly, to more or less adequately reflect what is real and not to impose a foreign intelligibility on reality. In having language, we "have" the world. But, as I have already argued, language is not simply a mirror held up to reality. The bond between language and reality is so close that Gadamer suggests that language does more than merely reflect reality; it also in a sense adds or contributes to the intelligibility of the world. Language can only do this for reality if there is already a fundamental "compatibility" or "kinship" between language and reality. Just as two lovers can only enhance each other's sense of self-worth and give a firmer direction to each other's character if there is a fundamental "compatibility" or "kinship" between them from the start—only so can they be "friends" and as equals desire what is best for the other—so language and reality must have this prior "compatibility" if language is not to impose itself on reality and insist on its own way like a false lover. Of course, language can exercise a negative influence. As we have already pointed out, language can draw attention to itself and block our access to the things themselves. But this is not its paradigmatic function. When language functions properly it reflects *and* enhances the reality of which it speaks. This "friendship" or deep compatibility of language and reality is what enables our own participation in the intelligible structure of reality. By language we not only comprehend what is real but we also have a role in enhancing the comprehensibility of reality. This is a task and goal of interpretation.

However, it should be pointed that although the "compatibility" of lovers is a condition of their finding fulfillment or wholeness in each other, such fulfillment is a limited fulfillment. The "kinship" between lovers enables them to experience a kind of satisfaction to their yearning for wholeness but that satisfaction is never total. The eros which drives their longing remains alive and points them beyond their own finite relationship. This well-known experience of lovers, who end up either tragically rejecting each other because their eros is not satisfied or who, more happily, come to view their love as a "symbol" of yet better loves (of which the *Symposium* tell us something important), has its analogue in the relation between language and reality. The compatibility of language and reality, which enables language to grasp and enhance the intelligibility of the world, is "finite" and incomplete. Although language is such that it can enable us to grasp truth, the longing of our linguistically mediated reason is such that we inevitably want more than any language can deliver. In finding the right words, words which truly disclose an aspect of reality to us, we want to know how this speech is related to other words in which we find truth and we want to know how this aspect of reality is related to other aspects of reality. In short, we want to know the whole. We seek a truly comprehensive understanding of reality and our place in it. Nothing else will satisfy the longing of reason.

The problem, however, is that there is no language of the whole. There is no one linguistic account in which we can give a coherent and comprehensive account of everything that could be truly said. Like frustrated lovers we are faced with a choice. We can either reject our linguistically mediated access to reality because of its limitations and vainly dream of some wordless apprehension of reality, like Aristotle's *nous* or Hegel's *absolute Wissen*, or we can accept it for what it is as a genuine but limited apprehension of reality, an apprehension which can, in principle, always transcend itself, but one which remains within language even as that language repeatedly points to realities that are extralinguistic.

For Gadamer, the fact that the compatibility of language and reality is limited is no reason to scorn the genuine insight that is made available to us. For this reason Gadamer describes himself as an advocate of Hegel's "bad infinite."[8] Again and again, language both discloses the world to us and in the process points us to further insights which impel us to revise, overturn, and reinterpret language's own accomplishments. Gadamer sees this unending process, which Hegel described as the "bad infinite" or an intellectual endeavor which repeatedly fails to grasp a definitive account of the whole as insurmountable. Yet for Gadamer this is not reason for despair. Rather the "bad infinite" of interpretation is the corollary to the inexhaustible intelligibility of the world and the inherent fecundity of human speech.

The thesis that language and reality "belong together" such that language limits, reflects, *and* enhances the intelligibility of the world is one of Gadamer's most important, provocative and "speculative" theses. By formulating this thesis in these terms Gadamer wants to steer between the Scylla of a naive positivism and the Charybdis of a subjective idealism. Embracing either horn of this dilemma is too simplistic to capture our actual experience of understanding and the role language plays in that experience. We are neither merely passive receptacles when we know, nor do we simply construct our own human, "all too human," reality. Rather, our linguistic intelligence "participates" in reality by both reflecting inherent intelligibility and by bringing out its many levels of potential meaning. In other words, the mind is both active and passive in its pursuit of understanding.

But how would Gadamer justify this parallelism between the intelligibility of the world and the intelligibility of language? Gadamer's claim that our linguistically mediated intelligence "participates" in reality is not a truth-claim guaranteed by any a priori insight into the necessity of such a "belonging-together" of language and reality. Rather, Gadamer seeks to justify it as the one thesis that does full justice to our actual experience as interpreters of the world.[9] In this regard, Gadamer is operating as a phenomenologist for whom the priority of our "lived experience" must take precedence over the demands of some extraneous criterion of theoretical justification that distorts the actual experience itself. It is Gadamer's contention that we actually experience language and its relation to reality in this dual role. We have all experienced, for example, the felicitous way in which finding the "right words" can open up a sphere of reality for us in ways that we could not anticipate prior to discovering the particular way in which certain ways of speaking have of disclosing the world to us. Finding the right words can open our eyes to what is before us. Similarly, we have all experienced what it is like to be trapped inside a language that distorts and frustrates our vision. Once liberated from such a language we realize in retrospect the powerful effect that language can have either to open us to reality or cut us off from it. Thus Gadamer's thesis that "Being that can be understood is language" is not a dogmatic or uncritical thesis, but one which is meant to attune us to the "things themselves" by offering us a theory of language's own relationship to the intelligibility of the world, a theory that recommends itself because of its faithfulness to experience itself.

Of course, Gadamer knows that in our actual experience the close connection between language and intelligible reality is also a source of profound problems. Language's ability to reflect and enhance, or, as the case may be, to distort the intelligibility of reality, gives rise to multiple interpretations of one and the same reality. This is not due just to the ever present possibility of false speech, but it also due in part to the fact that reality is not simple but extremely complex, multileveled, and unwieldy. This is reflected in the multiplicity of languages about or interpretations of any given reality. Gadamer is well aware that there is not one language of reality but only multiple languages or multiple interpretations of any one identifiable reality. Even though as a nonrelativist Gadamer does not think that all such languages are equally valid, his awareness of both the limits of any one language as well as his sensitivity to the deep complexity of the world lead him to conclude that there is no way to synthesize all these interpretations of reality into one grand interpretation. Moreover, even if we narrow our scope from reality as a whole to some particular reality like beauty or justice, Gadamer implies that there is no one definitive interpretation of these realities. There are only many interpretations of these realities. Whether they can be made to cohere with each other is a valid question, but it is a question whose answer must be sought in interpretation itself. In Gadamer's view such different interpretations need not all be valid. Nevertheless he thinks it is possible even for deeply conflicting interpretations to be reconciled at some level of deeper insight. This is possible in principle because these different interpretations can, despite their differences, reflect one and the same reality. Even so their compatibility and validity is not an a priori certainty and it consequently must be demonstrated wherever a challenge or conflict arises.

This is a version of the problem we already considered as "the one and the many." Plato often draws our attention to it by pointing out how there always seems to be one principle (or what he called an Idea) and many instances of that principle. For example, Plato maintained that there exists one Idea of beauty but many beautiful things. This is not just a "metaphysical" issue of the relation between "universals" and "particulars" but it is also a hermeneutical issue that involves us in interpretation. As the *Symposium* demonstrates, Plato was aware that the many beautiful things, like beautiful objects, persons, institutions, laws, or sciences all contain a different type of beauty that raises the questions of whether beauty as such exists and, if it does exist, just what it consists in. Accordingly, these many beautiful things compel us to say many different things about beauty. Just how it is that all the different things we are inclined to say about beauty reflect one and the same beauty is a very real question to consider. It is a matter for careful interpretation to determine just what kind of unity, if any, can be discerned in the many ways we encounter and speak about a phenomenon like beauty. Plato dealt with this issue under the rubric of "the one and the many" and Aristotle addressed it in terms of the *analogia entis* and the issue of *pros hen* predication. However, the same problem can also be posed as a problem of identity and difference. How can we speak of the identity of a reality like beauty when we encounter it in so many different things and when we speak of it in so many different ways? Perhaps there are just many different things and equally many different ways of speaking about them and no one reality called "beauty" itself.

Language as "Dialogue"

Gadamer thinks that language itself always confronts us with this problem of identity and difference, i.e., the problem of how the many different things we say about nominally identical realities are compatible with the real identity of the realities at issue. So close is this issue to the heart of language itself that Gadamer proposes that the essence of language is "dialogue" (*Gespräch*).[10] This is not a thesis that maintains that in order for language to really be language there must be a face-to-face encounter between speakers. Language as "dialogue" occurs even in the "soul's conversation with itself" (*Sophist*, 263e), which Plato defined as thought. Language is "dialogue" in the sense that in essence it presents us with a multiplicity of voices, i.e., with many complimentary and conflicting viewpoints on any subject matter. To understand what those subject matters are about we must "enter the conversation," we must become part of the dialogue by both listening to what has been said and by venturing to say something ourselves by taking a stand either pro or con about what has been handed down. The fact that we have access to reality only by entering the dialogue implies a fundamental insight into our condition as knowers. It is Gadamer's contention that we have no way to avoid the multiplicity of voices, the troubling ambiguity and lack of unanimity that inevitably arises in conversation. Such entanglement in multiplicity is a fundamental sign of our finitude as knowers that no intellectual method can finally transcend.

Gadamer sees this finitude as a phenomenon that Plato himself grappled with repeatedly. In the *Phaedo,* Plato's Socrates explains his disappointment with Anaxagoras's claim that "mind" (*nous*) is the cause of all things (97c–99e). What Socrates had hoped to find, he says, was a teleological explanation of the physical universe in which Anaxagoras had used his principle to explain how each thing in the world is ordered in the best way possible and how the whole world itself was similarly ordered for the best. Instead of an explanation which took the Good as the final principle of all things, Socrates relates how, despite his appeal to *nous,* Anaxagoras simply offered conventional physical explanations of things, which appealed to the typical pre-Socratic elements of air, aether, water, and "many other absurdities" (98c). Socrates goes on to explain how his disappointment turned him toward explanations in terms of *logoi,* discourses or theories (99e). This procedure followed a kind of hypothetical method in which Socrates began with the best theory or discourses about some subject matter he knew of and then tested its supposed assumptions and consequences by appeal to its adequacy and logical consistency. This procedure, Socrates relates, does not terminate in some version of the Ideas but presupposes it as its necessary condition. It's on the assumption of "the existence of absolute beauty and goodness and magnitude and all the rest of them" (100b) that Socrates works out his manner of inquiry. Socrates does not deduce the Ideas from some set of first principles but assumes it, in a fallibilistic spirit, on the grounds that it is necessary to make the best sense of the whole that he can.

As a presupposition, the Ideas are not presented as a way out of the *logoi,* a solution out of the conflict of "interpretations" or "theories," but as an assumption which enables us to see the multiplicity of voices as a positive condition of knowledge itself. As we saw in the last chapter, the only way to say what something is, to give its essential determination, its *logos ousia,* is to formulate an account of both its positive and negative predicates. To say what something is is impossible without also saying what it is not. To do this I must have a prior grasp of such formal categories as Being and non-Being, identity and difference, but also a grasp of more specific, substantive claims about the subject matter. Gadamer's point is that the substantive material components of our knowledge-claims arise from the *logoi,* which themselves only function with some prior grasp of the Ideas, including transcendentals like Being and non-Being. Interpretation occurs in "comparative" terms of specific accounts of the particulars which can only be compared to each other or be in dialogue with each other by virtue of a common ideal element shared by all these conflicting accounts. Thus interpretation is a mediation between different particular accounts made possible by general terms. Interpretation is the constant movement between these particular accounts and the general terms which unite them. Plato's thought on the Ideas, understood as an account of these general terms underlying disparate *logoi,* offers nothing like an escape from the *logoi,* but it does show, Gadamer contends, how such conversations are never mere conversations of difference, never a mere cacophony of sounds with no internal connections between them. Gadamer reminds us that all disagreements presuppose prior agreements without which there would be no way to identify disagreements as meaningful in the first place.[11] Such agreements have their bases in our shared experience of the world and our common involvement in language. Our involvement in both confronts us with the Ideas mediated by our entanglement in the *logoi.* Although such involvements often bring us to disagreements, Socrates's reliance on the Ideas shows how our entanglement in the *logoi* is not hopeless, even though such disagreements repeatedly remind us that truth is never wholly transparent and self-evident to all concerned. Nevertheless, Socrates's reliance on *logoi* is meant to suggest to us the fundamental promise of dialogue, as well as its unavoidable difficulties.

Finitude and Understanding

It is both the promise and difficulty of dialogue that Gadamer has in mind when he repeatedly reminds us that human understanding is always "finite." Gadamer offers a "strong" model of finitude as opposed to a more conventional, "weak" notion of our finitude as knowers. By a strong finitude I mean an inescapable limitation on our ability to know that cannot in essence be ameliorated. By contrast, a weak notion of finitude sees our limits as knowers as open to incremental and cumulative elimination.

To better understand Gadamer's strong notion of finitude it is helpful to consider a weak notion of finitude which we can find implicit in some models of the difference between divine and human knowledge. Many such models of divine knowledge are at base logical-propositional models. On this model, God knows *all* true propositions and has an exhaustive and infallible grasp of their various logical relationships. By contrast, we as finite knowers know only *some* true propositions and have only a very limited and fallible view of the logical interrelationships that obtain between them. Thus our knowledge and God's seems to differ only in degree and not in kind. If we can prescind from issues of time and timelessness here, it can be said that on this model God doesn't really know in a different way than we do; he simply knows more, infinitely more! This is the model of knowledge which one finds in its essential outlines in Descartes's *Meditations* and it is the model that has governed much modern thinking about human finitude. On this model, our finitude as knowers is steadily decreasing as we roll back our ignorance, one true proposition at a time. Finitude in the area of understanding does not really pertain to how we understand (via propositions and their entailment relations) or what we can understand but merely to how much we understand.

An important corollary of this model is that we are capable in principle of understanding each proposition on its own, of judging its truth in isolation from other propositions. So it is that Descartes thinks it is possible in principle to understand each truth-claim in isolation from others. Inasmuch as he makes this assumption he hopes to find a single indubitable truth from which other truths might be deduced. Only by seeking the certainty of each truth-claim in itself can we hope to avoid error and thereby gradually amass a body of undeniable truths.

Such a model of finitude is a "weak" model of finitude because on its terms finitude is not an essential characteristic of our knowledge but merely a contingent fact about it, which can in principle be overcome. Even today, computers have been built that approach "infinite" knowledge more closely than was ever imaginable before. Given this notion of a "weak" finitude, it is likely that such finitude will decrease as our knowledge continues to amass, as it doubtlessly will. In this sense, this kind of finitude is "weak" because we can, in principle, overcome it.

Yet even as the sheer number of valid knowledge-claims continues to expand there is a deeper sense of the limits of our understanding that we should consider. This type of finitude proves to be "strong" in a sense in which the "weak" model of finitude discussed above was not; it's not just a matter of how much we know, but *how* we know or the manner of our understanding that proves crucial here. In the propositional model of knowledge discussed above, it is taken for granted that each of the propositions involved is *meaningful* by itself. Under what conditions these propositions first become meaningful and thus become real candidates for truth-claims is left outside the scope of this notion of knowledge. Following Hegelian and Heideggerian initiatives, Gadamer has long relied on the now familiar "holistic" point that there are no meaningful propositions in isolation from the web of propositions, or semantic relations that are constituted by the "whole" language of which they are a part. Every proposition, every "bit" of language, every linguistic "unit" has a meaning only in terms of the whole range of semantic relations of the sphere of discourse in which it is formulated. Such holism does not imply that to understand one proposition in any given language one must understand all possible propositions in that language. No one obviously knows either all actual or all possible propositions in any language. Were it to imply such a competency we could not account for the existence of limited linguistic competencies, like that of children, for example. Rather it implies a notion of competency that suggests a pragmatic know-how in a certain *area* of language or sphere of discourse.

Gadamer refers to this interrelated web of relations that constitute every sphere of discourse and provides the warp and woof in which every meaningful proposition functions as a *logos*. There are, moreover, always a multiplicity of such *logoi* and our thought-life always involves at any given time multiple involvements in various *logoi*. Consciously relying on the multivocity of the Greek word *logos*, which can mean word, account, principle, reason, ratio, discourse or theory,[12] Gadamer argues that understanding always takes place within these *logoi* and in terms of their complex, many-leveled interrelationships. These *logoi* can be as simple as a "word" or a coherent point that one makes to someone with whom one shares a common interest, as, for example, when we say "I'd like to have a word with you" or these *logoi* can be as complicated as a poem or an integrated theoretical perspective or sphere of discourse worked out over time by many inquirers. As such, these *logoi* could resemble what Gadamer (or MacIntyre) calls a "tradition" or what Thomas Kuhn has called a "paradigm" or "disciplinary matrix." *Logoi* can be as simple or complex as these examples show, but they fall somewhere on this continuum from the relatively simple to the very complex.

The point, however, that Gadamer really wishes to make is a fundamental one about the nature of language, and he is not the first to make it. Like Saussure, Gadamer argues that language is not simply a list of words and their definitions. Language is not simply a lexicon and rules for using the words in the lexicon (*la langue*) but language, real human speech (*la parole*), is a dynamic power that consists of many overlapping spheres of meaning that cannot be reduced to a dictionary and a grammar.[13] For Gadamer, language consists of *logoi* that constantly challenge, amend, revise, expand, etc., the dictionary and the grammars which are mere abstractions from the dynamic flow of human speech. Each *logos* is such an evolving, limited "whole" of meaning, with both internal relations to itself and to other *logoi* and the world. In these many-leveled interrelationships—and only in these interrelationships—does meaning reside. Every *logos* is about some issue or subject matter and every *logos* includes within itself references to other *logoi* and other issues, references of both similarity and difference. Each *logos* includes within itself both claims about what the subject matter is and claims about what it is not.

> The *logos* is such a nature that whenever anything is meant by it, this is meant as identical to itself and, at the same time, as different from other things. Thus Self-sameness and Difference are always present in anything which is and is recognized as what it is. Only the interweaving of Self-sameness and Difference makes an assertion (*logos*) possible. In any assertion something which, in *being* what it is, is *identical* to itself, is linked to something *different* from itself. But it does not thereby lose its self-sameness. (PUD, 143)

Thus it can be said that for Gadamer all such *logoi* are both intentional and dialectical in nature. They are always about something, some aspect of the world, of ourselves and our relationship to the world. *Logoi* refer to this reality and they show us something about it in determinate ways. They demarcate and differentiate the world and thereby show us possibilities of meaning in it. Moreover, these *logoi* do this in a dialectical fashion or, as Gadamer would say, they are inherently *dialogical. Logoi,* like any genuine dialogue, contain within themselves both points of agreement and disagreement with other dialogue partners, both past and present. By being such a "dialogue," *logoi* are inherently open to other *logoi* and historically changing. Each *logos* is an ongoing locus of conversation not only with itself but also with other *logoi.* In this regard, *logoi* are porous and open to the world and to other spheres of discourse and yet *logoi* have a binding, limiting power as well.

Although *logoi* are open to other *logoi* and internal criticism and development, what makes them *logoi* is their unifying ability, their ability to disclose some range of phenomena as intelligible and meaningful in real but limited ways. What makes these *logoi* so powerful is that there is no access to the phenomena outside some specific *logos* about them. We have seen this already in our discussion above regarding the "symbolic" function of language. Although *logoi* can be transformed from within themselves and from the pressures of other *logoi,* their supersession is by no means a simple matter. In principle, each *logos* is capable of having its truth; each *logos* can offer an aspect of the real. Even when we move between different *logoi* on the same subject it is not an easy matter to either synthesize both into a new, better *logos,* or even to simply choose one *logos* over another. Not only are *logoi* disclosive of the phenomena, albeit in incomplete ways, but they themselves are never perfectly unified, conflict-free visions of the issues they reveal. At their fringes, *logoi* inevitably show signs of strain like ambiguity, limits of scope, even possible contradiction. For this reason, there is no *logos* that cannot be plausibly criticized on some grounds. Nevertheless, even when we are aware of the unique weaknesses of a specific *logos,* its disclosive function can still exercise a powerful hold on us. For example, we often find ourselves with a specific way of talking about an issue in which we are aware that we cannot say everything one might want to say by means of this *logos* and which we further know is not without its own internal problems but to which we are nevertheless drawn because, all things considered, it still remains the best way we know of speaking about the issue. Such attachments are not necessarily irrational but show both the power of the *logos* as well as the inherent need that each *logos* has to maintain itself as a "dialogue." To be such a "dialogue," each *logos* must both be open to the world and other *logoi* and it must also have something to say; it must assert itself by articulating what it has to offer in a way that simultaneously challenges itself and the other *logoi* in the discussion. Thus it is for Gadamer that all *logoi* are in constant interaction with themselves and other *logoi*. The result of this interaction is living speech, speech that can maintain itself in the identity of its meaning, but a speech that is also open to new insight and change. This process or conversation is in principle unending. There is no final *logos*. Just as no one can hope to have the last word, there is no perfect language toward which all spheres of discourse are culminating. In short, there is no final, definitive language of "the whole." There are "just" *logoi*, spheres of discourse in whose terms we come to understand ourselves and the world. Far from being a temporary or provisional turn, Socrates "turn to the *logoi*" represents the lasting condition of human understanding.

If we go back to our initial question of the finitude of human understanding and ask what Gadamer's notion of the *logos* character of understanding implies for human finitude, interesting conclusions suggest themselves. As I have already suggested, Gadamer has a "strong" notion of the finitude of understanding in that it's not just how much we know but the nature of what we know and how we know it that is marked by finitude. Such a finitude is a permanent and irrevocable characteristic of human thought.

To bring out more clearly just what Gadamer's strong account of finitude amounts to it would be revealing to compare Gadamer's notion of a strong finitude with that of Kant, whose own notion of human finitude can also be called "strong."

What we know according to Kant is phenomena and not things in themselves. How we know them is through the synthetic activity of the mind which constitutes reality for us by imposing a certain categorial form on the material given through the intuitive faculties of the senses. Do Gadamer's *logoi* function like Kantian categories? In some respects they do and in others they do not. In saying that we understand the world through the various *logoi* we inhabit, Gadamer is agreeing with

Kant that there is no unmediated view of reality. Plato already expressed the essence of the matter when Socrates describes how his disappointment with Anaxagoros lead him to conclude that there was no direct access to reality and that he could only proceed through examining theories or *logoi* (*Phaedo,* 99e). An unmediated view of reality is at best a regulative ideal that we can no sooner dispense with (given the inevitable conflicts that arise between *logoi* and the serious consequences which follow from them) than we can achieve. In this Gadamer and Kant agree and Gadamer himself has admitted this agreement.[14] But Gadamer's *logoi* are not Kantian categories. Gadamer's *logoi* are historically evolving and Kant's categories are not. What is more, necessity does not come with the *logoi* in any way like Kant claims necessity is grounded in the categories. *Logoi* are rich in historically mediated *possibilities* of understanding and their primary function is not to impose an a priori pattern of necessity on our experience. But even more fundamentally, Gadamer's *logoi* do not stand like an insurmountable barrier between us and reality. For Gadamer *reality* itself is understood through these spheres of discourse and it is not the case that they hinder contact with the true world by creating, as it were, a second world, a known world, whose relationship to the real world cannot be intelligibly explained.

In my opinion, Gadamer can only be understood as someone who sees no unbridgeable metaphysical gap in Kant's noumenon-phenomenon distinction. As a metaphysical thesis which purports to tell us about two spheres of reality, the noumenon-phenomenon distinction is unintelligible. As Hegel pointed out, one can no sooner posit an unbridgeable gap between reality-for-us and a reality-in-itself then one runs aground on the insurmountable problem of explaining the relationship between them in a nonquestion-begging fashion. The fact that our contact with reality is never unmediated but always through some *logos* does not change the fundamental fact that the *logoi* still refer to the one real world and have the power to disclose some aspect of that same world to us. The "parallelism" between language and Being, which is fundamental to Gadamer and assumed in such claims as "language and reality belong together," makes his understanding of the phenomenon-noumenon split relative. As we said earlier, "language contains the Ideas"; through language we can grasp essential truths about the one true world.

But if the *logoi* do not hinder contact with reality as such, they do affect the manner in which we know it. To say that we know reality *through* the *logoi* is to say that we never know it as a whole, all at once, immediately and exhaustively. Our finite knowledge is not like this at all. We only know "parts" or aspects of the world; we only know it discursively, mediated by a variety of rich, unwieldy, and historically conditioned spheres of discourse. Thus our view of reality is relative to these *logoi* and never a definitive or timeless perspective on the real: "There is no possible consciousness, however infinite, in which any traditionary 'subject matter' would appear in the light of eternity. Every appropriation of tradition is historically different: which does not mean that each one represents only a distorted understanding of it. Rather, each is the experience of an 'aspect' of the thing itself" (*TM*, 473, translation slightly altered). In this sense what we know is in a certain sense a distinctively human reality, a reality "for us." Reality in itself, understood as what Hegel calls "the whole," we can never know. In this sense, Gadamer agrees with Kant against Hegel that our minds are not capable of moving from the finite to the infinite. In this sense, the thing itself, unmediated and known all at once, is beyond our grasp. If noumenal reality is defined as "the whole," as it is by Hegel, Gadamer would agree with Kant against Hegel that such a grasp of reality is beyond us. But just because a grasp of the whole is beyond us does not mean that truth about the world is beyond us. Reality itself is in principle implicit in our different ways of speaking about it. The Ideas are implicit in language or one might say that noumenal reality—reality as an intelligible structure not constructed by our language—is implicit in phenomenal reality—reality as mediated by our language. Only on some such model as this can we see a phenomenal-noumenal distinction as regulative. Given that our knowledge of any phenomenon is not without internal tensions and external points of conflict with other *logoi*, such contradictions will always drive us on to seek ever better accounts of the things themselves. Even though such "better" accounts are themselves not without their own potential internal problems and possible conflicts with other accounts, human knowledge always moves forward by striving to overcome these conflicts with the guidance of an ideal of reality-in-itself. This ideal, however, has no metaphysical cash value, because its regulative function is limited to our quest for understanding and in fact its ability to function in this regulative way assumes that the noumena are not forever beyond the phenomena but already implicit in the varying accounts of the phenomena. Without this assumption, the phenomena cannot be thought of us offering us aspects of the real and instead float loose, as it were, as a surrogate for the one reality we experience and seek to understand through the many *logoi* we develop. But if the thing-in-itself is always already implicit in the thing-for-us, then we can see why the search to overcome contradiction makes sense as a permanent regulative ideal of human reason. Such contradictions need not imply that each of us or each community of inquirers develops its own phenomenal reality. On the contrary, if the conflict of *logoi* reflects the inherent complexity of reality, then each *logos* can in principle offer us an aspect of the real. Moreover, such conflict between perspectives or appearances of one and the same reality leaves intact the claim that reality at base is an internally coherent whole, and it is precisely this claim that implies that conflict resolution, however difficult, is possible in principle. Gadamer calls this task, following Hegel, the task of "infinite relation," i.e., the task of relating different *logoi* into a unified account of reality and he embraces this goal.[15] In fact, we sometimes do make genuine but relative progress in overcoming the limitations we perceive in specific *logoi*, but what does not change is the fact that as *logoi* evolve by becoming more nuanced and more comprehensive in their disclosive power, they still remain *logoi;* i.e., they remain *relatively* unified, intentional wholes that exist *in dialogue* with themselves and other such spheres of discourse.

However, once we accomplish such "limited" reconciliations of viewpoints, we are inevitably confronted with other limitations that arise as the dialogue moves forward, either by thinking itself more deeply or by encountering other spheres of discourse in terms of which it seeks to justify itself. Because all interpretations are interpretations of some aspect of one and the same reality ("the whole," as Hegel would say) there are no interpretive conflicts that cannot in principle be overcome. However, the fact that we can never grasp the whole all at once but only perspectively through some *logos* implies that we are never, in fact, in a position to bring about a reconciliation of all conflicts. To do this, we would have to be able to grasp the whole definitively and timelessly. Only then would we be able to say just how all partial interpretations "fit" into the whole and thus overcome all conflict. This very real limitation, however, does nothing to prevent us from seeking a more limited or finite reconciliation between specific *logoi* even though we know that the resolution of all conflict is impossible in practice to achieve. Overcoming conflict between two or more specific *logoi* is always possible in principle and sometimes even in reality as well. But all such "reconciliations" do not bring us progressively and cumulatively closer to overcoming all such conflicts. It is as if our involvement in multiple *logoi* has a "kaleidoscopic" effect on our ability to bring reality into a definitive and timeless focus. Every time we enter a new sphere of discourse our intimations of the whole and how the "parts" make up the whole can shift its focus. The multiplicity of *logoi* in their ever-changing historical interaction never allows any one *logos* about reality to offer access to more than "part" of the whole, a "part," moreover, that is itself a historically mediated perspective on some aspect of reality and is itself subject to contingent variations as it is brought into dialogue with various *logoi.*

Logos and *Aletheia*

One might legitimately wonder if anything like "truth" can maintain itself in this Heraclitean flux of *logoi*. What exactly would truth mean in this ever-shifting situation that Gadamer feels characterizes our involvement with the *logoi*? To answer this question more fully it is important to point to Gadamer's debt to Heidegger's account of truth. By turning to a "logos-centered" understanding of truth Gadamer is denying, in contrast to modern logic, that the proposition is the primary locus of truth. There are no propositions that are true as such or true in isolation from the *logos* of which they are part. "There can be no proposition that is purely and simply true. . . . Every proposition is motivated. Every proposition has presuppositions that it does not express. Only they who comprehend these presuppositions can really judge the truth of a proposition" (*HT*, 41–42). Thus Descartes's dream of discovering one indubitable truth at a time turns out to be an illusion. There is no proposition that can be judged in isolation to be true "by itself" or "in itself" without consideration of how it functions in the broader horizon of intelligible relations, which Gadamer calls a *logos*. The *logos* is the primary locus of truth.

To say, however, that the *logos* is the primary locus of truth is to invoke the Heideggerian notion of truth as disclosure or uncoveredness. "Truth," for Gadamer, means, first and foremost, "disclosedness."[16] Before we can speak of truth as "correctness," "adequation," "correspondence," or "coherence," the reality of which a *logos* speaks must stand disclosed *as* this or that determinate something. This event of disclosure Heidegger calls truth or "aletheia." In his essay on Heraclitus, "*Logos*," Heidegger explicitly says that *logos* and *aletheia* are the same.[17] In this context, Heidegger is speaking of the disclosive power of the *logos*, the power of speech to bring something before us as being this or that, as meaning an identifiable, determinate something. What Heidegger seems to be saying is something about the inherent power of speech to reveal the world. Each *logos*, each sphere of discourse, reveals a truth about reality, an aspect of the whole. It is only through these *logoi* that we can have access to what is real in the first place because it is only through these spheres of discourse that some aspect of the world shows itself as a determinate such and such, as meaning this or that and not meaning something else.

If it is the case that the *logos* (and not the proposition) is the primary locus of truth then "propositionalism," as a methodological strategy, falls short of capturing what rational thought is all about. By "propositionalism" I mean the thesis that truth finds its proper locus in propositions and their logical relationships to each other. But if no proposition has meaning and thus truth-value apart from its embeddedness in the sphere of discourse or *logos* of which it is a part, then truth cannot be discovered one proposition at a time, by simply grasping the meanings of propositions and their entailment relations to each other. What this implies is that making a judgment about truth is much more complicated than evaluating, with the help of modern logic, some set of propositions. This does not imply that logic is somehow dispensable for our inquiries, but it does imply that more than logic is involved in assessing claims to truth. If truth is relative to a *logos* then we must learn to use logic in the context of a conversation in which we participate on many levels in overlapping and complex spheres of discourse. In this regard, logic's results are more heuristic and preliminary in that it can help us "enter the conversation" with more awareness of what is at stake but it cannot function as a way to escape the "dialogical" process. While propositions entail other propositions and stand in relationships of logical consistency and inconsistency with other propositions, neither meaning nor truth is reducible to deductive entailment relations. Rather, both meaning and truth reside in the interrelated web of intelligible relationships that include, in addition to logical relationships between propositions, metaphorical associations, analogical connections, practical and aesthetic considerations, as well as ontological entanglements such as a metaphysical relation to the Ideas and the transcendentals. As a result, our judgments about truth need to be more tentative and open to other truth-claims whose finite context of disclosed validity may not be open to us at any given time.

One result of this "holism" is that it actually shows that we have less reason to be optimistic about a progressive accumulation of knowledge than those in the tradition of Descartes would have us believe. Far from guaranteeing the eventual termination of epistemic conflict through ever more refined methodological approaches to reality, the language-centered notion of finitude advocated by Gadamer forces us to recognize that our situation as knowers can never be free of conflict. Knowledge of the real is only possible in these *logoi* and their interaction. In their constant interaction, insight is generated into reality, but not in a way that guarantees the progressive accumulation of truth and the eventual extinction of dialectical conflict. While Gadamer thinks that any particular conflict between *logoi* can be adjudicated in principle because the *logoi* in question are about one and the same reality, he does not think that we are always in a position to actually bring about this reconciliation. The clash of *logoi* does not generate a progressive revelation of the real; they generate insight into an aspect of reality, an aspect whose contours cannot always be joined to another sphere of discourse of greater breadth and subtlety.

One effect of this constant kaleidoscopic interaction between *logoi* is that transitions between *logoi* do not necessarily follow a Hegelian logic of *Aufhebung*, of cancellation and preservation. Instead *logoi* generate insight by "highlighting" reality by raising an aspect of it into the intelligibility of an internally differentiated discourse. But as the notion of "highlighting" suggests, this process of "raising to intelligibility" takes place only by leaving much that is unsaid, much that is not raised to intelligibility, in the background. Thus thinking becomes, on this model, an endless process of grasping something determinate against an inexhaustible and insurmountable backdrop of indeterminateness. In this regard, thinking is like counting, as we have already pointed out above. Reality as a whole can only be approached through the "highlighting" of some *logos* that allows something determinate to emerge from the whole, but only at the cost of a certain inevitable distortion and one-sidedness. This points us to another sense in which our grasp of reality is "finite."

One way to speak about the inherently "finite" and "problematic" character of this disclosive or "highlighting" function of the *logoi* is to say that the truth inherent in the *logos* can only be had by paying the cost of a certain inevitable falsehood. If the locus of truth is always some *logos* so is, in a sense, the locus of falsehood this same *logos*. This is, of course, a key Heideggerian theme of the "common origin" "equiprimordiality" (*Gleichursprünglichkeit*) of truth and falsehood. Such a "common origin" does not imply that every *logos* must be as much "true" as it is "false," but it is to say that no *logos* is wholly true; no *logos* is so free of the limitations of the perspective on the whole that it could be smoothly integrated into a seamless account of the whole. Thus we find ourselves in interminable debate about the complete picture. This is not to say that every *specific* controversy is hopeless, without any possible resolutions of the difficulties which sparked it, but it is to deny that even as we resolve some conflicts between *logoi* (conflicts generated by the inherent weaknesses of the *logoi* themselves) we gradually move toward a *logoi*-free situation or a situation in which all the inherent weaknesses of the many different spheres of discourse are slowly transformed into a perfect, unequivocal *logos* of the whole. On the contrary, our grasp of the whole remains fragmented and indirect, even askew at various points. We have no way to bring the whole into definitive focus, once and for all.

However, this conclusion should not be mistaken for simple skepticism. Even though we can never know the whole definitively, each *logos* intends the whole inasmuch as it is open to the world and other *logoi* and each tests itself only in this openness. Far from implying a general skepticism that despairs of the possibility of any truth whatsoever, skepticism about definitive knowledge of the whole stops short of denying real "finite" truth. On the contrary, even though our access to the whole is incomplete and incompletable Gadamer never loses sight of the fact that a great deal of truth can be known about the world and our place in it precisely through the clash of *logoi*. One might say that we are constantly confronted by all kinds of truth in the clash of the *logoi*. Truth is the "light" generated by the dialogical encounter of *logoi*. As *logoi* interact or dialogue a myriad of insights into reality is generated, even though that "light" never lights up the whole once and for all. Instead we are always surrounded by truth, by many truths. Far from entailing skepticism, the conflict of *logoi* confronts us with a surfeit of truth. There is simply too much truth to ever synthesize into one definitive account.

The Conflict of *Logoi* and the Good

If the logos-character of understanding does not entail skepticism (far from it), this should not be taken to imply that Gadamer or Gadamerians are blind to other problems of our situation as knowers. If many truths are disclosed in the dialogue of the *logoi*, it must also be acknowledged that some of our most difficult problems as knowers arise from the conflict of *logoi*. These problems are not new. The signs of them can be seen in some of the earliest Western accounts of human inquiry, the so-called pre-Socratics, and, as I have already argued, it is not a problem that is likely to go away. Neither is the problem primarily an epistemological one, for at least two reasons. The first is that the problem really arises in its full difficulty only after obviously false *logoi* have been discarded. The conflict between *logoi* develops its full urgency only when we are dealing with *logoi* whose conflicts are brought to a head by the fact that both *logoi* make a compelling case for their respective truths. Second, it is not an epistemological problem in the sense of developing a *logos*-independent, neutral set of criteria for judging between *logoi*. All such criteria are relative to some *logos* or sphere of discourse, and invoking them to settle a conflict between *logoi* is rightly seen as question-begging. But if conflict between *logoi* cannot be settled in traditional, epistemological terms in what terms, if any, can they be settled?

Gadamer's contribution to this problem is an extension of the claim I already made about the formal or transcendental components like identity and difference which conflicting *logoi* presuppose. Not only do conflicting *logoi* presuppose such elements as Being and non-Being but they presuppose a shared practical reality. At base, what is at issue in these disputes is varying understandings of the Good. If this is so, it implies that conflicts between *logoi* present first and foremost a practical problem. Thus resolution of such conflicts is at bottom a practical matter. In this regard, Gadamer understands himself not only to be reasserting the priority of the Socratic search for the Good but the Kantian priority of practical knowledge over the theoretical knowledge as well.[18] There is no theory that allows us to escape from questions about the ethical implications of what we claim to know. Technical know-how and theoretical certainty do not allow us to prescind from such questions. In fact, the inevitable conflict between *logoi* presses this issue on us in an unrelenting and undeniable fashion.

Where such disagreements occur, "easy" and "hard" cases can be distinguished. "Easy" cases of conflict resolution can be seen where parties in a dispute come to an agreement about just what mistakes were made (perhaps on both sides) and just what changes have to be made to resolve the dispute. Such cases do occur, even if they are less frequent than we would like. We can also characterize other cases of conflict as "easy" when inquirers with different conflicting *logoi* agree to go their own ways. For example, they set up separate departments, organize different conferences, publish in different journals, and so on. This is not necessarily a reflection of a fundamental human failure to realize an epistemological ideal of unanimous agreement between inquirers, but a *rational* reflection of the fact that we only have access to reality through different *logoi*. Such arrangements do not necessarily signal a depletion of the human community's access to reality but are, in many cases, a fundamental enrichment of it. In modern societies, the right regarding freedom of speech has been guaranteed by law and corollaries to that right in the form of rules and norms for open speech have been set up in institutions of learning to further enhance and promote that right. This is how it should be. Both the proliferation of various spheres of discourse and the socially and legally protected rights to develop such *logoi* are signs of a healthy and *rational* intellectual atmosphere.

But for every such "easy" case of conflict resolution, there are countless "hard" cases where a practical solution of the kinds described above is not apparent. What then? It may seem that in these cases the only way such conflicts can be moved forward is by the arbitrary exercise of power. But is it the case that at bottom the difference between *logoi* come down to different programs of power? Are these theoretical differences themselves at bottom different expressions of what Nietzsche called the "will to power"? Gadamer resists this nihilistic turn, which tends to politicize intellectual discourse. His insistence on the practical horizon of such conflicts emphasizes that resistance. This may seem paradoxical if not naive to those who wish to equate the practical with the power games that characterize a great deal of human interaction, but Gadamer has another sense of "practical" in mind. For Gadamer, to be practical is to find ways of acting together in solidarity.[19] Gadamer reminds us that however sharp the conflict between *logoi*, exponents of conflicting spheres of discourse nevertheless share a common human concern for the Good. This fundamentally Platonic and Aristotelian motif is invoked by Gadamer to suggest a way out of these impasses that is neither epistemological nor naive by being either unaware of the deep and diverse disagreements behind such disputes or insufficiently cognizant of what is at stake in these controversies. What is at stake is nothing less than conflicting proposals about how to pursue some shared determinate good through a certain field of inquiry. In other words, each field of inquiry, in which conflicting *logoi* emerge, is itself an attempt to pursue and concretize a finite human good. This is not to say that all science is ultimately concerned with technological application. However true that may seem in contemporary society, it passes over the fact that prior to any questions of application of science, scientific inquiry and all theoretical inquiry generally is a form of practice, a way of acting together that always confronts the issue of what is best for this sphere of inquiry qua inquiry, i.e., qua *shared* activity. In this sense, the ultimate horizon of all theory is practical.[20] "Theoria itself is a practice" (*RAS*, 90). Thus Gadamer argues that "we can establish the priority of *theoria* on the basis of practical philosophy alone, without having to bring in the subject matter of theoretical philosophy. Practice itself is the all inclusive, distinctive characteristic of the human being. Thus, one must understand even theoretical activity as highest praxis [*Politics*, 1325b]" (*IG*, 175).

What this implies is that when conflict arises in these fields of inquiry between competing spheres of discourse what the exponents of these *logoi* must do is try to reidentify the good or goods that are commonly sought by each group. Conflict resolution can often only come about when each party is willing to examine itself in this fundamental way by making its agenda as explicit as possible and thereby opening itself up to critique and change in light of goods that are shared by both parties in the dispute. In the final analysis what brings about just such a determinate change in which the conflict is resolved is just such a "turn to the Good." Only by a shared commitment to what is good can the truth be advanced. This is a key implication of the ultimate practical horizon of theoretical inquiry. It is not a question of whose theory is superior in itself. There are no criteria of a superior theory that are independent of this practical horizon, this extrascientific concern about the Good.

Of course, such shared concern for the Good is not the same as agreement on the Good. Often this turn to the ethical moorings of theoretical practice only occurs (when it occurs at all) gradually and sometimes unconsciously over longer periods of conflict in which new proponents of the conflicting spheres of discourse often show their predecessors how their disputes presuppose deeper agreements in terms of which impasses can be dissolved and progress made. Often it takes new eyes to see the deeper commonalities uniting opponents in a dispute. This is by no means a simple or easy process. There is a great deal of room here for moral failure and all of us can point to innumerable cases of such failure. The fact that resolution of such conflicts is often carried out over generations and is never free from pain and change on both sides is indicative of the difficulties involved.

Nevertheless, the fundamental Gadamerian point is that such resolution is possible in ways that need not come down to a bald grab for power on the part of one side or the other; real resolution occurs only when each side is driven back to the common practical horizon which both sides share. Only by a reconsideration of what the real goods are can new pathways be found to realize them. In the final analysis, the real question in such disputes is not "What can I know?" but "What should I do?" It's a question of how to realize goods common to both parties. There is no formula or set of fixed rules for bringing such a resolution about but there is such a thing as practical intelligence, *phronesis*, as Plato and Aristotle remind us. It is a task demanding *phronesis* or practical intelligence that decides how best to move a community of inquirers forward. The realization that such conflicts are not merely "theoretical" but involve complex deliberations about what is best for a community of discourse at a certain time, in specific historical circumstances, does not make the task any simpler. Quite the contrary. But it does identify the deep foundations of the conflict properly and it helps us understand what is demanded of us in such situations.

What is even more important in the current intellectual climate is that Gadamer's insight suggests how changes from one sphere of discourse to another can be a function of reason, practical reason, and not necessarily an inherently irrational and alienating power play. This is not to turn a blind eye to the fact that power considerations can and often do enter into such conflicts, but it is to say that it is not in the nature of things for power necessarily to be involved in the resolution of such disputes and when it is determinative of the outcome, this situation represents a *failure* of practical reason, not an expression of its real foundations. Nietzsche's notion of the "will to power" is the logical outcome of the Enlightenment's fact-value dichotomy. Nietzsche sees the "interest-laden" nature of our theoretical concerns, but he has no way to account for the rational regulation of that interest. The result is that reason itself is swallowed up by the "arbitrary" nature of the interests that animate it. Gadamer's return to the Platonic priority of the Good to the true, or the primacy of practical over theoretical reason, implies a critique of the nihilistic consequences of Nietzsche's courageous insight. Gadamer reminds us that it is only by first pursuing the Good implicit in the solidarity of theoretical reflection that truth becomes possible for us. Considerations about the Good are not arational or irrational but are part of reason itself. It is the Good that provides the foundations or ultimate framework for our inquiries into truth.

The Good, the True, and the Beautiful

To elaborate on the connection between practice and theory, Gadamer appeals to the Platonic insight that the connection between the Good and the true is always mediated by beauty. This is a key motif that runs throughout the Gadamerian corpus. At the end of *Truth and Method* Gadamer states that "the Beautiful reveals itself in the search for the Good." Unlike "the absolutely intangible Good . . . it is part of [beauty's] own nature to be something visibly manifest. . . . It is the mark distinguishing the Good for the human soul" (*TM*, 481). Moreover this "beauty" is, according to Gadamer, something that always accompanies our experience of truth.[21] Citing Plato's *Phaedrus* myth of the soul's intermediary position between heaven and earth and its consequent struggle between the eternal vision of true reality enjoyed perpetually by the gods and the confusing medley of opinion and passions that characterizes mortal inquiry, Gadamer reminds us that it is beauty that gives us a first and insurmountable intuition of what truth means for us.

> At the vault of the heavens, the true world is revealed to view. There, in place of the disorder and inconstancy that characterize our so-called experience of the world down here on earth, we perceive the true constants and unchanging patterns of being. . . . It is by virtue of the beautiful that we are able to acquire a lasting remembrance of the true world. This is the way of philosophy. Plato describes the beautiful as that which shines forth most clearly and draws us to itself, as the very visibility of the ideal. In the beautiful presented in nature and art, we experience the convincing illumination of truth and harmony, which compels the admission: "This is true. . . ." The beautiful . . . gives us an assurance that the truth does not lie far off and inaccessible to us, but can be encountered in the disorder of reality with all its imperfections, evils, errors, extremes and fateful confusions. The ontological function

> of the beautiful is to bridge the chasm between the ideal and the real. (*RB*, 14–15)

Gadamer sees this myth as a profound indication of our finitude. Gadamer would argue that we have not outgrown this experience of beauty but that it continues to mark our experience of truth. Truth is not reducible to beauty, for Gadamer, but is always "attended by" and "announced" by beauty in a way similar to the fact, already mentioned, that questions of truth are always "accompanied" by questions about the Good.

To see the function of "beauty" in our apprehension of truth one need look no further than the function that intuitions of "order" or "harmony" have always played in the advancement of human knowledge. Consider the description of one marine geologist's own account of how she finally became convinced of the truth of plate tectonics:

> Seafloor spreading was a wonderful concept because it would explain so much of what we knew, but plate tectonics really set us free and flying. It gave us some firm rules so that we could predict what we should find in unknown places. . . . From the moment the plate concept was introduced, the geometry of the San Andreas system was an obviously interesting example. The night Don McKenzie and Bob Parker told me the idea, a bunch of us were drinking beer at the Little Bavaria in LaJolla. Don sketched it on a napkin. "Aha," said I, "but what about the Mendocino trench?" "Easy!" and he showed me three plates. As simple as that! The simplicity and power of the geometry of those three plates captured my mind that night and has never let go since. It is a wondrous thing to have the random facts in one's head suddenly fall into the slots of an orderly framework. It is like an explosion inside. That is what happened to me that night and that is what I often felt happen to me and to others as I was working out (and talking out) the geometry of the Western U.S. . . . The best part of the plate business is that it has made us all start communicating. People who squeeze rocks and people who identify deep-ocean nannofossils and people who map faults in Montana suddenly all care about each other's work. I think I spend half my time just talking and listening to people from many fields, searching together for how it might all fit together. And when something does fall into place, there is that mental explosion and the wondrous excitement. I think the human brain must love order.[22]

One thing that is striking about this passage is the nontheoretical naturalness of it. We are not reading the words of a philosopher poised for theoretical confrontation, but the words of an intelligent, sensitive scientist reflecting on her experience in the most natural and straightforward manner possible. Note how she describes her experience in terms of wonder and excitement. We come close here to the experience behind Plato and Aristotle's insight that wonder is the beginning of thought. Note, too, the metaphors of freedom and flying. Plato's myth of the winged soul has always captured something basic to our experience in such moments. But even more basic is how she describes the experience of simplicity and order that the theory of plate tectonics gave to their thinking. "The simplicity and power of the geometry of those three plates captured my mind that night and *has never let go since*" (my emphasis). As Gadamer reminds us, such beauty functions like "a lasting remembrance of the true world." Anyone who has done serious theoretical work knows immediately what she is talking about. We all have to agree with her that it is indeed "a wondrous thing to have the random facts in one's head suddenly fall into the slots of an orderly framework. It's like an explosion inside." This is the experience that Gadamer (and Plato) talk about as a "lasting remembrance of the true world; it is an experience of the beautiful, the experience of the convincing illumination of truth and harmony, which compels the admission: 'This is true.' " Moreover, it is this vision which sustains and guides the pursuit of truth, the experience that never lets us go and that continues to be the mark of new truths that we discover. Of course, she also speaks of how the theory fostered accurate predictions and how it enhanced an ever-increasing coherent account of the phenomena. Prediction and coherence are not to be denied in order to emphasize the more basic point of the "beauty" of the theory. Without invoking Plato or the tradition of the metaphysics of light which Plato appropriated and developed from Parmenides (and which Gadamer consciously invokes) this scientist has given expression to the transhistorical validity of this tradition. What is more, she has also borne testimony to the practical horizon of this experience. Not only does an immediately compelling order, an "aesthetic harmony" seem to be an important mark of truth here, but this truth has the further consequence of creating conditions of cooperation and communication between scientists, conditions which Gadamer describes as ethical conditions of solidarity and which she describes as "*searching together* for how it might all fit together" (my emphasis). In her mind, this "searching together" is "the *best* part of the plate business" (my emphasis). One does not have to be a trained geologist or a Platonist to recognize the far-reaching truth of this description of intellectual advancement that has been captured here. In it, we can see how the Good, the true, and the beautiful have always "belonged together."

But if we do turn to the Greeks again for further illumination in this matter this is no accident. The Greek "*kalos*," which translates as "beautiful," "noble," or "fine" is a word that was used to describe the wondrous, uniform motion of the cosmos as well as "right" or "noble" behavior. Here again the basic idea is order and harmony. The motion of the heavens is "*kalos*" or beautiful because of its unchanging order and inner harmony. Similarly, the virtuous person can be described as doing "beautiful" or "fine" actions because these actions are well-ordered (cf. *Gorgias*, 470e). Like the cosmos, they follow identifiable principles and lead to what is "appropriate" and "fitting" in the situation and the sum of such acts is a well-ordered life. Of course, a well-ordered life is never as ordered as the cosmos, never as unchanging, but is also subject to reversals and failures of principle. Nevertheless, the analogy is a strong one and both Plato and Aristotle recognize both its power and its analogical limitations. It is no accident that Plato argues in the *Republic* that the main purpose of primary education should be the inculcation of a pretheoretical sense of order and harmony in the soul, which is brought about in two fundamental ways: first, by repeated exposure to appropriate objects of beauty and, second, by the pursuit of physical health, or the "harmony" of the parts of the body, brought about by physical training. It is Plato's hope that an early but intimate appropriation of beauty will sensitize us to the higher-order beauties of reason, which we find in mathematics and ethics. Moreover, it is no accident that Plato's just person is characterized by a well-ordered soul, a soul that is led by reason, one whose passions are "measured" by reason's rule of what a well-ordered soul should be. In a similar way, Aristotle talks about certain actions as "fine" and in this he is tapping into the metaphorical reverberations of the Greek and Plato's Greek in particular. Even though Aristotle might argue that a "fine" action and the "fine" spectacle which we can witness nightly in the ordered movements of the sky are no more related in meaning than a "good" action is related to "good" day for sailing, his words seem unconvincing. In these contexts, Gadamer argues, he is more interested in his polemic against Plato's concept of the Good than he is in honestly tracing the common roots of their speech.[23] Be that as it may, order and harmony remain to this day indisputable hallmarks of both our ethical and theoretical experience. We cannot hermetically seal off our concerns with beauty from truth and goodness. In Gadamer's mind, as in Plato's, they "belong together."

But if beauty, truth, and goodness "belong together" in our experience how then can they be adequately distinguished? Certainly Gadamer is not saying that because all theoretical advances are attended by an aesthetic moment of beauty there is no difference between the beauty we experience in a theoretical breakthrough and the beauty of nature or a great work of art. The truth of a theory is beautiful because it is true, not true because it is beautiful. The beautiful "attends" and "announces" the truth but it does not supply an infallible criterion of truth. We can be mistaken in thinking that because a certain theory or discourse (*logos*) is beautiful it must be true. But no such necessity links beauty and truth in this way. Gadamer is well aware that although beauty often heralds truth, the truth of beautiful words must be tested in a wide variety of critical ways. Nevertheless Gadamer would have us see that these two realms of experience are actually closer than many people will be comfortable admitting. Gadamer's point here is that tendencies within modernity to ascribe absolute autonomy to each of these realms of experience is an abstraction from our actual experience, the result of which is an impoverishment of our appreciation of both beauty and truth. Great beauty in art or nature "presents itself as a pledge of order" (*RB*, 36). As a "pledge," it offers in effect a "promise" of something but it itself is not that something. "The beautiful . . . gives us an assurance that truth does not lie far off and inaccessible to us, but can be encountered in the disorder of reality with all its imperfections, evils, errors, extremes and fateful confusions" (*RB*, 15). Beauty is a "pledge" or "promise" of truth but it is not identical with that truth. I could use a metaphor I have already used and say that beauty in various ways "announces" truth.

Gadamer thinks of beauty found in great art or nature in these terms but he does not succumb to the Hegelian temptation of thinking that beauty can be supplanted by conceptual discourse.[24] In speaking about art as a pledge of order or truth Gadamer is *not* saying that what art promises, theory delivers. While beauty *promises* order, and *provokes* the search for meaning that often finds expression in theoretical reflection, the meaning of art does not culminate in reflection; beauty does not transform itself into theory without remainder. While it is true to say that beauty provokes thought and a search for order, it also *simultaneously* points to the limit of that search. While beauty "presents itself as a pledge of order" it does so by confronting us with a surfeit of meaning. A great artwork not only provokes us to thought by confronting us with palpable meaning and sense, but it also overwhelms us with a richness of meaning that cannot be exhausted. In great beauty generally and great art specifically we confront our own finitude in the tension between the inexhaustible richness of what stands before us and what we can think and say about it. In this sense beauty gives rise to thought but it does not complete itself in thought. Unlike thought whose identical meaning can be expressed in many ways by many individuals the meaning of great beauty stands, as it were, in itself. The meaning of a work of art is not in its ultimate depths translatable into conceptual terms. Thinking individuals cannot exhaust its meaning, transform it into conceptual terms and thereby turn it into a transferable reality. It is the singular facticity of great beauty, i.e., the fact that it is simply there, that "such a good thing stood among men," as Rilke said, that overwhelms and challenges us. "The work of art does not simply refer to something, because what it refers to is actually there" (*RB*, 35). Art speaks to us like the ineffable presence of a powerful individual, a "thou." It confronts us with its own meaning, its own depths, its own inexhaustible order and integrity and says to us "there is no place that fails to see you. You must change your life" (Rilke).[25]

It is this integrity of beauty or the fact that it finds its justification in itself, that it can never be a mere means but must be acknowledged as an "end in itself." Such intergrity gives beauty its transformative power in our lives. In confronting great beauty we are challenged to give our own fragmentary and inconsistent existence a meaning that can stand on its own, whose meaning can withstand critical scrutiny. This is a call not only to truth but to goodness as well. One thinks here of the life of Socrates whose integrity was so powerful that he readily made those around him feel shame at the inconsistencies of their own lives. This shame was provoked as much by the Socratic *elenchus* as it was by Socrates's "beautiful soul," by what Gadamer calls the "Doric harmony between *logos* and *ergon*"[26] in Socrates's life.

Beauty can function like this in our moral lives because it works in a way "to bridge the chasm between the real and ideal." What this means for us ethically is that it straddles the divide between the irreducible particularity of our ethical circumstances and the universality of moral demands. In this situation, "beauty" challenges us all to make our adherence to ethical principles as harmonious, as thought out and integrated into who we are as a beautiful thing is integrated in itself. When such a life is even approximated it has both an immediate reality like beauty as well as a character that is deeply compelling. In this sense, "beauty" bridges the gap between reality and ideality.

But if beauty functions like this in our ethical lives, it also performs a similar function in our theoretical lives. The gap between the real and ideal that "beauty" helps us bridge is the gap between the irreducible particularity of phenomena and the universality of meaning implicit in them. When we seek theoretical understanding we are actually always moving between a grasp of particular phenomena, qua particular, and a grasp of what the phenomena jointly share in as being phenomena of a common type. A key goal of understanding is to achieve this ideal mediation between particular and universal. Another way to put this would be to say that individuals cannot be comprehended without first being related to universals and universals cannot be seen for what they are wholly outside their relationships to individuals. Every "this" can be grasped only as a "what" and any "what" can only be grasped in relation to the full range of particulars that manifest the universal. Only in the back and forth movement between particular and universal is understanding generated. Thus at the level of conceptual determination there are no ontological atoms, no being by itself but only being in an infinite nexus of relationships. Once again, we are dealing with the "unresolved puzzle that the universal and the individual are entangled with each other, the unity of the many and the manifoldness of the one" (MD, 291). The role of beauty as halfway between the mere particular and pure universal is meant to stress the reciprocal interrelationship between particular and universal. Our theories need the harmonious kind of integration and attention to individual detail that we discover immediately in beauty itself. Beauty thus functions here as an exhortation for theory to recreate in its own activity the integrity of the aesthetic dimension of reality. At one and the same time, beautiful objects confront us with irreducible particularity and universally accessible meaning. Our grasp of such beautiful things always moves between these poles of the particular as such and its universal dimension. We can neither make the particular secondary by subsuming it under general terms, nor can we eliminate our reliance on this universally accessible side of the beautiful thing. Rather, we are dealing here with an uncomfortable or unstable reciprocity that forces us to seek understanding of the reality before us in a "movement" between its particularity and universality. What this implies is that our grasp of the thing is forever finite in the sense that the constant motion between particular and universal is unending, which gives rise to multiple interpretations or many possible viewpoints on the thing. None of these viewpoints is *the* viewpoint that is able to stop the movement between particular and universal by giving a definitive account of the thing itself in universal and timeless fashion.

We can better see what Gadamer has in mind by reminding ourselves what our search for understanding is like in the human sciences. In the human sciences the particulars demand to be seen as "individuals" in their own right and resist approaches that only seek to confirm, falsify, or further refine their general concepts for the purposes of use and control. Rather than subsuming the particulars under general concepts, general concepts are *schemata* that point us back to the particulars in order to better appreciate them as "special cases" or "individuals" or "ends in themselves." For example, if we were to undertake a study of Baroque music, we would need a general account of what the Baroque is and how it is similar to and different from other musical styles. The point, however, I wish to stress is that any general account of the nature of the Baroque is heuristic in principle. Its point is not to subsume or fully capture the difference in timeless terms between, say, the work of Haydn and Bach, but to point us back to the things themselves. In this sense the particulars, the specific works of Haydn and Bach, should be treated as "individuals" or "ends" and never as mere data meant to confirm some theory of "The Baroque." Each body of work and each work in the body of work of each composer is a "special case" which, although it doubtlessly bears real similarities to other works in the composer's corpus, can never be completely summed up and analyzed in general terms. Each work stands in itself and must be appreciated on its own terms. The point of such study is not subsumption under a theory but, to use a Heideggerian phrase, "to let Being be," i.e., to allow the full integrity and richness of these works to shine forth. The human sciences do not properly have their *telos* in ever more sophisticated accounts that enable us to master the phenomenon under consideration but in the appreciation and acknowledgment of "individual" phenomena, phenomena that have this kind of being which we typically find, not only in other persons, but also in great literature, poetry, painting, history, philosophy, etc. Such disciplines force us to acknowledge, in Gadamer's opinion, that our understanding of the realities that the human sciences investigate is only possible via a dialectical movement which keeps us suspended in a movement between the irreducible particulars and the universal meaning-claims which they anticipate and which we must rely on if we are to speak of them at all. There are no purely empirical accounts of these phenomenon. Neither can we substitute a universal generalization for our more direct contact with them. Instead, we find ourselves, when we hope to understand them at all, caught up in a movement between particulars and universals. Beauty, more than any other Idea, pulls us into this movement. In doing so, it bridges this gap between the real and the ideal.

It is Gadamer's view that Plato himself recognized the unending movement or reciprocity between particular and universal that "beauty" draws us into. This acknowledgment is signaled, in Gadamer's opinion, many places in Plato's works, but we see it very clearly in the fact that Plato incorporates "motion" into his account of thought, both in the *Phaedrus* myth of soul's "wings" being set in "motion" by beauty, and in the *Sophist,* where Plato includes both "motion" and "rest" in his list of transcendentals. Such an admission implies a further distancing from the two-world ontology that Plato rejects in the *Parmenides* and a further elaboration of the transcendental elements of Being. To put forth a metaphysics as a simple dichotomy between the static world of Being and the fluid world of becoming was never Plato's final intent. The real challenge was always to relate these realms of reality in an intelligible way. According to Gadamer, Plato was always committed to this goal. Gadamer sees in this incorporation of "motion" into Plato's ontology something fundamentally important for hermeneutics. For Gadamer the acknowledgment of motion as a constituent of ultimate reality is of fundamental importance because it enables Gadamer to argue that there are Platonic grounds for illuminating his own claim that change and variation in perspective are part of our experience of truth and, by implication, it opens the door to consider a more fundamental relationship between historicity and truth. With the incorporation of "motion" in a Platonic ontology Gadamer sees a way to bring about a marriage between Plato and hermeneutics, a marriage based not on the identity of the partners, but a marriage based on common intent or set of shared goals. In order to more fully explore the feasibility of such a partnership we now turn to this notion of "motion" as a transcendental or formal element of Being.

4

The Play of the World

"Motion" as an Ontological Principle

By rejecting the two-world ontology that is essential to both conventional Platonism and Aristotle's critique of the Ideas, Gadamer has suggested a fundamental revision in our understanding of Plato. If the Ideas represent an element within reality, rather than a separate reality in their own right, then the relationship between the Ideas and the changing temporal world must be rethought. As I have already claimed, Gadamer thinks that Plato was always committed to thinking through this issue and that the consequences of doing so began to show more clearly in dialogues like the *Sophist*, *Timaeus*, and *Philebus*.[1]

We have already pointed out how, according to Gadamer, Plato develops an understanding of the relationship between universal and particular that anticipates Aristotle's position on this issue. Plato clearly points in this direction in the *Sophist* (254d), where he includes the principle of motion (*kinesis*) and rest (*stasis*) in his list of the highest categories. The significance of the Idea of motion as one of the transcendentals is tied to the claim that the transcendentals themselves schematize the fundamental structure of reality. The inclusion of motion as a fundamental structure of Being suggests for Gadamer that "true" Being for Plato, contrary to the popular picture, need not be inherently changeless. Of course, as we already pointed out, Plato also includes "rest" among these transcendentals. For Gadamer, this is only to be expected given that Plato is putting forth a dialectical ontology, but it also signifies that whereas some elements of Being may be changeless, at least some elements of true Being are compatible with change. For a thinker like Gadamer who emphasizes historicity, particularly the historicity of human life, this is a fundamental admission. This enables Gadamer to see in Plato a tacit acknowledgment that some aspects of the "real" world do change.

The conclusion that change and Being are in principle compatible is already implicit in Gadamer's reconsideration of the *methexis* and *chorismos* problems. If appearances are precisely appearances *of Ideas* and thus are integrally related to Ideas, and never "mere" appearances on the order of deceptions or mere illusions, it seems plausible to infer that because change is an inseparable element of such genuine appearances, change must have a place in the order of Being itself. Moreover, if our knowledge of Ideas is dependent in important ways on particulars, which in turn cannot be adequately conceived apart from change, then change must have its place in our apprehension of at least some beings. And perhaps this admission even anticipates a modified ontological dualism like that of Aristotle, who saw, for example, the pattern of motion in the heavens as changeless, but also saw human ethical reality as no less real in its own right but also no less subject to a limited range of change. Plato approaches this insight in the *Philebus,* where he claims that some things are a "mixture" of Being and becoming, of "rest" and "motion," of change and permanence. This is particularly true, as we shall see, of the things that pertain to our moral identity as persons. This conclusion is embraced, according to Gadamer, by the *Philebus,* in which Plato includes *genesis* (becoming) as a real constituent of some beings, particularly our own moral lives.

In the *Philebus,* the issue of "becoming" in human life is raised through a consideration of the good life for human beings. Some, like Philebus, insist that the Good consists in the immediacy of pleasure, without reason or deliberation. His early departure from the dramatic scene and his extreme reticence in the dialogue is, according to Gadamer, indicative of his refusal to admit any role for rational reflection and public discourse in his commitment to pleasure as the Good.[2] Philebus's near silence is meant to suggest the claim that pleasure is simply an immediate good, not needing or allowing rational validation. Socrates, however, insists that even pleasure would not be good if we did not differentiate different types of pleasure. This means not only that there are good and bad pleasures—a point which Socrates repeatedly makes in many dialogues—but he also insists that in order for pleasure to be genuinely pleasing, I must, at least to some extent, be conscious of how a particular pleasure was pleasing and how it fits into my life in a justifiable way.[3] In short, it is only because we can give an account (*logos*) of how certain pleasures at certain times are good that it is possible for them to find their proper place in human life. It is our constant task to be discerning about our pleasures, i.e., to make decisions about them by distinguishing, among other things, what is an appropriate pleasure from what is not. This includes not only distinguishing between various types of pleasures as such and their respective values, but also considering such factors as the time, place, and manner of procurement as integral to what differentiates good from bad pleasures. For this process of distinguishing and differentiating pleasure Socrates uses the metaphor of a "mixture."[4] A good life is a "mixture" of reason and pleasure in that only reason can properly distinguish the value of different pleasures as such, as well as the contextual issues of which pleasure to pursue in which circumstances or to what degree a certain pleasure should be sought or by which means it may properly be obtained.

Not only is the value of pleasure dependent on reason, but Socrates also claims that reason itself involves a kind of pleasure. Only reason or knowledge which can be "enjoyed" is worth having.[5] The usefulness of knowledge is obviously pleasurable, but knowledge is also desirable or pleasurable for its own sake. In the *Republic*, knowledge is one of the examples that Socrates gives of the highest types of good, i.e., those goods we desire both for their own sakes and their results (357b). This pleasure in the value of knowledge is not, however, immediate; it requires articulation in language, a *logos*. Without such a *logos* we cannot distinguish genuine knowledge from empty words, mere trivia, or useless information. Without this "appreciation" of its value—this "pleasure" which is mediated by a *logos*—knowledge itself would not be worthwhile.

What this says about the role of "becoming" in our lives is significant. If our life is a "mixture" of reason and pleasure this "mixture" is not "mixed" once and then thereafter possessed for all time. On the contrary, inasmuch as we live the "mixed" life only when we distinguish good from bad pleasures and "useful" from "unuseful" knowledge, the metaphor of "mixture" is a metaphor for choice and deliberation. As such it points to something that is always in process, or always becoming. Not only is it not the case that all pleasures are always good, regardless of circumstances, but even in the realm of knowledge, the "usefulness" of knowledge is also relative to context. Thus our relation to the Good in these spheres of human life is never fixed and settled. We must always deliberate and make choices. In other words, we must use our practical intelligence if we hope to live well. Only so can we consistently choose the right thing in the right way in the right circumstances. Only humans make such choices informed by reason. "Knowingly preferring one thing to another and consciously choosing among possible alternatives is the unique and specific characteristic of human being" (*RAS*, 91).

Plato calls this process of choice "a mixture of the limited and unlimited," i.e., combination of our finite circumstance with the "unlimited" nature of the Good.[6] The Good is called "unlimited" here because the different ways in which it can be manifested in different circumstances is infinitely variable or at the very least its variety is, in practice, innumerable. The key point regarding the metaphor of life as a "mixture" is that our very selves, our very being as it were, is a product of our awareness of our situation mediated by our grasp of what is good. What comes out of this mixture is the "good for us," a genuine good, i.e., a good which genuinely reflects the Good (albeit imperfectly) as it shows itself in our contingent circumstances. We are a "becoming" in that our relation to the Good is never fixed in a timeless intuition that would make this process of deliberation and "dialogue" superfluous. We must always deliberate and allow a "dialogue" to take place within us and with others regarding our real ethical alternatives, because our knowledge of the Good is never clear enough nor complete enough to make the answers to the questions we face as we pass through life self-evident. If we hope to lead a good life we must learn to think, to deliberate, to weigh options and choose the better course among a finite range of historically limited options. In other words, we must attempt to grasp the one Good in its many different specific aspects that confront us in the many different circumstances of our lives and make decisions that accord with that particular knowledge. As Gadamer reminds us, we never stop being learners here. We never know definitively how to live and choose. Rather we have access to the Good only in the process of choice with which change confronts us. In terms of the ontology of human beings, who we "are" is inseparable from the process of deliberation and choice, and thus there is a sense in which it can be said that our being is inseparable from "becoming."

The claim that what a human being is is inseparable from "motion" or "becoming" is also suggested elsewhere in Plato. The very nature of the soul itself points to the role of motion in the order of reality. As the *Phaedo* tells us, the soul is the principle of life and life itself is characterized by self-motion (105cd). It is well known that for many Greeks what distinguished the living from the nonliving is self-motion. The soul, however, is also that by which we think. Thought itself is thus marked by "motion." There is no thinking without the soul and there is no soul without motion. Thus there is no thought without motion. This can be seen plainly in that thought is always discursive; it runs through one idea (or a limited set of ideas) at a time. We do this primarily because our thought is linguistic in nature. We must articulate our thought in language and the process of articulation is a process or a movement. But if our thought is a process or a movement and is nonetheless capable of grasping the true order of reality, then that true order of reality must, at some level, be compatible with this movement. Thus Gadamer argues that

> the petrified tranquility of a cosmos of Ideas cannot be the ultimate truth for Plato. For the soul, which he coordinates with these Ideas, is motion. Thus the *logos* which thinks the relationship of the Ideas to one another

> is necessarily the movement of thought and consequently a movement of what is thought. Even though the sense in which motion is supposed to "be" might not be thinkable without contradiction, the dialectic of motion . . . cannot keep us from recognizing that motion and being necessarily go together. That is clearly the conclusion reached in the *Sophist*. (*HD*, 14)

What is more, thought is motion, not only in the fundamental sense of being discursively linguistic but also because it is inherently dialectical. As we saw in Chapter 2, Gadamer points out how Plato claimed that we cannot say what something is without at least implicitly comparing it to what it is not. All positive predication implies a denial in the sense that certain predicates are implicitly ruled out. Thus all positive predication implies a process of differentiation and as such is dialectical or characterized by "motion."

But we have also seen how "motion" is tied to thought in yet another fundamental way. As we pointed out above, thought involves a constant movement between particulars (*tode ti*) and general or universal concepts (*ti esti*). This movement between a particular "this" and a universal "what" is integral to thought itself. It is our "soul" or, to use a more contemporary idiom, our linguistically mediated reason that constantly moves between the "this" and the "what" and thus reflects the relationships that obtain here. As such, the soul itself, according to Gadamer, is involved in a "participation" of sorts.

> Thus we have a threefold *methexis* (participation) here: (1) the *methexis* of the individual in the Idea, (2) the *methexis* of the soul in the Idea, but ultimately, (3) the *methexis* of the Ideas in each other—for any thinking of something is a delimiting from and a combining with (cf. the *Sophist* on *dihairesis* and *synagògè*). My thesis, then, is this: these are three aspects of one and the same relationship. To think of "this here" as "what" it is, is always at the same time to differentiate the "what" from the "this." But to differentiate the "what" is always to differentiate one "what" from another "what": the impurity in the appearing "this" is in truth the existence of some other pure thing in it. (*IG*, 88)

All thinking involves this unending motion between the "what" and the "this," between the particulars and the different Ideas or "whats" that lend it its essential character. This motion is reflected in the very conversation in the soul that Plato and Gadamer call "thought." What is so fundamental about this "motion" or process is that both particular and universal are defined by it. This process is their common medium in which both develop over time. This insight is essential to grasping Gadamer's position and it is one to which we will return below.

"Motion" and Interpretation

In pointing out this "transcendental" function of motion in thought, Gadamer has the nature of human understanding as interpretation very much in mind. When we interpret a text there is a similar movement between a "this" and a "what," between particular things and experiences, on the one hand, and, on the other hand, general accounts or Ideas which explicitly or implicitly make claims to universality. We always look to particular things or experiences when we interpret, but we also attempt to relate a particular "this" to a general "what." "A person who speaks—who, that is to say, uses the general meaning of words—is so oriented toward the particularity of what he is perceiving that everything he says acquires a share in the particularity of the circumstances he is considering" (*TM*, 429). By moving back and forth between the particular thing and general concepts both are actually enriched and extended in important ways. Gadamer argues that

> the general concept meant by the word is enriched by any given perception of a thing, so that what emerges is a new, more specific word formation which does more justice to the particularity of that act of perception. However certainly speaking implies using preestablished words with general meanings, at the same time, a constant process of concept formation is going on by means of which the life of a language develops. (*TM*, 429)

This ongoing process of concept formation is integral to interpretation itself.

As an example, take the text we referred to above, Plato's *Republic*, to make a point about the inherent interconnectedness of Ideas. When we interpret this text we are involved with universal truth-claims that are mediated at a number of levels with various particularities. Not only are we concerned with general Ideas like "justice" or "moral rectitude" but we must also understand Plato's particular uses of this term, and we must consult our own grasp of these issues as well. As we have already seen, Gadamer maintains in general that all interpretation involves mediation between universality and particularity. But the various levels of this mediation can and should be more precisely distinguished. There are, in my opinion, at least three levels of particularity that mediate our grasp of any text. They are the particular language of the text itself, i.e., what the words say in their historical and textual context; the particular historical situation of the interpreter, i.e., the tradition from which she approaches the text; and lastly, the particular, potentially unique experience of the interpreter herself. Let us look at each particularity in somewhat more detail.

All interpretations should begin with the particularity of the language of the text itself, i.e., what it literally says. What a text like the *Republic* actually says is indispensable to what it means. But these two aspects of the text, what it says and what it means, are not at all synonymous. We look to what the text says, its particular use of a particular natural language in order to understand what it means or, in other words, what truth-claims it is making about a variety of subjects, e.g., justice, equality, merit, human nature, virtue, education, responsibility, truth, goodness, etc. The language of Plato's text makes claims about the nature of these universals. The meaning of these universals, as understood by Plato, is found in the particular language of the text, but their meaning as such is not synonymous with this language. If it were, translation of his work (or any work for that matter) would be virtually impossible. As it stands, however, the meaning of a text is closely tied to the particular language of the text, but it is in principle possible for it to transcend that language. The language points beyond itself to these extralinguistic meanings. This is why it is possible to translate the text's meaning from one language to another or even to talk about the same meaning in different words, either in another natural language than that of the text or in the same natural language of the original text. Of course, we know particularly from our dealing with texts that were not written in our native language that this separation between language and meaning is relative and sometimes very difficult to carry out. Nevertheless, such a separation is possible in principle and we invoke it implicitly, even when we work fluently in the original language of the text, in order to separate the true meaning of the words in this particular textual context from everything else these words could mean in the natural language of which the text is a part.

Understanding a text like the *Republic*, however, is not just a function of gaining linguistic competence in its language. Another kind of "translation" must take place as well. In order to really understand how Plato's language points to a universal meaning-claim I must also relate that language and its meaning to my own experience. This implies not only that I must translate Plato's Greek into English (or whatever language I speak) but I must relate the truth-claims he makes to my own experience. This, too, is a kind of translation, which even a Greek of Plato's day would have to perform in order to understand his text. After all the philological and historical work has been done, I still have to ask myself how what I seemingly understand Plato to be saying squares with what I know about these subjects. Unless these subjects already have some meaning for me, unless I have a "preunderstanding" of them, i.e., some sort of grasp of them prior to reading the text, a text like the *Republic* will make no claim on me. Unless I already have some understanding of this subject matter I will not be able to follow Plato's meaning as it unfolds, either in agreement or disagreement with him. This fact is part of what Gadamer has in mind when he claims that interpretation is always mediated by a "prejudice" or "preunderstanding" regarding the very things themselves.[7] This preunderstanding is a "prejudice" not in the sense of a dogmatic bias but in the sense of a prejudgment (*Vor-urteil*) which gives me a preliminary and provisional understanding of the realities of which the text speaks and against which the text can begin to articulate itself in its own distinctive outlines. Of course such "prejudices" can and do change, but this fact makes them no less indispensable for interpretation.

But even our particular "preunderstanding" of the things themselves has levels of complexity and particularity that should be carefully articulated here. On the one hand, there is the particularity of my own more or less direct experience with the realities of which the text speaks, and, on the other hand, there is the particular history of my culture which always in part mediates my own experience. Both these particularities mediate my grasp of Plato's text. Although my experience and the tradition of which I am a part are logically distinct, in actual contexts of understanding they are always interpenetrating. In a way that is difficult to untangle, my own experience is always, in part, a product of my culture and its tradition, but it is also always my own experience and as such it may be different in some ways from that which has been handed down by tradition. Let's look at this relationship a little more closely.

One key source of the preunderstanding with which we approach a text is our own historicity. Our prior understanding is not a timeless and wordless intuition but is itself formed in a complicated way by factors such as the natural language in which we think, the practices we engage in and take for granted, and the other texts we have read. Our natural language is itself a repository of experience and perspectives on the meaning of the issues of which the text speaks. Our language may, in part, even be affected by the text itself that we study. For example, texts like Plato's *Republic*, Descartes's *Meditations*, the Bible, or what have you, have all affected our historical and linguistic situation in Western society. All of these texts, and many more, have left traces in our everyday speech and practice. When we turn our attention to these texts themselves, we are singling out an aspect of our very own history, on which these texts have had their own complicated effects. We are part of this ongoing history and our interpretation is both affected by it and has a potential effect upon it. Moreover, the more we study this history and trace its effects on our language and practice, the more we bring to our study of any text on which we have not previously focused our attention. Here we are not simply dealing with a preunderstanding as an unconscious effect that our discourses and practices unwittingly exercise on our attempts at interpretation, but our preunderstanding is itself now more conscious of itself. In both these ways, we can see why Gadamer insists that all interpretations come out of a tradition of inquiry, whether we are less aware of that tradition as uncritical speakers of various culturally mediated discourses or somewhat more aware of that tradition as more or less self-conscious researchers. In both senses, our preunderstanding is the locus and carrier of that tradition. In this sense, we are, in part, this history of various effects. This is what Gadamer calls a *Wirkungsgeschichte* or history of effects.[8] But Gadamer stresses that we are at best only relatively aware of all the effects that this history has had on us. So closely are we tied to this history, which provides the constant, unspoken background against which our study of any text takes place, that we can never make all its effects conscious and an object of critical scrutiny. Of course, we can accomplish this task to some relative degree. Nevertheless we remain, vis-à-vis our *Wirkungsgeschichte*, "more being than consciousness" ("*mehr Sein als Bewusstsein*"), as Gadamer reminds us.

When I try to understand a text like the *Republic* I bring this history with me as part of my preunderstanding. It is only by entering into a "dialogue" with Plato's text that I come to understand him at all. This "dialogue" is a movement between the understandings I bring with me about these issues, as well as the understandings of these issues offered by Plato's text. What arises from this dialogue is an interpretation of Plato, which itself is neither a simple reiteration of the text nor a product of the tradition of interpretation in which it and the interpreter are embedded, but a "mixture" or mediation between Plato and the complex situation of the interpreter. Gadamer calls it a "fusion of horizons" (*Horizontsverschmelzung*).[9] It is an understanding *of Plato*, but an understanding that is related to the historically mediated concerns I bring to the text. Such an understanding "fuses" the horizon of Plato's text with that of our own experience.

But such a "fusion" is not in principle a corruption of Plato's text or its original meaning. Even though Gadamer insists that all interpretation involves this "fusion of horizons," not all such fusions involve an essential alteration of the text's meaning. In other words they need not involve an arbitrary projection of my horizon of concerns on to the so-called *Ursinn* or original meaning of the text. Of course, such unjustifiable "projections" can occur, but it is Gadamer's provocative point that not all "fusion of horizons" involves an arbitrary act of violence against the text's own integrity. Gadamer can make this claim because he insists that neither Plato's text exists as an impermeable meaning *an sich* nor does my own experience exist hermetically sealed off from the tradition in which the text participates. Both Plato's text and my experience "belong together." In principle, they share the common horizon of time or the historical tradition of which both are parts. Both the Ideas which are the final referents of Plato's meaning and my own historically mediated experience share a common connection or involvement with each other. Thus Gadamer can argue that I understand the very things themselves, things like the Ideas of justice, equality, merit, etc., and that this same understanding is never a timeless, definitive intuition of the whole web of Ideas, in which these things exist. Our choice here is not between a meaning in itself, which we can somehow intuit or reconstruct, or an arbitrary projection of the interpreter's horizon unto the text. Such a choice presents us only with a false dichotomy. The reality is that both text and interpreter "participate" in a common process which defines them both. So it is that history and tradition do, in fact, limit my grasp of the Ideas; they make my understanding a temporally relative understanding and not a definitive, timeless vision of reality. But it is also the case that within this temporal horizon I can grasp something true about the Ideas. History does not mechanically dictate my understanding. Our involvement in history does not imply that we are caught in a closed circle or a hermetically sealed sphere in which no contact with transhistorical reality is possible.

A good example of such a "fusion of horizons," in which the things themselves are genuinely grasped via the historicity of the interpreter, is Plato's "feminism" in the *Republic*. Of course, earlier interpreters and certainly Plato himself would never have used the term "feminism" or even understood its meaning (hence the need for scare quotes). Nevertheless, from our vantage point in history, "feminism" is an appropriate way for us to mark the first sustained argument in Western culture that gender should not be used as the basis to judge ability to perform certain tasks or to determine eligibility for education. Plato argues for a limited functional equality in principle between men and women in a narrative context filled with regular misogynistic asides. We see this clearly, perhaps more clearly than Plato himself. There is no reason to deny this inconsistency in Plato's text. Moreover, Plato's "feminism" is not a feminism in the modern sense of the word in that it is not informed by a prodemocratic ethos which values the individual and her development as ends in themselves. All of these differences and qualifications can and should be made, but it still remains the case that we are understanding *Plato himself* even when we see him through the prism of our awareness of the tortuous history of gender inequality in our culture. Plato couldn't have possibly had that particular historical awareness, and yet it is still possible that our experience is connected to his own and to his text. Such a connection provides us a real access to the things themselves, the things that make up the focus of his text and our interest in it. The fact that we inevitably see Plato through our own contemporary eyes does not mean that we cannot see Plato at all. Gadamer would insist that what links Plato's experience (and his text) to our experience (and our language) is a common participation in the Ideas. We share a common reality, intelligibly structured by the same principles, even though this rational structure is historically mediated in different ways in different contexts.

Such a common access to the Ideas, however, should not be taken to mean that we are simply destined to repeat Plato. In fact, we can even grasp things about the Ideas that were not grasped before. Here we are confronted with another level of particularity that is involved in our grasp of a text. Despite the fact that we are, in part, our "history of effects," a *Wirkungsgeschichte*, this does not preclude the possibility of something genuinely new emerging, either from our own grasp of the past or from our experience of realities like justice, equality, merit, etc., of which Plato's text speaks. We are not *only* our past and we are not merely "products" of that past. Tradition is the background against which the new and unique may emerge. My particular experience, which need not be dictated to me by the past, might suggest a new, critical perspective on the text itself. This would not mean that this new perspective was itself immediate, untouched by the influences of our past. Our preunderstanding would still be integral to understanding the text, but it does point to a sense in which history is not a straitjacket but the arena for historical possibility, i.e., for something genuinely new and different to emerge in our ongoing experience, and this same new insight can even affect how we understand our past. In this sense, interpretation would also involve the mediation of a "what" with a "this." The "this" of my particular historical circumstances constantly changes as the constellation of factors that make it up shift in the course of time. As these shifts occur, we bring our traditions of speech and practice with us, and it is in terms of them that we initially try to come to terms with our new situation. But sometimes the old words fail us and sometimes established practices are found wanting. In such contexts, we must "reinvent" ourselves if we are to do justice to the reality which our new historical horizon has opened up to us. Of course, we can never totally reinvent our language or practice, but we can introduce innovations that are more adequate to what is now before us. We do this frequently when we reinterpret the great texts of the past. As our situation changes, how we interpret these texts must change as well. We must somehow relate their universal meaning to particular circumstances we find ourselves in. When we do this, however, such changes are always enframed by a background of "tradition," which continues to support us and supply our point of reference, even as we modify it in one way or another. In this respect history or tradition is like Neurod's ship on which we all remain passengers even as we gradually change the very traditions that make it possible for us to understand the world and ourselves in the first place.

Grasping this complicated relationship between our various levels of particularity and the universal of thought is essential to understand how Gadamer meets the charge that talk of tradition and historicity precludes any sense whatsoever of a universal truth. Talk of tradition in this connection is not only meant to point to inherent limits in our grasp of things, but it also tells us something about the relation of "Being and time." Charges of subjectivism leveled at thinkers like Gadamer who point out the historicity of interpretation make certain uncritical assumptions about the being of the universals which are the focus of all interpretations. As I have already pointed out above, we often fear charges of subjectivism because we assume that we should be able to grasp the being of these universals "*an sich*," apart from their relations to our particular language and historical circumstances. We fear that our language and circumstances are not essentially related to them but somehow alienated and inimical to them. But this assumption implicitly invokes a two-world ontology of Being-in-itself that exists "separately" from us, from our language and our experience. If these universals, however, do not exist in a second intelligible world but are an aspect of our temporally and linguistically mediated reality, then it should come as no surprise that we grasp their being through time and not apart from it. Gadamer's notion of "tradition" is meant in part to stress that time is not inimical to true knowledge but the medium of truth itself. Time or history is the medium of truth because these realities are temporal in nature. Thus, when we approach texts from the past, like Plato's, it is not a matter of extracting ourselves from our circumstances in order to grasp the meaning of the text, which supposedly exists in a separate, intelligible reality, but it is a matter of relating what Plato says in his context and in his language to our circumstances in our language. This is possible in the first place only because Plato's concerns and ours belong to the same ongoing stream of "tradition."

The act of relating the text to my circumstances is called by Gadamer the act of "application."[10] Application is the constant process of "mediating between the then and the now, between the thou and the I" (*TM*, 333). Only by engaging in this mediation can I begin to grasp these realities themselves as they really are, i.e., as realities whose meanings are connected to our language and experience in essential ways and which evolve over time in constant dialogue. Thus Gadamer writes that "the meaning of Being itself emerges and as always it completes itself through its temporalization [*Verzeitlichung*]" (DNS, 368). "Temporalization" implies that one and the same meaning unfolds itself into different historical possibilities over time. Far from signaling a depletion of an original meaning or the destruction of its identity, Gadamer says that the process of one meaning unfolding its many different historical possibilities actually signals an "increase in being" (*Seinszuwachs*).[11]

To better understand what Gadamer means by "application," "temporalization," or "increase in being" it is helpful, in my opinion, to turn to an important trend in modern culture, which Charles Taylor has called "expressivism." In my opinion Gadamer shares a great deal with this "expressivist" tradition and in this respect he can be seen as a representative of the "Romantic" tradition, despite the fact that Gadamer would probably not identify himself in these terms. I would argue that these Romantic elements in Gadamer's philosophy are very much a part of his *wirkungsgeschichtliche Bewusstsein* or "historically affected consciousness." Even though Gadamer has not expressly identified himself with these Romantic roots, he does claim that one's historically affected consciousness is always more being than consciousness. In other words, how we are affected by history always exceeds our grasp of its effects. But what is "expressivism" and, more to the point, how is it integrally related to what Gadamer means by interpretation as "application," "temporalization," and an "increase in being"? It is to these questions that we now turn.

"Expressivism" and Interpretation

Taylor points out that the key ideas of expressivism can be traced back to figures in the generation immediately succeeding Kant.[12] For these thinkers, men like Herder and Hegel, there was a new challenge to somehow combine three central concerns: they attempted to combine (1) the Kantian notions of human beings as autonomous or self-defining with (2) their emerging awareness of the many different ways history enters our self-understanding, along with, particularly in the case of

Hegel, (3) the older idea that human beings are reflections of a pregiven nature, analogous to that which we find in Aristotle's philosophical anthropology. These three concerns, autonomy, history, and nature, all figured prominently in their attempts to give a philosophical account of human self-understanding. What emerged from this attempt was a theory of meaning or, more specifically, a theory about how meaning emerges, particularly the meanings which are integral to our self-understanding as human beings. In the case of self-understanding—which Gadamer's hermeneutics takes as his model for understanding in general—what emerges is a theory of meaning formation that, so to speak, splits the difference between "finding" and "making." Taylor points out how these philosophers did not want to say either that the meanings which are integral to self-understanding are simply pregiven, waiting to be found and adequately described, or simply invented, made up in response to the personal and historical contingencies of our lives. The first alternative would not only be contrary to the Kantian ideal of self-definition but also contrary to the role that history plays in contributing to the varieties of human self-understanding. But the second alternative, the alternative which maintains that we simply define ourselves, that we project a complex meaning onto our circumstances contingent upon the exigencies we face, was equally unpalatable. Not only are we always in part "products" of the historical circumstances, of which Herder had begun to make his generation so sensitive, but there is also something to be said for the older idea of "nature." Our being is always also governed in part by a "nature" that is not of our choosing. Of course, the key question is whether these varied concerns can all be reconciled. Could these thinkers (including Gadamer) split the difference between self-discovery of one's place in the order of things and self-creation as a complex act of will?

To find their way between the horns of this dilemma, these thinkers relied, in part, on Aristotle's distinction between potentiality and actuality. They frequently appealed to the idea that things have a potential that becomes actual over time. But they could only rely on this general idea up to a point. As is well known, Aristotle's account of human potential is in a certain sense both ahistorical and unidimensional. Although human beings only develop over time, history, in all its concrete particularity, does not in Aristotle's view play an integral role in defining that potential. Our potential is given to us as a *telos* which defines our lives by virtue of the fact that we can either live up to it and realize it, make it actual, or, as the case may be, fail in some respects to make it actual. Although we either realize or fail to realize this potential in time, which includes the concrete social circumstances of our lives, the *telos* itself is pregiven. In short, there aren't essentially many ways to be fully human, which in part always depend on my choice and historical circumstances. There is only one way to be fully human, and neither history nor my choice has anything to do with defining the nature of that *telos* as such. Such a conception of the human *telos* was simply not compatible with any strong sense of human autonomy or any strong insight into the way history enters our very identities. On the other hand, they found it equally implausible that human beings could simply define themselves through the exercise of their rational wills. Not only did their awareness of history suggest that such rational wills existed, contrary to Kant, in time, embedded in many particular historical contingencies, but they also thought that there was something like a "nature," not just human nature, but a pregiven order of things in which they had to find themselves. They were convinced that there had to be a *telos* for human life, even a *telos* that was in some sense pregiven, but also one that could accommodate human history and human freedom.

In response to these seemingly conflicting intuitions they developed a theory of meaning, which sees meaning emerging from potential to actual, but one whose account of the potential allows it to develop in concert with history and freedom. Taylor calls this theory "expressivism." In the terms of this theory, meaning is "expressed" in a dual sense of both "making manifest" what is latent and pregiven and "defining" or giving further shape to this potential. To make a meaning manifest in this sense does not imply that what is made manifest "was already fully formulated beforehand."[13] At best it was inchoate, only partially formed. In some sense, it requires my contribution to bring it about.

In such contexts meaning emerges in a way analogous to the work of an artist. An artist can bring to expression a meaning that was inchoate and partially formed, but in bringing it to expression, the artist also adds something to it; she forms it a certain way and puts her own stamp on it. One might say that she brings to expression one of the possibilities inherent in the inchoate form. Other meanings may have also been latent but this particular artist helped define—and not simply find—this potential to which her work gives expression. But neither is it the case that this act of creative definition was, as it were, a creation ex nihilo. The artist was dependent on what she found in the preexisting form. This dependency is not such that she is condemned merely to slavishly imitate what she finds. Her work is never merely *mimesis.* Nevertheless, her genuine creativity was informed and made possible, in part, by what was pregiven. We might say that on such a model the artist's creativity is real and free but is nevertheless limited by a "nature" that supplies a potential for meaning which itself is also limited and yet much richer in different possibilities than thinkers like Aristotle ever supposed. Moreover, on this model, not only does freedom for self-definition or self-expression find a place but history does as well. The many-sided potential inherent in "nature" is brought out in different ways by different artists depending on the historical circumstances of its manifestation. Not only is this "nature" open enough to allow the freedom of self-expression, but it is also open to historical contextualization. "Nature," "history," and "freedom" work in concert to "express" the artist's meaning.

Although Gadamer never uses Taylor's term of art, "expressivism," to identify his theory of hermeneutical understanding, he relies on some of its key components, which it seems plausible to suggest that he, like Taylor, found primarily in Hegel. Key to understanding Gadamer's "expressivism" is his oft-repeated claim that "a thought first attains determinate existence in being formulated in words" (*HD*, 94). This means that the thought is neither found preexisting the words, which would make the words a mere "casing" for thought, nor is it the case that the words themselves produce the thought such that the thought is "mere words." Rather, word and thought are intimately linked. Language is necessary to make thought complete, to bring out its inherent potential.

Gadamer would, however, add a Heideggerian twist to his appropriation of this tradition. Unlike Hegel, Gadamer does not think that thought can ever become transparent to itself. For Hegel all expression "remains tied to the idea of total objectification of self and (thus it) fulfills itself in absolute knowing" (*HD*, 95). But Gadamer is clear in his contention that Hegel fails to be sufficiently sensitive to how an "insurmountable limitation becomes manifest in our experience of language. What makes it possible for language to speak is not 'Being' as the abstract immediacy of the self-determining concept. Rather, it is much better described in terms of the Being which Heidegger refers to as a clearing. A clearing, however, implies both something disclosed and something still enclosed" (*HD*, 95). In other words, all unconcealment through language always also conceals something. Thus any "expression" can never be complete. All such speaking involves a finite disclosure of reality. Nevertheless, if we keep the features of expressivism, which I pointed to above in mind, as well as the key Heideggerian qualification that Gadamer insists on, this will provide us important clues to what Gadamer means by "application," "temporalization," and "increase in being."

"Application," "Temporalization," and "Increase"

Gadamer frequently appeals to Aristotle's notion of *phronesis* or practical wisdom to help his readers grasp his general understanding of how meaning can emerge over time without destroying the underlying identity of that meaning.[14] *Phronesis* is paradigmatic for interpretation, according to Gadamer, because it involves a constant movement between a universal meaning-claim and particular circumstances. This movement comes about in part because it is the nature of the ethical universal itself to be somewhat inexact. Although the best thought out ethical principles are conclusions arrived at by the most exact and consistent scrutiny of concrete cases, such principles are never "complete" in the sense of grasping all the possible meanings that confront us in such cases, despite the fact that they have genuinely abstracted something important of what is common to these cases. In short, they remain "abstractions" and as such they stand in need of being fleshed out in concrete cases. Their lack of "completeness" implies that such universals must constantly be tested against new cases and revised accordingly.[15] In other words, they must be applied to the particular situations where they are relevant with an eye to the particular contingencies involved. Only then is it truly possible for the right thing to be done in the right way and for the right reasons. When, however, a person of practical "wisdom" revises a universal ethical norm in light of new circumstances, this does not show that the identity of the universal itself has simply changed, but rather it has been "applied" in a new way to new circumstances. This does not imply that we are now dealing with a new and different universal; it shows instead the possibilities of meaning inherent in the universal itself. Application of the universal is an application of one and the same universal in many diverse situations. In diverse situations over time different aspects of the universal's meaning show themselves. In terms of expressivism, this process of meaning formation both brings out a latent potential and helps define it.

In my opinion, this is one sense in which Gadamer speaks of a "temporalization" of meaning and an "increase in being." The being of the universal is increased in application to a particular set of circumstances because its meaning becomes, in principle, fuller, more complete with each genuinely defensible application of it. In this sense, too, interpretation of ethical norms is dependent on the "this" of particular circumstances for their full, concrete meaning to be realized. Similarly, when we interpret a text, we follow the very things themselves as they show themselves in the text, in our tradition, and in our present experience, and what comes out is a reading of the text, which is not identical with some "*Urtext*" or "pure" truth, but an application or concretization of the meaning of the issues involved. As an application, this is not in principle a depletion or destruction of an original, perfect, or pure meaning, but an "increase in being" of the things themselves. Something which is given or found to have a relatively determinant nature that is not of our making is "extended," "added to," or "increased" in the act of application. By this act we contribute something to what the universal itself is. Such acts are more than mere reports of the way things are; they are also acts through which these same things are "increased." What we have here, in terms of the expressivist model of meaning, is a meaning whose pregiven potential is both made manifest and further defined in the act of application or interpretation. The meaning of the text is not only reflected in acts of valid interpretation but it is also "enhanced."

This process of "growth" or increase in being is, in Gadamer's view, infinitely expandable. Unlike *techne*, the plying of a craft, in which one definite *telos*, the finished product, is always in view and signals the practitioner that she has reached her goal, *phronesis* (and interpretation modeled on *phronesis*) knows no such determinate end. The only goal of *phronesis* is good action itself. The process of applying ethical principles to ever new circumstances does not come to an end in some discrete and reproducible product. Instead, Aristotle insists that this process of intelligent application is its own end. Such a process involves a process which is in principle endless. Inasmuch as this process continues to bring out and shape the inherent meaning of the universals, the universals themselves have a kind of unlimited meaning.

Such an "increase in being" also can come about when the judge interprets a law in light of both its past applications and the concrete complexities of the case at hand.[16] By looking to past precedents, the judge is not only looking to a history of applications of one and the same law, but she is also searching for an application of the law that is relevant to the concrete case before her. If the case is genuinely difficult, which means that it does not neatly fit the pattern of past cases, but is truly ambiguous in showing both similarities and dissimilarities with past cases, then the judge has a genuine problem of interpretation before her. If she finds a successful solution to this problem, the judge will neither subvert the original law, nor merely report on what it says, nor simply reiterate past precedents. Instead, she will extend the law further by showing how her decision is consistent with both what the law says and with important past precedents, as well as showing that her solution addresses the relevant particular facts of the case at hand. In doing this she is doing more than simply repeating what is already known. She is pointing out that this decision is a defensible decision because it conforms to real *possibilities* inherent in the original law and its past applications. She need not assert that her solution is the only possible solution in order to defend her decision. It is enough if she can show how her decision is consistent with the law and past practice and how it "fits" the case, even if it is not strictly entailed by them. For this kind of interpretation of the law to be valid this type of consistency and adequacy must be found. Otherwise the decision is indefensible and liable to be overturned. But if it is successful, the law has been "increased," made fuller and richer by this application. This is possible because the law exists in time and is an ongoing process of interpretation. Talk of the law "in itself" apart from this historical process of concrete interpretations would be nonsense. But as a temporal reality the law evolves, which does not mean that every new application gives us a new law but one and the same law is "increased" over time. Its meaning is both drawn out and made manifest from its own preexisting resources and defined and actively shaped by the judge's decision.

As we can see from the example of law, a model of interpretation which insists that application is essential to it and even talks about this interpretation bringing about an "increase in being" is not without critical resources. While such a model does accommodate the possibility of different valid interpretations, it stops short of endorsing the equal validity of all interpretations. In modeling textual interpretation on interpretation of the law, Gadamer avoids both an uncritical subjectivism as well as a dogmatic objectivism. The notion of interpretation through application presupposes a notion of validity or reasonableness in interpretation. Not all interpretations are valid either in ethics, law, or textual analysis. It is worth digressing a bit here to briefly consider how Gadamer understands validity in interpretation, because it will shed more light on the idea that interpretation involves an "increase in being."

Gadamer argues that two important criteria of validity in interpretation are consistency and completeness.[17] Interpretations must be internally consistent with themselves and with what the text says. Moreover, they must be "complete" in that they address in principle all the salient issues in the text. No issue can, in principle, be ignored or not be able to find a place in a valid interpretation. This does not mean that a valid interpretation would address literally everything in the text. No interpretation is explicit about everything. But Gadamer's point is that a valid interpretation can be tested against everything in the text, and if it is a valid interpretation it will be "complete" in the sense that it can be shown to shed light on all the real issues of the text, either explicitly or implicitly. Moreover, such a complete interpretation will be complete in that it can withstand critical scrutiny. This implies that a "complete" interpretation has the resources within itself to answer criticisms raised against it. Of course, no interpretation can anticipate all criticisms. However, a truly valid interpretation has a kind internal coherence and obviousness about it, such that it is implicitly equipped to handle criticisms as they arise. Thus such interpretations tend to endure. They become classics and remain touchstones of rational interpretation, even though other interpretations are offered that may also recommend themselves on similar grounds. So, too, lasting precedents of legal decision withstand criticism and continue to recommend themselves as valid models of legal interpretation.

This brings us to another related criterion that is equally important for understanding what distinguishes reasonable from unreasonable interpretations. Gadamer argues that a valid interpretation is a self-effacing interpretation in that it lets the text speak about the very issues which it addresses. Valid interpretations confront us with the things themselves and allow them to become manifest. Consequently, such interpretations do not draw attention to themselves qua interpretations by means of inconsistencies, by being one-sided, by raising peripheral issues, by being overly concerned with issues of method or what have you. The best interpretations have a kind of self-evidence to them that brings us face to face with the issues that are the focus of the text. There is something almost obvious about such interpretations in that they disappear, as it were, behind the issues that they make manifest. When we read these interpretations we cannot help but become more involved with the very realities of which the text speaks.

Such criteria of validity in interpretation are by no means merely formal criteria appended to Gadamer's ontology of understanding. On the contrary, "completeness," "consistency," and "self-effacement" are all related to Gadamer's thought about the transcendental elements of Being, particularly the one, the Good, and the beautiful. The first two characteristics of a valid interpretation, consistency and completeness, are more familiar ways of expressing the more general ideal that any reasonable interpretation must be unified. It must be "unified" by being both logically consistent or "one" with itself, and it must be unified in that it leaves no dangling pieces, as it were, no parts of the text unaccounted for. But "unity" is another way of speaking about the Good itself. "The idea of the Good," Gadamer says, can be understood "as the unity of what is unitary." As such, "the idea of the Good would seem to be presupposed by anything ordered, enduring and consistent" (*IG*, 31). Thus, only interpretations which have this kind of unity are "good" interpretations, i.e., they are expressions of the Good itself.

But as we said in Chapter 3, the search for the Good always "takes flight into the Beautiful" (*Philebus*, 64e5; *TM*, 481). What this means generally is that the Good is recognized by us as the beautiful or as that which has a self-evident type of immediacy about it or what Gadamer calls a "radiance" (*TM*, 486). Now, in the context of our discussion of validity in interpretation, it is precisely the "self-effacing" interpretation which has just this immediacy. Such "radiance" or "beauty" is present in these interpretations in that they bring us face to face with the things themselves. The things themselves "shine forth" from them and, as we said already, such interpretations have a way of involving us with the very things themselves and not with their own technical scaffolding. Qua interpretations, such interpretations are self-effacing in that they disappear, as it were, behind the "radiance" of the things themselves. In some sense such interpretations can be described as the self-presentation of the things. This idea, that things *present themselves* in valid interpretation, is central to Gadamer's overall ontology. As such, we will return to it below. For now is suffices to point out that in grasping a good interpretation we come face to face with the things themselves without being forced to pay undue attention to the interpreter's intentions, style, commitments, or other idiosyncracies that often interfere in a bad interpretation with the interpretation's ability to "deliver the goods," i.e., to bring us into a deeper understanding of the issues that the text addresses.

The fact that such interpretations are "good" and "beautiful" in this special sense also helps shed light on the claim that interpretation involves an "increase in being." Just as there are many good things that are good in related but not identical ways and just as there are many beautiful things that do not undermine the identity of the beautiful, but actually add to its richness, so Gadamer argues that various interpretations of any issue can, in principle, add to our sense of the issue without the identity of the issue itself being dissolved. On the contrary, the fact that interpretation expands an issue's meaning by historically mediated application shows the kind of historical identity that such realities have. Gadamer speaks of an identity that "presents itself so differently in the changing courses of ages and circumstances," but he continues to argue that such an identity "does not disintegrate into the changing aspects of itself so that it would lose all identity, but it is there in them all. They all belong to it. They are contemporaneous with it" (*TM*, 120–21). Such an identity is much like that of a person who carries her identity with her into her future. Moreover, this identity does not dissolve and get formed anew every time she acts or "applies it" toward her future. It is there in these acts of "application," it is contemporaneous with them, like the Good and the beautiful are there in their various historical presentations. By being there in each of these presentations, neither the person, nor the Good, nor the beautiful is depleted. Rather, the reality of each one is increased with each new manifestation.

To further illustrate his point about an "increase in being" Gadamer appeals to the idea of an image, or picture (*Bild*).[18] A successful portrait of someone is a "picture" or "image" of that person. As a "picture," it is not a mere copy that could readily be duplicated or destroyed without any loss. Rather, a "picture" goes beyond the function of a copy in that it makes a "presentation" of the thing it images. This implies that the image functions to make the thing itself present in a certain way. In a successful portrait, the person portrayed is presented in a certain "essential" light. Something essential is shown to us about that person, and, perhaps, even to the person herself. Sitting for such a portrait makes one very vulnerable; something of genuine insight might be made manifest that I didn't fully realize about myself and which the artist "expresses" for me. It is always possible that this revelation is less than flattering. Be that as it may, the point is that we are confronted in such cases of portraiture with the expressivist insights of "making manifest" and "defining."

Gadamer gives further sense to these notions by appealing to the neo-Platonic metaphor of emanation.[19] Because good portraits present something essential of the person one can say that the portrait "emanates" from the person, not only because the portrait is dependent on the person as its original, but also because the portrait plays its own role in defining who this person is. The portrait gives a more definite and fuller meaning to the person and thus has an effect on the original. In this sense, a good portrait enhances the reality of the person portrayed, it signifies an "increase in being." By representing that person in a certain way the essence (or part of the essence) of that person becomes accessible in a new way. There is a sense in which this truth about the person is there for the first time in the portrait; only as portrayed is this truth made accessible.

In a similar way the concept of a "representative" under the law suggests an analogous event. Gadamer points out how under canon law a "representative" of someone was seen as a substitute who acts on behalf of the person represented. The one represented, however, gains in their standing as a person, i.e., a bearer of rights, by virtue of having someone else represent them before the law.[20] Even though it is the case that the representative has their standing as a representative only because of the person they represent—whether they were chosen by that person or delegated by the court for that person—it is nevertheless true that qua representative they also contribute something essential to the person, even though they give to the person only what they are supposed to possess already, i.e., their rights. Nevertheless, without this act of representation, the person represented could not have effectively realized these rights. It may sound odd to say that the legal representative contributes something essential to the being of the person represented, but the fact of the matter is that in all likelihood the person represented would not have had their full rights and standing as a person recognized without their representative. Their fuller standing as a person was brought about and thus made more real through the act of representation. In this sense, the representative has an essential effect on the person represented, just as the portrait has an effect on the person who is presented in it.

Gadamer also turns to christological sources to make a similar point.[21] In Christian theology, Christ is frequently said to be humanity's "representative" before God. As our representative he is said to "reconcile" believers to God, thereby making them "sons and daughters" of God, and as sons and daughters, also "heirs" to the kingdom of God. Through this legal and familial language what is implied is that through Christ's mediation we come into our own proper inheritance, or our own proper relationship to God. We thereby fulfill our calling or purpose as human beings. By fulfilling this purpose for us, Christ's act does not threaten to deplete who we are, but it "increases" who we are.

But Christ is also said to present God the Father to human beings. Christ can make this presentation because he is "one" with the Father in the sense that he "proceeds" from Father like an "emanation" or "overflow" of God the Father. In this "emanation," God the Father is not depleted or essentially changed, but rather what God is for us is supposedly made clearer, fuller, and richer for us through Christ's revelation. God is "increased," in a sense, through the mystery of the incarnation.[22]

Gadamer, of course, is not a theologian and he is not interested in making a contribution to christology, but his point is that we have many accessible models to grasp what is meant by talk of an "increase of being" occurring through the presentation of some reality in a temporal process of interpretation.

Not only can we find models for thinking about interpretation along these lines in ethics, law, and theology, but the very idea of interpretation as an "increase in being" can be illuminated by appealing more directly to its organic foundation. "Increase," or in German "*Zuwachs*," often means growth. Its literal meaning connects the idea of an "increase in being" to a natural organic process. Gadamer asks us to consider whether "presentation" as a kind of "emanation" or "overflow" might not be noted in the very nature of biological life itself.[23] "Self-presentation" for Gadamer "is a universal ontological characteristic of nature" (*TM*, 108). In this he is also following the Romantics, for whom organic metaphors were just as central. Gadamer points out that when we watch young animals play, it makes sense, in his opinion, to say that we are watching an "emanation" or "overflow" of their very being. Of course, we know that this behavior is logically distinct from what these animal are, but their play (*Spiel*) is their self-presentation and as such it is a behavior that profoundly affects what these animals are. Without play, they will never become what they are meant to be. In this sense, "play" brings about a transformation in their being that cannot be described as a change of essence but rather as a realization of their essence that takes place as a gradual "growth" or "increase" in what they are. In this regard, the notion of an "increase in being" is not simply an accretion added on to something but an integral organic development within it.

In a similar way human parents recognize the same necessity of self-presentation in play for their children's well-being. Human parents constantly encourage their children to seek out socially appropriate vehicles of self-assertion or self-presentation, i.e., to play. In keeping a child to itself, one might spare it the risks associated with self-presentation, but such a parent would do irreparable damage to a child. A child's play is its own self-emanation that actually redounds to what it is and what it might be. Thus play is an ontological event in which the child's being evolves. The child does not simply become "aware" of itself in play; play brings about more than a change in the child's self-awareness or subjectivity. Play actually develops what the child is and it is this objective change that in no small part brings about a subjective change in the child's self-awareness.

Moreover, such "play" is not simply the child's action or decision, as if the child "decides" to play and "decides" how she will evolve through play. "Play" is much more the child's passion or something in which the child feels quite naturally caught up. As such the child does not merely decide to play but, in a sense, the child *is* its play. No fundamental choice or alternative exists for the child. The child must play to become who she is. She must allow herself to be swept up, as it were, by her circumstances and to thereby put herself in a position to explore its many possibilities for her. Play is only play when it is spontaneous in this way. All such play is beyond deliberation. In this sense, the child does not make herself through self-conscious choices, but in playing she nevertheless "increases" herself by realizing possibilities inherent to her in unique ways.

Gadamer insists, however, that such self-presentation or play does not cease with childhood. Even as adults we "play" in this sense and continue to develop who we are. Not only do we become who we are in the complex act of responding to the many different possibilities of meaning found in the historical circumstances of our lives, but such acts define us before any "decision" to show ourselves in a certain light. In other words, we don't "play" in the primary sense of the term when we decide to play a role or put on a certain mask for someone. If we played only when we had first decided to show ourselves to others in a certain predetermined way this would imply that we had full access to ourselves prior to such play. Such a model, which is not really a valid model of play as Gadamer understands it, but merely a model of "play acting," implies a transparency of self-knowledge and a mastery over our acts of self-presentation that we simply do not have. Rather, in real play I am swept up in the game, in the force of circumstances, in the vortices of meaning, and I find myself responding to these circumstances in unforeseen ways. In such a structure I become who I am both for myself and for others. Of course, I make decisions within the game. I am involved in "applying" myself to my situation, but such acts of self-assertion are not prior to the meaningful events in which I find myself entwined and to which I am compelled to respond. Like a chess player who becomes who she is qua chess player only by responding to immumerable possibilities inherent in the rule-bound game of chess, human beings become who they by taking up a dynamic of meaning, a play of possibilities that is never entirely of their making and within which their decisions take on their own meaning both for themselves and others. In such a game I both respond to conditions in which I already find myself carried along and, in part, I give them shape and definition as well.

The Play of the World

Gadamer's notion of "play," however, is not intended simply to make a point about the connection between our historicity and our individual development. Rather, it is a basic ontological insight which informs Gadamer's whole enterprise. It is not only humans and other animals who "play" throughout their lives and so become who they are through repeated acts of self-presentation, but Gadamer wants to say that there is a sense in which reality or the world "plays" and becomes what it is through its own acts of self-presentation. The "first and last insight," Gadamer writes, "is that Being is self-presentation" (*TM*, 485). One might say that for Gadamer Being itself is play. But how and where does this "ontological play" occur?

One place where this "ontological play" occurs is in the movement between language and the many things of which language speaks. We pointed out above that Gadamer suggests that interpretations are best seen as "presentations" or "emanations" of the things themselves. Gadamer is suggesting once again that there is an intimate relation between the words in which things are reflected and the things themselves. This relation is as intimate, in fact, as the relation between child's acts of self-presentation and herself. In this regard, Gadamer appeals to this ontological notion of play to illuminate the relation between language and the universals of thought. Just as there is an inseparable relation between a child's acts of self-presentation and herself such that she cannot really separate herself and her identity from her play, there is also an intimate connection between the self-presentation of things in language and the things themselves. On this model, language is the self-presentation of the things themselves, the "play of the world," as it were.

As we have already pointed out, in play there is an "overflow" of the player that does not signify an emptying or loss of the player but an enhancement of the player in the sense that the player comes into her own through play, i.e., she discovers for herself and manifests to others more of what she really is. Moreover, this self-presentation is not an isolated act of will and subjectivity, but a response embedded in the nature of the game itself. In giving oneself over to the game, the self is made more manifest. But just as the player is not only made known in her various acts of presentation but also present in all of them, the things themselves are not only made known in the many ways they are spoken of, they are also present in the many types of discourse we use when we speak of things. In the many different ways we talk about the realities that are our common focus of thought, these same realities are presented in many variations in many different contexts. Such a presentation of reality is, on Gadamer's model, a self-presentation or emanation of the same reality in which its true richness is revealed in time. Like a great work of music or drama that exists only in its many presentations and presents itself in its infinite richness only in and through its different presentations, so the world presents itself through language. Such "play" is by no means frivolous but a genuine event in which the world unfolds itself to us in the medium of language. Such language does not flow from an arbitrary decision to talk in this way or that way but is a response to the things themselves and emanates from them. For Gadamer language is this ontological event. In language we find the play of the world itself.

Once again, Gadamer tries to make this ontological event clearer and more plausible for us by comparing it to what goes on in our experience of art, particularly dramatic art.[24] There are some things that are characteristic of our experience of a theatrical presentation (*Schauspiel*), some of which I have already alluded to, that are key here. The first of which, mentioned above, is that such works of art exist first and foremost in and through their performances. For example, Shakespeare's *Hamlet* is not simply a text to be read and imagined; it is meant to be performed and it only fully exists in its various performances. There is no "silent" substitute which can match the fullness of the real, spoken *Hamlet;* its being is only fully found in its presentations. The fact, however, that there are many such presentations of *Hamlet* would not lead Gadamer to say that there are many, distinct "*Hamlets.*" On the contrary, one and the same *Hamlet* exists in its many performances. *Hamlet* itself is contemporaneous with them all, despite the fact that each performance may be significantly different as well. In fact, Gadamer wants to say that it is precisely the type of being which a play like *Hamlet* has that enables it to be what it is as a temporal reality whose being is always in some sense different in each of its discrete presentations, while at the same time maintaining its identity throughout them all.

In a similar way the meaning of things is inseparable from their many different presentations in language. Just as *Hamlet* does not exist apart from its many presentations or the law does not exist apart from its history of different applications, the meaning of things is inseparable from the medium of language in which they present themselves. The thing itself is present in its many linguistic formulations. In any one of these formulations, I can, in principle, find the thing and come to really understand it in some respects. Of course, such understanding is not exhaustive of the thing's meaning, any more than any one performance of *Hamlet* exhausts its meaning or any one legal decision encompasses the whole law. Nevertheless the things themselves are found in the words in which they are spoken.

Gadamer says when we are fortunate enough to find things in words something happens, an event occurs, which can be illustrated also by an appeal to dramatic presentation. When a play is performed well something happens to all involved—text, actors, audience, etc.—which Gadamer calls "transformation into structure" and "total mediation."[25] When the actors do their jobs well the text speaks to us about the realities which are its focus. Both the language of text and the speech, actions, gestures, and movements of the actors point beyond themselves to the meaning which is the heart and soul of the play. Gadamer calls this transformation "transformation into structure." What emerges from the performance is a meaningful whole, a structure of articulated meaning, which is there in its repeatable identity in all the performances of the play, despite the fact that it shows itself differently in different performances. That such a transformation occurs is clear when we reflect on what is often the key difference between a good and bad performance. A bad performance hinders this transformation from occurring. In such a performance we are distracted by what is actually happening on stage—either by the inept articulation and movement of the actors or by a bungling production crew or what have you. But in a good performance all the historical contingencies of the production do not literally disappear but they are effaced, and the structure of the play, its meaning, shines through. In short, the play itself is present: it presents itself, its meaning becomes available for us.

When we are fortunate to witness such a performance something else happens as well that Gadamer calls "total mediation." Not only do the actors and various other aspects of the production withdraw behind the self-presentation of the play but we, the audience, are also caught up in this event of meaning. Gadamer calls it a form of "participation" in which we are "present" to the realities which the play is about. Such "presence" points us to the original Greek concept of *theoria* in which the "*theoros* means someone who takes part in a delegation to a festival" (*TM*, 124). Although such a delegate does not necessarily perform any of the ritual that might be integral to the festival, his presence is not indifferent to the festival's identity. Just as his presence is part of what makes the festival what it is, so too the presence of the audience is essential to the play's identity. The audience's presence makes it possible for the meaning of the play to emerge, to be real, by having an effect and being affected by them. "In the same way," Gadamer argues, "Greek metaphysics still conceives the essence of *theoria* and of *nous* as being purely present to what is truly real" (*TM*, 124). *Theoria* and *nous* are not the same as the realities they are present to, but *theoria* or *nous* are essential to their full presence to emerge because *theoria* or *nous* provide the conditions for this emergence. For Gadamer, this act of presentation is made possible by language. He argues that Plato, too, saw this "in his theory of *anamnesis* [which] combined the mythical idea of remembrance with his dialectic, which sought the truth of Being in the *logoi*—i.e., the ideality of language" (*TM*, 114). Gadamer's general point here is the point I attempted to make above, namely, in language the world presents itself, the meaning of things as they really are can, in principle, shine through the linguistic medium and catch us up, as it were, in its own dynamic performance, i.e., in its own play. When language speaks in this way, we not only recognize something that is real but we also "participate" in its meaning, maybe even contribute to this meaning in our response to it. In short, we are caught up in "the play of the world" and carried along various paths of meaning.

"*Spiel*," "*Aufhebung*," and "*Ereignis*"

By now it may have struck some readers that in speaking of the "play" as "the clue to ontological explanation"[26] Gadamer is consciously steering a path between Hegel and Heidegger, and he is doing so by consciously relying on his insights into Plato's reliance on understanding through the *logos*. It is helpful, I think, to explore this claim more fully.

Gadamer's "first and last insight that Being is self-presentation" (*TM*, 485) is strongly reminiscent of Hegel's concept of *Geist.* Compare, for example, this altogether typical Hegelian statement from Hegel's *Lectures on the Philosophy of Religion:* "Spirit's essential character is *to be altogether active.* More exactly, it is the activity of *self-manifesting*" (Hegel's emphasis).[27] Inasmuch as Gadamer insists that reality presents itself in "play," in "self-presentation," Gadamer is a good Hegelian. But as Hegel's many writings attest, the "self-manifestation" of Spirit follows an immanent logic which Hegel sees as both necessary and evolving through history toward its culmination in "absolute knowledge." As many commentators have described this process, it is one characterized by *Aufhebung* in which the weaknesses of previous understandings are eclipsed while at the same time preserving their inherent strengths. At the end of this logical process the possibilities inherent in the whole are adequately articulated and finally exhausted by being definitively actualized in their own proper and necessary end state. Inasmuch as this is so for Hegel, Gadamer's notion of play wants to stress in contrast the "unnecessary," "unpredictable," "spontaneous" nature of these events of ontological self-presentation. For Gadamer, there is no necessary logic or end state to this process of "play." "Play," as the self-presentation of reality, can carry us off in many directions and its inherent instability, or movement, knows no definitive rest. "*Aufhebung*" as the cumulative process of Spirit's self-correcting, self-manifestation, is not a process that finds a clear parallel in Gadamer.

But this is a point where Gadamer's close relationship to Heidegger is important. In substituting "play" (*Spiel*) for *Aufhebung,* Gadamer actually moves closer to Heidegger's notion of *Ereignis.* By *Ereignis* Heidegger designates the "appropriative event" of meaning whereby Being shows itself differently in the major epochs of human history. Like Heidegger, Gadamer stresses that *reality shows itself,* its "play" is its own act of *self-presentation.* Moreover, like Heidegger, Gadamer stresses that the result of this process over time is that reality shows itself differently at different times. But if we focus on the nature of this difference in Gadamer and Heidegger important differences between these two thinkers begin to emerge, differences which will occupy us further in the next chapter. But for now it can be said that, for Heidegger, the difference between the different events of meaning approaches what we might call—if I might use a non-Heideggerian idiom—"incommensurability" or—if I choose to use a Hegelian idiom—"non-identity." By this I mean that for Heidegger there is a real sense in which these events cannot be critically compared so that their underlying "identity" or common source can be made more manifest. Although Heidegger insists that such events are events of Being, one and the same Being, he repeatedly stresses that this Being "withdraws" and "withholds itself" behind these revelatory events. Thus the underlying identity which makes each of these events self-presentations of one reality remains shrouded in mystery and unknowing; the actual events themselves remain "incommensurable." For Gadamer, on the other hand, such diverse events of meaning contain within themselves an identity that is discernable in principle. In fact, one might say that their differences are, in principle, commensurable. Such an identity falls short of revealing to us an immanent logic of the self-presentation of reality à la Hegel, but it also promises us more than the "oblivion of Being."

The Conflict of Propositions

To better see what these claims actually amount to, it is helpful to turn to a problem that we have previously encountered and with which we are all familiar. One way in which "the play of the world" is more concretely manifested is in the unwieldy multivocity of natural language. On a Gadamerian model, language has so many possible meanings because the inherent richness of reality is reflected in it. If language is a kind of mirror of reality and what we find in the mirror is an unwieldy play of meaningful possibilities, then by learning a language we too come to participate in this play. Another way to say this is that by virtue of being language users we have ready access to the world and its many possible meanings.

Of course, this kind of access in language to the play of the world is anything but unproblematic. The many possibilities of meaning in it create not only the possibility of agreement and concord but it also provides endless opportunities for disagreement and strife. The many meanings or interpretations of nominally identical realities confront us with issues of identity and commensurability which so fundamentally divide Hegel from Heidegger. Not only "continental" philosophers grapple with these problems, but many philosophers in the analytic tradition have also responded to the incommensurability of meaning in various discourses with the attempt to create formal languages whose meanings would be so unequivocal and precise that ambiguity and misunderstanding would be minimized and, ideally, eliminated. Gadamer is skeptical of these attempts not because the problem to which these attempts to formulate a formal language is a pseudoproblem, but because of what they wrongly assume about our relation to language.

Behind the dream of an unequivocal system of signs stands an instrumentalist view of language. On this model, language is *primarily* a tool or instrument we use and control for our ends. Gadamer would not deny that we use language or that language is a tool, which human beings can manipulate to some extent for their ends. Not only the reality of sophistry, ancient and modern, makes this fact plain, but any creative use of language supplies ample evidence that language is a powerful tool. But the limited degree to which we are able to manipulate language makes Gadamer skeptical that the dominant model of tool-use is appropriate here. Language is not *primarily* a tool. At best language is only secondarily a tool because it is the very medium of thought itself. As a medium, Gadamer wants to say that it provides the conditions and thereby limits the possibilities of what can be thought. Moreover, we have no other medium for thought, and all attempts to master and control the medium are inevitably undercut by its pervasive and somewhat unwieldy assertiveness. Language has a way of asserting itself, of insisting on its own meaning, and we must follow it if we hope to understand at all. This assertiveness of natural language is seen in the fact that all formal languages never really supplant natural languages because when we use a formal language, and ask what it is saying, we inevitably fall back into a natural language to make its meaning clear. Natural language is the medium of every formal language, and thus even formal languages cannot supplant our dependency on natural language in all its multivocity.[28]

Of course, Gadamer is not insensitive to the fact that the multiplicity of meanings inherent in every natural language is a source of constant problems of communication and solidarity. When the world "plays" in language what emerges is a complex mix of ostensibly compatible and incompatible interpretations. Here we come back to the problems of "commensurability" and "identity," which we encountered above. If such occurrences only issued in interpretations that were consistent with each other Gadamer's metaphor of the play of reality would be less troubling and provocative. As it is, however, "the play of the world" seems to issue in interpretations, some of which are consistent with each other, and some of which are not. Given this fact, how can Gadamer plausibly contend that the play of interpretations issues from one and same reality? How can he maintain that the plethora of interpretations is evidence of the inherent richness of a reality that is internally consistent with itself and unfolding itself over time? Isn't Heidegger's view that such conflicts at best obscure their common source more defensible? Or even better, shouldn't we follow the neo-Nietzscheans in seeing the many conflicting interpretations as nothing more than human constructs that do not reflect an original richness but only reveal the conflicting interests of the interpreters?

Gadamer responds to this challenge by making a far-reaching point about the nature of language in all its multiplicity of meaning. Any natural language is multiple in its meanings because it is a repository of the many questions asked and answers given over the course of its development.[29] This takes us back to his basic "Platonic" claim that the essence of language is dialogue. This means that language is not primarily propositional in nature but dialogical. Language is first and foremost a "dialogue" and not a "proposition" in the sense that "if one wants to grasp a proposition in its truth then there is no proposition that can be comprehended only in terms of the content that it presents. Every proposition has presuppositions that are not asserted" (*HT*, 42). The "motivation" presupposed behind every proposition is the "question" to which it is a response. No proposition has meaning as such or in itself. As Gadamer argues, "there is no possible assertion that cannot be understood as an answer to a question and it can only be so understood" (*HT*, 43). If every proposition is an answer to a question, and every question presupposes a viewpoint of inquiry or another set of questions, then there are no pure propositions. The ideal of a purely formal system of propositions whose meaning exists in itself, in isolation from all historically mediated questions, is an empty ideal. In reality, such a formal language is no language at all because it exists apart from the only context of inquiry that could give it meaning. In truth, however, so-called formal languages are themselves never unmotivated. They are themselves responses to complex sets of questions. Scratch the surface of any formal language and a whole ontology reveals itself, usually an ontology of a highly mathematicized concept of nature.

Be that as it may, what the priority of the question over the proposition tells us about a hermeneutical response to the conflict of interpretations is revealing. We have multiplicity of meaning in language and multiple interpretations in large part because we ask different questions of reality. If we encounter different, logically incompatible interpretations of some issue, this does not necessarily imply that such interpretations cannot both show us something true about the one and the same issue and are instead best understood as stemming from the conflicting interests of the interpreters. We can have different interpretations of the same phenomena, even interpretations that are on the propositional level logically incompatible, if we keep in mind that the contradiction in propositional content may be due to the fact that each interpretation is really asking different questions of the things themselves. If this is so, then preserving the truth in both accounts does not violate the law of noncontradiction. Such contradictory claims are only apparently contradictory because they can be understood to assert "A" and "not-A" of the same thing in *different senses*, i.e., as different "answers" to different "questions." Such an approach, however, presupposes that the conflict of propositional content does not reflect a lack of identity in the subject matter itself. In other words, if such conflict of interpretation is merely a disagreement of words, of propositions, the unity of the thing itself is not threatened. This implies that such propositional conflict should be resolvable in principle.

Gadamer relies in part on the Augustinian notion of the "inner word" or "word of the heart" (*verbum cordis*) to further elaborate on how such a resolution between conflicting interpretations is possible, at least in principle. Jean Grondin has brought this aspect of Gadamer's thought to our attention and rightly argued for its importance.[30] Following the Stoic distinction between each word uttered (*logos prophorikòs*) and what lies behind each uttered word (*logos endiàthetos*), Augustine developed the distinction between the *actus signatus,* the spoken word, and everything implied or pointed to by that word, the *actus exercitus.* Gadamer uses this distinction to point out that it is a very basic fact about language that in order to understand any proposition or utterance it is not enough to know the meaning of the words involved, as one might find them in a dictionary. One must rather be able to "fulfill" or "complete" the meaning of the words spoken or written by going beyond the mere words themselves to everything that is implied or referred to by them. Such acts of "completion" are never really finished in the sense that each "word," or each unified use of language, is always involved with an infinite web of meanings all of which we never succeed in making fully explicit. Interpretation is indeed an endless enterprise. Nevertheless, when we understand someone or another text we do so precisely because we know how to think along with them, we know what they mean by following the movement or direction of meaning that their words propel us toward. By following this direction of meaning (*Richtungssinn*) we engage in a further movement that "completes" their meaning, albeit relatively. This is seen in any genuine dialogue where a respondent demonstrates that she understood what was said, not by a parrotlike reiteration of the point made, but by developing the issue further. This means that she has grasped something of the "inner word" that animates the "outer word" of the statement. This inner word is indeed endless. Gadamer says it involves "thinking through the subject matter to the end" (*TM,* 422) and who, indeed, is ever really finished with this process? Nevertheless, the thoughtful dialogue partner or thoughtful reader must find this inner word and supply it for herself if she hopes to understand anything at all. But this is especially so when we hope to understand the issues in dispute between conflicting interpretations. In the case of conflicting interpretations we often find evidence of a failure to have "thought through the subject matter to the end." Had one or both sides thought through the issues more carefully, mistakes could have been avoided, mistakes that lead to the contradictions dividing interpretations. By "thinking along with" each interpretation such mistakes begin to show themselves. Or alternatively, by dealing with the subject matter itself in a fuller, more complete fashion the differences which divide interpretations are seen as only "apparent" because they stem from the simple but important fact that the issues involved were approached with fundamentally different questions in mind. If this is the case, a basis for a more far-reaching agreement can begin to show itself.

The Augustinian nature of the "inner word" makes it possible for Gadamer to offer a two-pronged response to deep conflicts of interpretation. As we saw in Chapter 3, Gadamer provides us grounds for arguing that incompatible interpretations are resolvable in principle because all such interpretations presuppose a grasp of such transcendentals as identity, difference, one and many, beauty, truth, goodness, etc. Such a "participation" in the transcendentals allows interpreters to rediscover common ground and in light of this common ground to work out their differences. However, Gadamer also points to another possible avenue of conflict resolution—the inner word. Here one need not appeal directly to the transcendental elements of being implicitly shared by different interpretations. One can turn instead to the explicit issues that divide interpretations—the things themselves—and propose a resolution that recommends itself because it is more "complete," i.e., it has genuinely thought through the issues involved in a more adequate and comprehensive way.

These two aspects of Gadamer's thought—the appeal to transcendentals and the inner word—point us, once again, to Plato and Heidegger, respectively. Gadamer's appeal to the "inner word" presupposes the internal relations between Ideas which enable them to function as an infinite web of meaning that "moves" in accord with each meaningful utterance. But Gadamer also relies on Heidegger here, despite his critical reservations about Heidegger's notion of *Ereignis*. Not only did Heidegger precede Gadamer in relying on Augustine to develop his notion of "complete" meaning of the statement (*Vollzugssinn der Aussage*)—a fact which Gadamer readily acknowledges[31]—but, as we have already seen, Gadamer's notion of "play" as an ontological event in which reality presents itself through language is an explicit attempt to critically appropriate what is meant by the Heideggerian notion of *das Ereignis*. By critically appropriating aspects of Heidegger's position, Gadamer hopes to demonstrate that Heidegger's increasing emphasis on the complete "forgetfulness of Being" is not inevitable. By stressing that in language we have actual contact with multiple events of meaning, which shape us and which constantly "dialogue" with each other, Gadamer is suggesting that our prospects in the order of things is fundamentally different than Heidegger suggests. The "event" of meaning, as it turns out on Gadamer's reading, is more accessible to us than Heidegger would allow. While such "accessibility" does not imply that human beings can completely fathom these events of meaning in ways that make us sovereign masters of our own knowledge and understanding—as Hegel hoped to guarantee for us—Gadamer nevertheless suggests that we can grasp the underlying identities of such events. By doing so, we cease, in principle, being merely passive vis-à-vis these events and begin instead to see ways around our differences. In short, the possibility of grasping the identity underneath the different manifestations of one and the same reality gives us a ground for a solidarity that is missing in Heidegger. Moreover, our common concern for the Good, although not unproblematic, nevertheless shows that our situation is not without grounds for hope. We are not consigned to a "thoughtful waiting" for a time beyond Western culture's current crisis of meaning. Instead, if Gadamer's critique of Heidegger is compelling, we are called to a more active and critical appropriation of tradition itself. To see why Gadamer thinks that this conclusion is warranted we need to look more closely at some aspects of his understanding of Heidegger. The next chapter is devoted to a more detailed examination of this complex, fruitful, and tension-filled relationship.

5

"Beyond Being": Gadamer and Heidegger

Gadamer, Heidegger, and "Metaphysics"

In 1922, Paul Natorp gave his young doctoral candidate a manuscript of Heidegger's on Aristotle.[1] This unpublished manuscript contained Heidegger's ideas for a new interpretation of Aristotle, which he submitted to the faculty at Marburg as part of his candidacy for the position he eventually received.[2] Even then, Gadamer thought that "Heidegger brought superb powers of phenomenological intuition [*Anschauungskraft*] to his interpretations and, in so doing, freed the original Aristotelian text so thoroughly and effectively from the overlay of the scholastic tradition and from the miserable, distorted picture the critical philosophy of the period had of Aristotle . . . that he began to speak in an unexpected way" (*HW*, 32). This initial impression of Gadamer's grew into a fundamental respect for and solidarity with Heidegger's philosophy, one which developed and deepened as he attended Heidegger's lectures and studied the publications that slowly emerged from his hand.

Gadamer's respect for Heidegger, however, manifested itself initially in silence, in a refusal to write on Heidegger, a fact that might strike some as puzzling, to say the least. Although Gadamer continued to be influenced by Heidegger and this influence showed itself in his lectures and in his *Habilitationsschrift*, Gadamer remained reticent to write about Heidegger for nearly forty years. Gadamer's reticence was not due to the fact that he thought that what Heidegger had to say was "beyond words," but because he saw from early on that Heidegger's thought was of such originality and importance that it was best served by not taking part in the trendy adulation or equally trendy controversy that always seemed to follow Heidegger. Rather, Gadamer hoped that by allowing Heidegger the time to develop his own thought we would thereby gain the distance needed to take a truer measure of his achievement. Moreover, Gadamer has always maintained that a profound intellectual debt, like the one he has to Heidegger, is not best honored by a facile imitation or repetition of a thinker but by developing one's own thought. Finally, in 1960, with the publication of both *Wahrheit und Methode* and an introduction to the Reclam edition of *Vom Ursprung des Kunstwerkes* (which Heidegger asked Gadamer to write), the silence was broken. Gadamer not only began to assess Heidegger's achievement in print, but he also began to respond to various interpretations and criticisms of Heidegger by others. This response has continued to the present day.

When we read the various remarks scattered throughout many of Gadamer's later works, as well as the series of essays that explicitly treat aspects of Heidegger's thought, once again the overwhelming impression is one of fundamental respect for and solidarity with Heidegger's philosophy. Thus when I provocatively suggest that Gadamer's thought points "beyond Being," i.e., beyond Heidegger and Heidegger's relentless pursuit of the question of Being, this cannot be taken to mean that Gadamer at any time has renounced his indebtedness to Heidegger and changed his fundamental Heideggerian orientation. Gadamer consistently refuses to treat Heidegger "like a dead dog." In fact, Gadamer explicitly credits Heidegger's account of *Dasein*'s "facticity" as the fundamental impulse that oriented his own thought toward the problems of historicity.[3] Moreover, Gadamer's dialectical account of truth, which embraces both "unconcealedness" and "correctness" as undeniable elements of the phenomenon of truth, is explicitly Heideggerian. And Heidegger's thesis from the "Letter on Humanism" that "language is the House of Being"[4] finds a deep resonance in Gadamer's reflections on the "belongingness" of language and reality. Surely, this list of Gadamer's intellectual debts to Heidegger could be considerably lengthened. Given these facts, Gadamer's move "beyond Being" is not to be understood as a pronouncement about the irrelevance or invalidity of Heidegger's thought, but as an important corrective or adjustment in the direction that Heidegger's philosophy took, particularly from the early thirties on.[5]

One reason why Gadamer thinks that such a reassessment of Heidegger is necessary is because the Heideggerian legacy is not univocal. This is so not only because Heidegger's thought leaves us, like all great philosophical achievements, with the question of how we are to appropriate it. Of course, we must interpret Heidegger's work in light of our own historical horizon, a horizon that does not exactly correspond to Heidegger's own. But Heidegger's thought needs critical reassessment also for the more fundamental reason that Heidegger's own thought underwent significant change. If one wants to understand Heidegger one must assess these changes critically—as Heidegger himself constantly tried to help us understand his own development by offering us his own critical commentary on it. Nevertheless, we cannot rehearse all the changes in Heidegger's development, either acknowledged or unacknowledged by Heidegger himself. The subject would simply take us too far afield for this essay. But, neither can we simply take Heidegger's own self-assessment at face value. For our purposes, we are put on the right track if we look at Heidegger's own development (and its relation to Gadamer's thought) with the awareness that Gadamer's thought takes issue with several key issues in Heidegger's own self-assessment of his development. By understanding what these issues are and how Gadamer reacts to them we get important clues to their major philosophical differences.

With the gradual publication of Heidegger's early lectures in the *Gesamtausgabe* it is slowly being recognized how, at the start of his career, Heidegger was more open to metaphysics and its potential for "fundamental ontology" than he was in his later writings. When Heidegger began his teaching activity he understood himself as a philosopher who sought a better way to do metaphysics, i.e., as someone who sought to make the rigid metaphysical categories "fluid" (*verflüssigen*) again by bringing back the centrality of the question of the meaning of Being for metaphysics.[6] Many of the writings from this period are concerned with metaphysical problems. For example, his *Habilitationschrift, The Doctrine of Categories and Meaning in Duns Scotus,* dealt with metaphysical issues in the medieval doctrine of transcendentals and the analogy of Being. And in his last lectures at Marburg from the summer of 1928, *Die Metaphysische Anfangsgründe der Logik im Ausgang von Leibniz,* he even refers regularly to his own work as a metaphysics which combines a fundamental ontology with something he calls there a metontology.[7] Even *Sein und Zeit,* which does not describe itself as metaphysics, presupposes the vitality of metaphysics in its proposal for a "*Destruktion*" of metaphysics.[8] "*Destruktion,*" which Heidegger understood as a dismantling or de-constructing (*Abbau*) of the metaphysical tradition in order to liberate the vital insights that had become encrusted within the dead language of dogma and ossified scholasticism, only makes sense if there is something valid about this type of thought to be recovered in the process. In *Being and Time,* Heidegger is concerned to uncover just how the metaphysical tradition failed to do justice to some of its own best insights into the phenomenon of time and its relation to Being. This process allowed him to be discerning in his assessment of metaphysics, pointing out not only its failures but also its potential resources for a recovery of this problem.

After the so-called turn, however, Heidegger's stance toward metaphysics begins to change. Not only does the strategy of "*Destruktion*" play less and less of a role in Heidegger's methodology, but he begins to talk more of an "overcoming" (*Überwindung*) of metaphysics. Of course, we should qualify what he means by this "overcoming" by saying that it must be understood in terms of "getting over" (*Verwindung*), in the way, say, that one gets over a major disappointment not by forgetting it but by coming to terms with it and finding constructive ways to respond to it. This is a point Gadamer is fond of making. But even with this qualification, Heidegger's thought increasingly seeks a place "beyond" metaphysics, a "beyond" that is understood variously in different writings. In some cases, Heidegger seeks a critical distance from the metaphysical tradition, but there can be no doubt that his writing is still deeply informed by metaphysics. In other instances, however, Heidegger takes this search to a point where he can even say that "our task is to cease all overcoming and leave metaphysics to itself."[9] There is, it seems to me, a growing tendency to get "beyond metaphysics" in a more final way—a tendency to want to move into the place of "thinking" where metaphysical thinking has been definitively transcended. This trend in Heidegger's thought is motivated, in my opinion, by the fact that increasingly Heidegger comes to see all metaphysics as the same; it all culminates in various versions of "subjectivism" or "humanism," all of which in one way or another attempts to subordinate Being to human beings and their projects. Metaphysics, as Heidegger understands it, is increasingly forgetful of the fundamental ontological difference; i.e., that Being is not a being or even merely "the Being of beings." For Heidegger, all metaphysical thinking necessarily leads to nihilism or what Heidegger calls the "forgetfulness of Being" (*Seinsvergessenheit*), and his later thought increasingly emphasized the near total and irreversible nature of the oblivion to which Being has been assigned (or assigned itself). His famous statement from his 1976 *Spiegel* interview that "only a god can save us" points to this predicament of blind forgetfulness that Heidegger increasingly sees as our irreversible fate.

Gadamer has many critical reservations about Heidegger's attitude toward metaphysics and its supposed culmination in nihilism. At the very least, Gadamer finds these antimetaphysical tendencies in Heidegger as untenable exaggerations. While they may contain a kernel of truth, they simply go too far in rendering a one-sided reading of what metaphysics has been or might yet be. While a certain dogmatic, nondialectical reading of the metaphysical tradition may lead to the "complete forgetfulness of Being," metaphysics as such need not. There is, for Gadamer, no "near necessary" or "fateful" link between metaphysics as such and *Seinsvergessenheit.* While it is true to say that Heidegger never goes as far as Hegel in attributing strict necessity to his reading of the history of philosophy, his talk of the fate of metaphysics as nihilism or *Seinsvergessenheit* suggests a much stronger connection, or predisposition within metaphysics itself toward its supposed end. Gadamer rejects this rhetoric of "fate" or "near necessity," but he still understands himself as a Heideggerian, albeit a Heideggerian who is concerned to revive elements within the metaphysical tradition. Gadamer's own lifelong preoccupation with Plato (and Hegel) is evidence enough of this, as is his claim that hermeneutics, properly understood, "leads us back into the problems of classical metaphysics" (*TM*, 460). Gadamer is in some respects more sympathetic with the earlier Heidegger, the Heidegger who wanted to dismantle and reconstitute the metaphysical tradition in order to infuse it with new life than he is with the later Heidegger who wanted to "leave metaphysics to itself." In short, "*Destruktion*" always remains a vital and valid strategy for Gadamer, but in Gadamer's opinion we can never reach a point where metaphysical questions can simply be left behind. This is perhaps one reason why Gadamer often relies on his knowledge of Heidegger from the Marburg years and seeks to interpret his real intentions in light of his "thought experiments" from this time, which understood themselves to be much closer to metaphysics than the later Heidegger would allow.

Gadamer's appreciation of the potential of metaphysical thought is also a key reason why Gadamer rejects the idea that there is such a thing as *the* language of metaphysics.[10] There is not *one* language of metaphysics for Gadamer. Instead, there is simply language, i.e., the many discourses, we engage in. Such discourses lead us inevitably to raise metaphysical questions. For Gadamer metaphysical questions are implicit in all language. For example, all language uses general terms to refer to particular things and events. How this can be is just one of the questions language inevitably confronts us with. Such questions may be answered insightfully or poorly, but there is no *one* language of metaphysics and more fundamentally there is no way to develop a language of thinking which avoids metaphysical issues. Gadamer maintains that Heidegger's later attempts to develop a distinct language of thinking, whose closest neighbor is poetry, leads to what he calls Heidegger's *Sprachnot* (linguistic crisis/poverty).[11] While Gadamer acknowledges that the later Heidegger can still offer us brilliant insights, it is simply a mistake to think that he occupies ground that is really beyond metaphysics. Metaphysical questions are implicit whenever we speak. If we are thoughtful, we simply cannot avoid them. In light of this realization, Gadamer never adopts, like Heidegger did at one time and others like Derrida have done, the practice of writing metaphysical terms like "*Sein*" with an anachronistic spelling (*Seyn*) or "under erasure." Even if one writes "*Seyn*" or "*~~Seyn~~*" or "*Sein*" or "*~~Sein~~*," one still has to ask what these terms mean written in just these ways in just these contexts. To answer these questions there are no clever techniques that we can employ but we must instead use natural language and say what we mean as best we can. To fail to do just that is to risk mere meaninglessness.

Gadamer, however, not only resists Heidegger's growing alienation from the metaphysical issues implicit in natural language, he also particularly takes issue with his claims about the "forgetfulness of Being." As early as 1961, Gadamer wrote to Leo Strauss claiming that his (Gadamer's) "point of departure is not the *complete forgetfulness of Being*, the 'night of Being,' rather, on the contrary—I say this against Heidegger and Buber—the unreality of such an assertion."[12] *Wahrheit und Methode*, as well as Gadamer's other writings, are replete with references to other thinkers who demonstrate that this "forgetfulness of Being" has never been complete. Beyond Gadamer's reading of Plato (to which we will return subsequently), Gadamer could cite Aristotle on *phronesis* and the *analogia entis*, Plotinus's doctrine of emanation, Augustine's reflection on the *verbum cordis* and his Trinitarian speculations, Aquinas on the difference between *logos* and *verbum* and the incarnation, Nicholas of Cusa on language, Cajetan's *De Nominum Analogia*, the later Schelling and Fichte, Hegel's speculative logic, and even Husserl's doctrine of categorial intuition from the sixth *Logical Investigation* and his perceptive analyses of time and its relation to the problems of constitution as evidence against the "complete forgetfulness of Being." The fact that Heidegger was familiar with all these instances (and more) from the philosophical past should have warned him against his thesis about the "oblivion of Being." Gadamer repeatedly protests that what I would call Heidegger's "negative eschatology" or "reversed eschatology"—from Being to the near-complete forgetfulness of Being—is not an irreversible consequence of even the most sober reading of the history of philosophy. In fact, Gadamer's writings on Heidegger often point out the proximity of Heidegger's insights to various positions worked out by various thinkers in the metaphysical tradition. Gadamer is fond of pointing out how Heidegger missed opportunities for a deeper exploration of his question in terms of the history of philosophy.

But behind these attempts to achieve a more balanced appreciation of Heidegger's thought and its relationship to the past there is a deeper concern. By maintaining that the "forgetfulness of Being" has never been complete Gadamer wishes to show that there is reason to believe that the history of metaphysics does not lead to the kind of nihilism that Heidegger says is the fate of metaphysics in the West. How Gadamer proposes to avoid this nihilism will occupy us below, but for now it is important to stress that Gadamer's disagreement with Heidegger is not a mere academic dispute about how to read the history of philosophy. From a Gadamerian perspective, Heidegger's distortion of the metaphysical tradition leads to a distorted view of the conditions of human thought. Nothing less than our prospects for ethical knowledge, broadly construed, i.e., knowledge of who we are and how we should direct our lives, is ultimately at stake. Could it be that by repudiating metaphysics as such what is lost is nothing less than a basis for human solidarity and ethical deliberation? It seems to me that Gadamer is worried about just this problem. In short, Heidegger's thesis about the complete forgetfulness of Being threatens to obscure and undermine the very foundations of normative discourse. Without such a language of normative speech, a speech which is in a strong sense rational and rooted in what is, a truly meaningful human life becomes deeply problematic. It's important to stress this point because it is this fundamental human issue that is ultimately at stake between Heidegger and Gadamer. Failure to see this amounts to a failure to give this critique its proper seriousness.

Gadamer bases his critique of Heidegger in large part on the latter's reading of Plato. Gadamer begins here because he knows that Heidegger equated metaphysics with Platonism.[13] Quite straightforwardly, Gadamer hoped to show that if Heidegger was wrong in his assessment of Plato, the "founder of metaphysics," then he might very well be wrong about metaphysics and its fate. But if Heidegger is wrong about the inevitable destiny of metaphysical thought then a fundamental reassessment of his own thought will be required. Nothing less than such a reassessment is at stake in Gadamer's encounter with Heidegger's philosophy. The specific point of departure for Gadamer's understanding of Heidegger's legacy is the claim that Heidegger's critique of the metaphysical tradition rests on a serious misunderstanding of Plato's notion of the Good. Not only does this imply that Plato did not inaugurate the "forgetfulness of Being," of which Heidegger repeatedly accuses him, but it also implies a profound ontological point about our available ethical resources, resources necessary for coming to terms with our fundamental question of how we should live. Simply put, what this difference amounts to is that Gadamer maintains that human beings have never been without the ability to know something essential for their lives about the Good, whereas Heidegger's analysis of the "Event of Being" increasingly undercuts the possibility of this knowledge. To see how Gadamer makes this case we need to turn first to a brief account of Heidegger's reading of Platonism and its connection to the metaphysical tradition in the West. We will then turn to Gadamer's confrontation with the nihilistic tendencies in the thought of the later Heidegger.

Heidegger and Plato

Heidegger maintained that the early Greeks thought of Being as *phusis*, the "event" or process in which things emerged out of concealment to become what they are and to maintain themselves as what they are.[14] *Phusis* was seen as this movement of un-concealment or *a-letheia*. Thus *phusis* was what "truth" (aletheia) meant for early Greek thinkers like Heraclitus. But, as Heraclitus pointed out, Being or nature (*phusis*) also "loves to hide" (*phusis kruptesthai philei*). What this means, according to Heidegger, is, in part, that Being's unconcealment is never univocal. This is so in that *phusis* is the process of Being's emergence which, while showing itself truly, may nevertheless show only a side or view (*Anblick*) of itself and not its whole reality. Thus Heidegger says that this "truth" or unconcealment is also a concealment. But what is more, *phusis* is also the process in which Being may show itself falsely as a mere appearance or semblance (*Anschein*) of itself, which is really an illusion. In this sense, the concealment that may accompany any movement of unconcealment may be profound. This is why any acknowledgment of truth is always fraught with risk. The possibility of grasping what is genuinely the case (even if it is a limited, perspectival grasping), as well as being duped by an "appearance" that appears true but is really false, are both marked in similar ways. They both have a kind of "radiance" or self-evident appearance (*Schein*) to them that makes it difficult to tell them apart. It is in the nature (*phusis*) of things themselves that their appearance or "unconcealedness" has this duplicity attached to it. Even when the appearance is genuine the unconcealment or truth may very well be one-sided and incomplete. Surprises, qualifications, and reversals are inseparable from our quest for truth. Truth, on this model, is a kind of constant tension between unconcealment and concealment, emergence and withdrawal, motion and rest.

So far Gadamer and Heidegger are in accord about the origin of our concept of truth. But it is from this perspective on truth that Heidegger thinks he can grasp the negative implications of Plato's ontology for later thought and it is this attribution of these negative implications to Plato that Gadamer wishes to question.

Heidegger claims that Plato found this earlier notion of truth as *phusis* intolerable. Its tension-filled ambivalence between unconcealment and concealment, its constant "becoming" between Being and non-Being, truth and falsehood, supposedly led Plato away from stressing the relationship between *aletheia* and *phusis* and compelled him instead to interpret truth in terms of his notion of *idèa*. This is a subtle but decisive shift in our understanding of truth, according to Heidegger. Simply put, it is a shift from truth as a "process" of emergence and concealment to truth as a "product" of emergence; it is a shift from "motion" to "rest," from change to changelessness, from becoming to Being. Plato thought of the *idèa* of something as the "what" of something. A thing's "whatness" or essence is its *idèa.* The "whatness" of something or its essence is what emerges from the process of its unconcealment; it is the end-product of this process. As an end-product it is fully formed and determinate; it is now at rest, not in motion; it is now changeless, not in change; it has now ceased to become and it now finally "is." As such what it offers us is a changeless look or vision of itself. Inasmuch as this look is changeless the notion of a *process* of emergence drops out of the story, according to Heidegger. On his reading, Plato merely stresses the "whatness" or essence of a thing as a thing's true being. Heidegger thinks that Plato could ignore the process of emergence, because he thinks of a thing's "Idea" as its unchanging presence. Thus, for Plato, Being is supposedly continuous presence, a presence which leaves no room for "absence" or "withdrawal." Instead of seeing Being as a process of emergence *and* withdrawal that exists somewhere between presence and absence, Plato opens the way to see Being as a being, or an Idea as pure presence. This Idea is "produced" by the Good in the *Republic,* which Plato calls the "cause" (*aitia*) of all Being, and in the mythical language of the *Timaeus* the *demiurgos* takes on this role. In Heidegger's mind this sets the stage for Aristotle's doctrine of the four causes, as well as for the later Christian doctrine of creation ex nihilo and its even later transformation into Nietzsche's will to power. But this is jumping ahead of ourselves.

This tendency to see Being as the presence of a "what" or an "essence" is suggested by the fact that an *idèa* is connected to vision (*idein*) or how a thing looks or how it presents itself to be seen. What is seen, i.e., really seen, is a presence that stays put and does not constantly change but remains the same throughout its many different appearances. Thus metaphors of vision, perception, and light become central to Plato's account of what thinking is. According to Heidegger, this same emphasis on vision leads him increasingly to stress the importance of correct (*orthotes*) changeless vision. This is the fundamental change in Plato's thinking that Heidegger stresses. "In *orthotes,* the correctness of the look, lies everything,"[15] says Heidegger. According to Heidegger, Plato changed the primary emphasis in our experience of truth from *aletheia* to *orthotes,* from unconcealedness to correctness. This emphasis on vision, light, and correctness is supposedly evidenced very clearly in the "Allegory of the Cave," where the person emerging from the cave receives an ever more correct vision of the Ideas the closer she moves toward the light of the sun or the Idea of the Good (*tou agathou*). Slowly, ever so slowly and painfully, the philosopher learns to bring her vision into conformity (*homoiosis*) with the Ideas. Slowly she sees the things that have true presence or true Being without a trace of movement or "becoming" about them.

For Heidegger, this subtle shift in emphasis has profound and ultimately ironic consequences. The shift from Being as *phusis* to Being as *idea* or presence—a shift from understanding Being as a movement to understanding Being as a static being or Idea[16]—may have been motivated by a desire to serve truth by making its access more secure, but this subtle shift in emphasis actually lead to a radical undermining of truth over the centuries. This is supposedly demonstrated by the logical culmination of this theory in various "humanisms" or philosophies of the subject. Without rehearsing Heidegger's interpretation of the history of this development in detail, it can be pointed out that his general line of reasoning rests on the premise that once truth ceases to be *aletheia* and comes to be correctness, the emphasis shifts from truth as an ontological event to truth as a judgment made by a subject. In other words, it is the thinking subject that decides which "visions" or "perceptions" of truth are correct and what is to count as conformity. Not only must truth be seen as the presence of the Idea, but the *I* must *recognize* that it is the presence of the Idea. The subject's own recognition of this presence to her mind becomes the basis for truth's existence. Thus we have, centuries before the emergence of a philosopher like Descartes, the seeds of his claim that truth is certainty, self-certainty. And if we divorce Descartes's account of certainty from his doctrine of the *lumen naturale* (a claim which, in the minds of many, fell with his theology) human beings become the final measure of truth. In this context it is a short step from Descartes to Kant's defense of the *autonomy* of reason, *human* reason, by an appeal to the a priori elements in our experience. But if the unchanging nature of the a priori falls away because it is no longer seen as a necessary given, behind which we cannot question, but is seen as a contingent product of a long line of ever more subtle human *decisions* about how best to manipulate and control the world for our purposes, then the stage is set for Nietzsche's doctrine of Being as the will to power. Whereas the Good supposedly "produced" presence in the *Republic*, human beings become the "producers" of meaning in the blind pursuit of power in various ingenious guises. It is this line of development that leads Heidegger to argue that the "beginning of metaphysics in the thought of Plato is at the same time the beginning of humanism,"[17] or the tendency to be able to think Being only in terms that serve human goals. Ironically, nothing could be further from Plato's intentions, but such is the consequence, according to Heidegger, of Plato's fateful decision to think truth (*aletheia*) as correctness (*orthotes*).

This history links Plato with Nietzsche in a line of development that is continuous enough for Heidegger to refer to its whole course as "the history of metaphysics." It is this continuous history that enables Heidegger to equate metaphysics with Platonism. If this history's development is as "necessary" or "fateful" as Heidegger claims then it makes sense that Heidegger would refer to Nietzsche as the "last metaphysician" and even the "most unbridled Platonist."[18] Nietzsche is the "last metaphysician" and even the "most unbridled Platonist" because he logically brings to a close a movement of thought initiated by Plato, who, in all likelihood, would have been repulsed by its consequences. Not only did it result in an "humanistic" or "subjectivistic" account of truth, according to Heidegger, but this account of truth, which makes human beings in various ways the final arbiters of truth, is also of a piece with the tendency of technology to bring all aspects of reality under human control.

This is the last phase of metaphysics, the "technological phase." With "technology" comes not only the widespread degradation of the natural world and the equally well-known social and psychological strains that come with the industrial and postindustrial revolutions, but also a sharp division in human thinking between fact and value. Whatever cannot be investigated and controlled by the techniques and methods of science is relegated to a "private" or "subjective" sphere, from whence it is unable to exercise significant influence on the serious business of extending an ever-increasing technological control over the natural and social world. "Truth" no longer extends over both realms of "fact" and "value," but is instead confined to the realm of fact ascertained by the natural sciences. The very fact that our age is characterized by this dichotomy (a false dichotomy in Gadamer's opinion), is indicative of the metaphysical history that Western society has been living out. In fact this "end of metaphysics" is the nihilism that results when the criteria or standards we use to differentiate reality and give it sense and order are seen as nothing more than the various techniques which the will to power ingeniously employs. If such is the position we are in, we are indeed "beyond good and evil" and even beyond truth and falsehood. In short, we have arrived at an age of nihilism, a nihilism that Nietzsche foresaw and sought to hasten in the hopes of overcoming it by passing through it like an illness that cannot be avoided but may be lived through.

Heidegger was genuinely disturbed by what his reflections on the history of philosophy were revealing. So seriously did he take the risk of "subjectivity" that he increasingly worried that even *Sein und Zeit*, whose project of fundamental ontology stressed that human *Dasein*, as the "clearing" in Being, was necessary for truth, ran the "risk of reinforcing subjectivity."[19] This is undoubtedly one important factor that led to the so-called turn in his subsequent thinking in which human beings play an ever-decreasing role in the revelation of Being and Being itself moves to the fore and assumes the initiative, so to speak. In making this "turn," Heidegger did not hope to reverse, at one fell swoop, the nihilism that is the supposed fate of metaphysics, but to both acknowledge nihilism as our fate and to begin to prepare the ground for its possible overcoming.

In Gadamer's opinion, Heidegger was surely right to see that the emphasis on subjectivity, even transcendental subjectivity of thinkers like Kant and Husserl, was vulnerable to Nietzsche's doctrine of the will to power. In our own day if we think of how the distinction between necessary and contingent truths has been rejected by pragmatists like Quine and Rorty this thesis seems born out. Such distinctions are, it is claimed, nothing more than relative linguistic distinctions between what we in our present context find indispensable for description of our experience and what we find optional. Of course, what is emphasized by these philosophers is that the line between the indispensable and the optional is fluid; it may in fact change as our context changes and this is precisely the point. Such distinctions are simply relative to our needs. Rorty is even bold enough to confess that his position and Nietzsche's are in fundamental agreement.[20]

But Heidegger was no pragmatist and he also wished to avoid a position like Nietzsche's. In Gadamer's view it is a mistake to see Nietzsche as having already reached a position that Heidegger's own thought eventually embraced.[21] Certainly Gadamer is right about Heidegger's intent, but it remains a valid question, in my opinion, to wonder if the implications of what Heidegger says do not undermine this intent. Does Heidegger's reading of the history of metaphysics offer a way out? As a young philosopher, Heidegger had often turned to the Greeks precisely because their emphasis on the ontological foundations of truth were so much more congenial to him than the then-prevailing neo-Kantian emphasis on transcendental subjectivity. But a critical and creative return to the Greeks, particularly Plato and Aristotle, was cut off for him by his own claim that those beginnings inevitably lead to the impasses he wished to escape. Moreover, inasmuch as metaphysics was tantamount to philosophy for Heidegger, he became increasingly alienated from other thinkers from the past as well. Heidegger tried to go back before Plato and Aristotle into the pre-Socratics to search for the origins of our predicament, origins which he hoped would show signs of other possibilities for "thinking." But even in the pre-Socratics Heidegger increasingly saw only near-necessary prefigurations of "metaphysics" and its nihilistic outcome.[22]

Gadamer's Challenge

Gadamer sets out to overcome this Heideggerian reading of metaphysics and its consequences. As we will see shortly, his challenge to Heidegger is complex, but its foundation is surely Gadamer's rereading of the Platonic corpus in light of Heidegger's criticism. In general, Gadamer hopes to show that Heidegger was wrong about Plato's unqualified substitution of *aletheia* for *orthotes.* "It is conceivable," Gadamer writes, "that one could find in Platonic philosophy one possible way to get behind the question as formulated in Aristotelian and the post-Aristotelian metaphysics, so that the dimension of self-manifesting Being, the Being of *aletheia* that articulates itself in the *logos,* could be recognized in the dialectic of Ideas" (*HW,* 160). If Gadamer is right about this fundamental point there is no inevitable path of development for metaphysics. This critique sets the stage for a deeper criticism of Heidegger. In general it can be said that Gadamer not only uses Heidegger's insights on truth against Heidegger's Plato interpretation but he also uses Heidegger's insights into *aletheia* to critique Heidegger's insistence that metaphysics leads to nihilism and the loss of a foundation for ethical solidarity. This reconnecting of Being and truth leads Gadamer to reconnect Being to other transcendentals as well. This leads in turn to a relativization of the ontological difference, which suggests that Being is not as inaccessible to beings as Heidegger increasingly thought. Let us begin to examine this multifaceted challenge by looking at the important issues in Gadamer's Plato interpretation which tell against Heidegger's own reading of Plato.

Key to Gadamer's effort to resist this Heideggerian reading of Plato is his denial that Plato banishes "motility" or "motion" (*Bewegtheit*) from the web of Ideas. As we saw in the last chapter, Gadamer argues that Plato incorporated "motion" and "rest" into the inner structure of Being. This is important for Gadamer's understanding of Heidegger because, as Gadamer stresses, it is "precisely the point at which the later Heidegger takes up the question" (*HW,* 84). If Gadamer is right that it is a misreading of Plato to ascribe to him the denial of a key place for "motion" in his ontology, then a real question arises as to whether Plato really was an unequivocal advocate of what has been called the "metaphysics of presence." If Ideas always withdraw and conceal themselves in some ways whenever they simultaneously reveal themselves in others there would be no pure presence and consequently no static vision of the Ideas. If there is no changeless presence of the Ideas there can be no final, definitive, changeless vision of them, and consequently there can be no final certainty or control of them. Certainly the fact that Plato himself never gave what he purported to be a definitive account of *any* of the

Ideas in any of the dialogues is suggestive of this conclusion. Instead of an unchanging look we must depend more completely on the things themselves and how they present themselves variously in various contexts (which is precisely what the dialogues do) and less on the subjective quality of our "vision" of them. In other words, we must develop a more ontological account of truth and look less to criteria generated by our own demands that the things reveal themselves in certain ways—like with the marks of clarity and distinction—if we are to take them seriously at all. Instead we should follow Aristotle's advice and only seek "as much clearness as the subject matter admits of."[23] In doing this we acknowledge that it is ultimately the things themselves that make both what we grasp and how we grasp it possible for us.

In order to further the case for an ontological account of truth in Plato, Gadamer focuses on the nature of the Good as Plato describes it in the *Republic.* But before we get to what Gadamer says about this text it is useful in my opinion to outline his general strategy in the following inference: If the Good is the Idea of Ideas, the paradigm of all Ideas, or what gives Being to all other Ideas, then it seems likely that what holds for the Good, would hold, mutatis mutandis, for the other Ideas. Although the Good is in some important ways distinct from other Ideas in its transcendental function, Gadamer insists that the Good communicates something of its openness to the other Ideas in their various historical determinations. In other words, if "motion" or concealment and unconcealment is inherent to the Good and, consequently, no definitively correct account of the Good is possible, then it is plausible to infer that motion is inherent to at least some of the other Ideas as well. Just as it would be misleading to speak of any final account of the Good, so it would be misleading to speak of a final account of these Ideas. The point here is not that truth has nothing to do with correctness but that "correctness" is relative to the context of inquiry shared by dialogue partners. Truth for Plato is always more than "mere" correctness; it is "always already" *aletheia.*

In order to make this point, Gadamer begins by reminding us "that Plato uses only the word *idèa* and never *eidos* for *agathon*" (*IG,* 27). This implies, Gadamer thinks, that the *idèa tou agathou* is somehow distinct from other *eidai* or forms. According to Gadamer, its distinctness lies in its singular transcendence, or the sense in which it is "beyond all Being" (*epekeina tès ousias*) (*Republic,* 509b). Gadamer understands this transcendence in terms analogous to Heidegger's notion of the ontological difference, i.e., as the denial that the Good is in any way a being. It may be copresent with all beings but it is not itself a being.

> The fact that Plato never speaks of the *eidos tou agathou* (form of the Good) indicates that the Idea of the Good has a character all its own. *Eidos* always refers only to the object, as accords with its being neuter. In following the natural tendency of our thinking to objectify, the feminine form, *idea*, can certainly designate an object too, as do *doxa* and *epistèmè*. But in *idea*, taken as a "view of something," the viewing or looking is more pronounced than in *eidos*, taken as "how something looks." Consequently, *idea tou agathou* (Idea of the Good) implies not so much the "view of the good" as a "looking to the Good" as numerous turns of speech such as *apoblepein pros* show. (*IG*, 27, 28)

Gadamer is saying that in Plato's own text there is a suggestion that whereas a thinker may strive to look *at* the other forms (*eidai*) one may only strive to look *to* the Idea of the Good.[24] Gadamer thinks that this is more than a trivial difference of the prepositions "at" and "to" or an equally trivial etymological nicety. Instead the difference in grammar is significant because it suggests that the Good was never thought of by Plato as a continuous presence that one can definitively grasp. Certainly the difficulty of grasping the Good once and for all is strongly suggested by Socrates's fear of being able to speak straightforwardly about this subject in the *Republic*, and his subsequent attempt in the "Allegory of the Cave" bears out this difficulty by pointing out that the Good is the hardest of the Ideas to comprehend, even for one who has made the journey out of the cave.

The upshot of this insight for the Heideggerian interpretation of Plato is plain. The Good, for Plato, does not show itself as continuous presence, but as the general "movement" of simultaneous unconcealment and concealment. The Good is difficult to comprehend because it cannot be directly comprehended at all. It is never a "pure presence," a static Idea, whose intelligible structure can be captured in a carefully articulated theory, but instead it is only given to us indirectly, in the contexts where we discern what is best through dialogical questioning. The transcendence of the Good even suggests that the Good shows itself *more* as concealment than unconcealment. Nevertheless, it is important to remind ourselves that Plato says that the Good is "beyond Being" but never, like Plotinus, "beyond all thinking" (*epekeina noèseòs*).[25] What this transcendence bespeaks is a *relative* difference between the way the Good is manifested and the way the other Ideas are manifested. This point will occupy us again below, but suffice it to say that the transcendence of the Good implies the most important point against Heidegger's reading of Plato, namely, that motility or movement is not absent from Plato's ontology. Thus there is no one-sided emphasis on "correctness" (*orthotes*) or "presence" (*parousia*) rather than *aletheia* in Plato's account of truth, and consequently there is nothing in principle fateful and irrevocable in Plato's various accounts of the Ideas for subsequent accounts of philosophical thought. If subsequent philosophy focused merely on the issue of the correct vision of the *eidai* and thus set a course for subjectivism and nihilism, there was nothing inevitable in that development, even though it may be understandable after the fact. For Plato, truth is *both* "correctness" (*orthotes*) and unconcealment (*aletheia*).

But before we explore further how Gadamer's critique implies a rejection of nihilism itself there is also another criticism of Heidegger that stems from Gadamer's insistence that truth, as understood by Plato, includes *aletheia.* Gadamer is fond of pointing out that if the motion of concealment and unconcealment is always operative in any revelation of reality then we must learn to pay more attention to the contextual factors of any truth-claim. No truth-claim or proposition would be purely or unequivocally true. Its truth would depend on the context in which it is able to reveal some aspect of reality to us. Only within such a context could we speak of a proposition's "correctness." As we already pointed out, this context, for Gadamer, is a context generated by historically mediated questions. Thus all truth is relative to these questions and there are, consequently, no definitive, acontextual, or final truth-claims.

The implication of this insight is not subjectivism in a historicist guise. Gadamer's claim is not that every historical individual or generation has their own, unique truth, inaccessible to other individuals or generations. His point is that we have access to the truth of other individuals from other times and cultures, if and only if we enter into the process of inquiry with them. In order to do this we must learn that our access to truth is rooted in *dialogue* or a *shared* questioning into reality and not in the private vision of the individual who strives to confirm his sight to the changeless presence of the timeless Ideas which are the true Being of reality. But neither is truth primarily discovered by the solitary Heideggerian thinker. Instead, truth is a function of "dialogue," not only with the great minds of the past but also with other human beings with whom we share our lives. Gadamer sees the Platonic dialogues themselves as key evidence for the "dialogical" nature of all truth. Truth does not occur primarily in solipsistic inwardness but in shared contexts of inquiry, which presuppose a common past and which point us toward a common future. By talking with each other, i.e., by critically responding to our own attempts to understand, as well as those of others, we come to better understandings of reality. There is no substitution for this dialogue, not even an immersion in the thought of the great thinkers of the past. As invaluable and indispensable as this experience is, it cannot take the place of our own voices trying to articulate our understanding to ourselves and each other.

For Gadamer the Platonic dialogues are not actual historical accounts of conversations that really took place, but they do mime the true nature of dialogue by demonstrating that insight into reality can only occur in conversations, conversations that are very relative to the conversants and their context. In Heidegger, by contrast, there is almost no emphasis on dialogue as such. Despite his extensive scholarship, his thought is increasingly a soliloquy on Being and its fate or at best it is a dialogue with other great minds of the past. But there is little or no emphasis on shared inquiry into a common reality or critical questioning of each other. It is almost as if Heidegger's own methodology is highly individualistic, despite the fact that he does emphasize the "wordly" character of thought and the fact that *Dasein* is always also a *Mitsein*, i.e., that *Dasein* is always in-the-world-with-others. For Heidegger, dialogue with these others is simply not integral to the experience of truth. This is somewhat ironic because Heidegger does frequently make the case for living speech (*die Rede*), speech about particular things disclosed in a specific context. It is his contention that such speech often brings us closer to reality than the dogmatic adherence to the conceptual schemes that often dominate academic language. Nevertheless, this emphasis on real speech never really evolves into a sustained emphasis on dialogue as the locus of truth's disclosure. Real, everyday speech is intrinsically dialogical; it always revolves around common understandings, concerns, and questions. Even the most banal speech about the weather can remind us that we share a common fate under a common sky.

Gadamer's constant emphasis on "dialogue" as the place where truth occurs is, in my opinion, a key example of how he appropriates Heidegger's insights and in a very telling way turns them against Heidegger himself. By claiming that dialogue is always made possible by the questions that motivate it, Gadamer does more than argue that the truth that can emerge from such dialogue is always a relative, partial truth. Of course, it is a truth relative to the context of questioning and never "the whole truth." Such truths both reveal and conceal in exactly the way that Heidegger claims that truth itself is a constant movement between unconcealment and concealment. Thus we can see how central Heidegger's account of truth as *aletheia* is for Gadamer. But truth also occurs in a *shared* context of questioning in *dialogue.* Truth is not primarily a private event in the inner life of the singular thinker but an insight confirmed in and through dialogue with others.[26] Truth for Gadamer is only possible in solidarity with others. Only because we can share a common context of inquiry or questioning can truth emerge as an answer to these questions, questions which are generated in dialogue. Thus truth presupposes solidarity. This is a claim that is almost completely missing in Heidegger and which Gadamer intends to correct by his emphasis on dialogue.

It is fair to say that at least part of Gadamer's critique of Heidegger can be understood as an attempt to employ the notion of truth as *aletheia* against certain tendencies in Heidegger. This is, of course, an attempt to use Heidegger against Heidegger, but there is no inconsistency in critically employing one aspect of a thinker's thought against other aspects, especially if a body of thought evinces inconsistencies. But this appeal to a certain concept of truth in the service of a critique of Heidegger has broader ramifications than those we have already considered. We have already seen how Gadamer turns his understanding of *aletheia* against Heidegger's Plato interpretation, and we have seen how it also leads him to stress the connection between truth and dialogue against Heidegger. But there is a third, more profound criticism of Heidegger, that is implicit in Gadamer's reading of Plato. Simply put, Gadamer intends to resist the nihilistic implications of Heidegger's later thought by reorienting us toward the experience of truth, which is itself suggestive of a different ontological project.

To see how this might be the deepest intent of Gadamer's Heidegger critique, consider once more the following important quote:

> The philosophical stimuli I received from Heidegger led me more and more into the realm of dialectic, Plato's as well as Hegel's. Decades of teaching were devoted to elaborating and testing what I have called here the Platonic-Aristotelian unitary effect. But in the background was the continuous challenge posed for me by the path Heidegger's own thought took, and especially by his interpretation of Plato as the decisive step toward "metaphysical thought's" obliviousness to Being [*Sein*]. My elaboration and projection of a philosophical hermeneutics in *Wahrheit und Methode* bear witness to my efforts to withstand this challenge theoretically. (*IG*, 5)

This text clearly suggests that Gadamer's lifelong challenge is to withstand the inevitability of *Seinsvergessenheit* and the nihilism that is supposedly its result.

But why would Gadamer have worried that there were nihilistic implications in Heidegger's own thought, implications that may even have been at odds with some of Heidegger's own philosophical concerns to somehow overcome nihilism? To see how Gadamer might have very plausibly worried about the possible nihilistic implications of Heidegger's later thought it is helpful to look briefly at one of Heidegger's own characterizations of his own development. In *Vier Seminare* Heidegger describes his own development as having involved three phases: the first phase concerned itself with the meaning of Being (*Sinn von Sein*). The second phase was occupied with the issue of the truth of Being (*Wahrheit des Seins*). And the third phase focused on the topology of Being (*Topos des Seins*).[27] In light of this schema, I think Gadamer's critique of Heidegger can be described generally as an attempt to subject Heidegger's third phase to a criticism based on the first two phases, and more specially as a critique which takes the second phase as its point of departure against the third. In short, Gadamer attempts to employ Heidegger's insights into truth against the later Heidegger, particularly the later Heidegger's tendency toward nihilism implicit in some of the key impasses of Heidegger's later thought. As I hope to show, the result of this is a fundamental rethinking of Heidegger's ontological project.

The reason Gadamer is prone to offer this resistance certainly has something to do generally with the fact that the question of truth remains fundamental and inescapable for Gadamer, whereas for Heidegger, it gradually loses its grip on his thought.[28] In these same *Vier Seminare* Heidegger even goes so far as to say that "*aletheia* has nothing to do with *Wahrheit* (truth)."[29] This statement is indicative of the deeper difference between Gadamer and Heidegger. In saying that "*aletheia* has nothing to do with *Wahrheit*," Heidegger shows that in the last phase of his thought he understood *aletheia* in terms that are less dialectical than he had previously and that are certainly less dialectical than Gadamer. One might further characterize this change by pointing out how for the early and middle Heidegger (and Gadamer) truth involves a movement or dialectic between "correctness" and "unconcealment." This dialectic shows itself as a partial revelation of a determinate truth (a what) that is also a concealment because it is relative to a context involving particular things and events. Evidence for this understanding of truth can be found in *Being and Time*, section 44, where Heidegger does not reject the traditional notion of truth as *adequatio* but tries to relate it to a more "originary" notion of truth as unconcealment. Heidegger never really explains this relationship in *Being and Time* and this is perhaps why the later Heidegger no longer focuses on this relationship between what is revealed and the particular manner of that revelation. Instead, what he focuses on might be called "the movement as such" or the process itself rather than the dialectical moments of this process in their interrelatedness. Thus the later Heidegger focuses almost exclusively on *das Ereignis* or the "appropriative Event" in which Being gives itself to us. We can say that Heidegger gives priority in this thought about this Event to the process *and* consequently assigns the "what" that emerges in it to a secondary status. It is in this spirit that he contends in the *Beiträge* that "it is no longer a question of discussing 'about' something and of exhibiting something objective, but of being conveyed to the e-vent."[30] Instead Heidegger focuses on the process as such and even insists that any attempt to understand the event of "giving" or "there is" (*es gibt*) in terms of *what* is given confuses the process itself with a determinate such and such. In other words, it confuses Being with beings, the very difference that Heidegger repeatedly claims is forgotten by metaphysical thought. To avoid this fateful confusion we must not think of this process in terms of any determinate something but as the process or "waying" (*Wesung*) in which determinate things come to be taken for what they are.[31] This process is the "there is" (*es gibt*) whereby all the distinctions of thought and action are made possible and as such it is not a definite thought itself; it itself is beyond all definite standards of thinking and acting. Because all standards depend on this Event, we have no way to assess its significance, but we must simply accept it as our fate. As Heidegger says, we are "conveyed" by this Event, swept along with it, as it were. It is determinative of what we can think, say, and do, and our wills and minds are its products and not in any substantive sense its critical partners.

Gadamer's critical remarks on Heidegger's last phase imply, in my opinion, two fundamental problems with this tendency in Heidegger's philosophy. The first problem we have already alluded to above. Gadamer is best understood in my opinion as claiming that the priority of process over content in the Event, which is the direction that Heidegger's later thought takes, is an abstraction that threatens the Event itself with meaninglessness. In other words, one cannot really grasp the nature of the revelation of truth apart from what is revealed in the process of revelation. To think of this process simply as a "way" (*Weg*) and not also in terms of a "what," or the determinate something that emerges from it, gives us no purchase on the process itself. To think process as process is void of meaning. To have meaning the process of revelation must be understood in terms of *what* is revealed. Otherwise the result is at best meaningless and at worst it implies nihilism.

This points us to an even deeper problem with this late Heideggerian line of thought. If the Event just occurs and we are subject to this occurrence as our destiny, regardless of how it occurs or what emerges from it, then there is no ground or standard implicit to this occurrence to which we can appeal to understand our situation and how we should respond to it. Any response at all seems compatible with this Event. There is nothing intrinsic in the Event that points to any kind of normative response to it. One might as well acquiesce in the present as resist it with all one's strength. Despite the fact that Heidegger was appalled by the nihilism of contemporary civilization it is not at all clear that he avoids it or prepares the way for its eventual overcoming.[32]

I think that in the final analysis Gadamer's thought struggles at its deepest levels with nihilism. For these purposes he appeals to elements within Heidegger's own thought. But Heidegger himself does not leave us with an unambiguous response to nihilism. Thus, Gadamer finds that at certain points, he must use Heidegger against Heidegger, i.e., he must look to certain aspects of Heidegger's legacy to resist tendencies in other parts of Heidegger's thought. For these purposes Gadamer not only returns to Plato's notion of the Good in order to save truth (*aletheia*) from Heidegger's one-sided historical account, but also to save some of Heidegger's own insights from a nihilism to which they were prone. Gadamer tries, first of all, to show that Plato did not reduce truth to mere correctness but maintained the relativity of correctness to the process of inquiry or dialogical questioning. Second, and more importantly, Gadamer's thought implies, contrary to Heidegger, how it is that in taking our experience of the Good as paradigmatic for our experience of Being we have an experience that both calls us to critique and provides within itself the immanent standards that govern that critique. In other words, Gadamer would give us hope for being "critical partners" in the Event and not simply its pawns. Is this perhaps what Heidegger himself had in mind when he talked about our need to become "Shepherds of Being"?

But how is it that if we take Plato's account of the Good as paradigmatic for our thinking about Being we learn of an experience that both draws us into critical conversation and, at the same time, helps us discover the normative guidelines of that conversation? To answer this question we must look again at the relative ontological difference between the Good and the other Ideas. This will lead us to what I call the "withdrawal of the Ideas" and their unique regulative role in our discourse.

The "Withdrawal" of the Ideas

Gadamer's account of the relative difference between the reality of the Good (and the other transcendentals) and the other Ideas is emphasized with a great deal of clarity and consistency in his writings. The advantage of this is that it enables Gadamer to preserve something of the plausibility of Heidegger's account while distancing himself from Heidegger's more radical conclusions. In other words, it enables him to suggest that Heidegger was right to think that "Platonism," as understood by philosophers like Aristotle and those who follow him in his Plato critique, does lead to *Seinsvergessenheit,* but Plato himself and much of the metaphysical tradition need not be interpreted in this light. I would say, however, that the transcendence of the Good and the other transcendentals may be overemphasized by Gadamer in order not to undermine Heidegger's account too much. I think that there are reasons both in Gadamer's account of the theory of Ideas and in the Platonic texts that suggest that the *relative* difference between the transcendentals and the other Ideas, although real, is nevertheless not as sharply demarcated as Gadamer sometimes suggests. In other words, I think that Gadamer was in a position to make an even stronger case against Heidegger's Plato interpretation and to draw even more important consequences from it. It is to this case and its consequences that we now turn.

If the Good is transcendent in that it is "beyond all Being," this is to be understood, Gadamer thinks, in the sense that the Good is not a being but that which somehow bestows Being on things. Such transcendence implies that the Good could never be the changeless object of vision because, like the sun, it is what makes vision possible in the first place. This is to say that it is the Good which is the source of the unified intelligibility of things. At best we become aware of the Good indirectly; it is copresent in things and we discern it as what is best in this or that specific context, but it is never present by itself as a changeless object of sensuous perception or intellectual vision. In short, the Good may be discerned in various contexts and even govern our cognitive access to the ethical nature of the situations we find ourselves in, but it itself never can become the object of changeless theory. We grasp it "in context," "with other things" and never by itself, alone and pure, but always mixed with the confusions of contingency that are part and parcel of our finitude.

A similar kind of transcendence, however, holds for the other transcendentals as well, i.e., for unity, truth, beauty, Being and non-Being, and difference, motion, and rest, etc. All of these transcendentals are ways the Good is found in all things, even the other Ideas. These Ideas, as well, are never pure objects of theory, but we do have an indispensable understanding of them nevertheless. In this sense, all the transcendentals are not beings but are "beyond Being." They are ontological principles that determine everything that is, but they are not themselves discrete beings or things, even ideal things. Human intelligence is able to discern their common presence in physical things and in other Ideas without confusing that copresence with the presence of a being in its own right.

Certainly a two-world version of the *chorismos* is not necessary to this theory of ideal reality.

But if the transcendentals are "beyond Being" in this sense what then is the relationship between the transcendentals and the other Ideas? The essential features of the relationship can be expressed as follows: All the transcendentals are always copresent with the other Ideas, but not all Ideas are copresent with the transcendentals or each other. For example, if I am to think about identity and difference I do not need to understand what the principle of triangularity is, but in order to think about the nature of triangles, I do indeed draw upon notions of unity, truth, identity and difference and the rest, but need not draw upon all the other Ideas such as circularity or justice. In this sense, the transcendentals are more "transcendent" by virtue of their ubiquity.

But there is nevertheless an important sense in which not only the transcendentals are "beyond Being" but the other Ideas are as well. The Ideas, Ideas like triangularity, justice, human nature, etc., are "beyond Being" in that they, too, are not beings or things in their own right but ontological principles inherent in things. Gadamer does not stress this transcendence of the more frequently discussed Ideas as much as he stresses the transcendence of the transcendentals, especially the Good, but he could have and it seems to me that it would have strengthened his case against the Heideggerian reading of metaphysics. Ideas like triangularity and justice are not beings, anymore than goodness, beauty, truth, unity, etc., are. That an Idea like triangularity is not a being can be readily seen from the fact that the ontological principle instantiated in all triangles is itself not *a* triangle. Triangularity is the principle of all three-sided plane figures, but it is itself neither a plane figure nor three-sided. Moreover, whereas all real triangles have sides of some determinate length, and interior angles whose sum is always 180 degrees, triangularity has no sides or angles and consequently no dimensions at all. Analogous observations could be made of the other Ideas. The properties which reside in things by virtue of an Idea do not necessarily apply to the Idea itself. We know the common properties of different things, like two or more triangles, by recognizing the common principle that informs them all, but the principle itself is not necessarily an instance of these same properties. To think otherwise is to involve ourselves in the infamous regresses of the so-called third man argument, a danger of which Plato himself was well aware. Might we say that Ideas have Being, but cannot be conceived as beings? It seems to me that what Plato says about the Ideas is suggestive of the ontological difference so central to Heidegger's thought, but the scope of this difference is much broader than Heidegger supposed.

In my opinion, Gadamer implies such a "transcendence" of the Ideas on the basis of his reading of the *Parmenides*, in which Plato articulates the infinite regress problem that results from thinking of the Ideas as discrete instances of themselves, instead of as interrelated ontological principles. Gadamer claims that Plato intended the *Parmenides* to give instruction on how *not* to think about the Ideas.[33] Moreover, the conclusion that Ideas are not beings or things can be drawn as an inference from Gadamer's claim that the Ideas do not exist as discrete ideal entities but exist in an ideal web of logical or dialectical relationships. Gadamer claims that the Ideas were never intended by Plato to be thought of as a collection of discrete, static, noetic particulars, but were rather intended to be thought of as a noetic fabric of interrelated strands, no one of which could ever be analyzed in complete isolation from the others.

Although Gadamer does draw these conclusions it seems to me that he does not apply them as clearly and doggedly against Heidegger's reading of the history of metaphysics as he could have. If the Ideas themselves and not just the transcendentals are not beings to be "looked at" but ontological principles to be "looked to" in our attempts to understand, there would be even less reason to give credence to the claim that Plato initiated the so-called metaphysics of presence, thereby fatefully equating truth with mere correctness and setting us on the inevitable road to subjectivism.

By stressing that we are always "looking to" the Ideas without ever being able to make them changeless objects of vision in their own right, we can speak of how these Ideas are regulative for our inquiry in a unique sense. Such Ideas are *not* regulative in the sense that our inquiry is coming ever closer to them by a process in which we repeatedly correct our vision to approximate the motionless presence of the Ideas. Such a notion of the regulative nature of the Ideas would assume that the Ideas stand still, as it were, and present a changeless target for our inquiry.[34] But if motility is inherent to these Ideas, then they cannot be regulative by virtue of their changelessness. Instead, their regulative character has to have something to do with the inherent motility. In Gadamerian terms, one could say that their regulative character of the Ideas and the transcendentals is not rooted in the fact that these realities are changeless, motionless ideals to be asymptotically approached but in the fact that they "withdraw" or "move" with changing contexts of inquiries. What is regulative about this "withdrawal" has at least as much to do with the "process" of inquiry as with the "product" of inquiry. By constantly withdrawing, the Ideas do not so much give us an endpoint we can finally reach but they draw us again and again into further inquiry, into new questions, into new ways to draw connections to previous lines of inquiry and to paths of questioning that are other than our own. In other words, when different conclusions are reached by different inquirers questioning the *same* realities we are naturally inclined to ask why. It is the logical assumption that if the realities we all speak about are in fact common to us all, and yet different, competent inquirers come to different conclusions regarding these realities, then there ought to be a way to explain and overcome those differences, at least in principle. The repeated occurrence of these differences is the experience I am calling the "withdrawal of the Ideas," their fundamental transcendence that draws us along with it into further questioning.

This "withdrawal of the Ideas" is, in my opinion, the Gadamerian analogue to Being "conveyed" by the Event of Being. But it is an analogue with a key difference. We are drawn into this process precisely because it is always governed by the transcendentals. This is suggested at the very least by the experience of contradiction. Contradiction draws us into thought because it calls into question the "oneness" of reality, which must be one and internally harmonious (*kalon*) if it is to be taken as meaningful and true at all. Thus contradiction itself draws us into the issues of the one, the beautiful, and the true. But it also has a way of confronting us with the Good as well. When we are faced with the presence of contradiction in a dialogue whose subject matter we share with our conversation partners there is always more on the line than the logical unity of our thought. We are also faced with the fact that contradiction threatens our ability to act together on the basis of our insights. At the very least, the possibility of moving forward in the conversation will be stymied by these contradictions. It may even force us to rebuild a foundation for common discourse and action. Questions about what the Good is in this context or, in other words, questions about what is best to do next, once these contradictions have been unearthed, simply cannot be avoided. One might say that our *Mitsein* is never reducible to mere spatial or temporal contiguity with each other, or even a *Mitsein* that stops with the socially mediated practice we share, but it is an "ontological *Mitsein*," i.e., who we are is determined by our common involvement in the same reality which makes common resources available to us for dealing with our common destiny. Thus it is the case that even though we never know the one, the true, the beautiful, or the Good as such they nevertheless regulate our thought and determine the general guidelines of inquiry. In short, our common search for them draws us into the process of inquiry and this process is, in principle, endless. Hence it is the case that any successful attempt to overcome the disagreement between lines of inquiry is provisional and not final. Other questioners may arrive at different conclusions and the need to find new ways to reconcile conflicting insights will be on us once again. The Ideas, in other words, continue to withdraw. But their withdrawal is not a consignment to oblivion, to a realm completely unconnected to us and, therefore, completely irrelevant to us. Despite their withdrawal, the Ideas continue to govern our *Mitsein.* For this reason, Gadamer can say that we are always called upon to engage in the task of "infinite relation" (*TM,* xxxvi). This task of "infinite relation" is nothing less than the task of unending dialogue. We are never in a position where the way in which Being "withdraws," i.e., presents itself differently in different contexts of inquiry, does not call upon us to seek new understanding. We seek this understanding not only from the epistemic motive of wanting to know how conflicting viewpoints can be reconciled but also from ethical motives which stem from the awareness that we must live and act together, and that ability assumes that we do indeed share a common world, even though that commonality is never a transparent given but must be won "hermeneutically" on each occasion.

Being and the Good: Relativizing the Ontological Difference

By way of an attempt at a summary it can be said that this connection between truth, solidarity, and participation in a common reality grounded in the transcendentals is missing in Heidegger. Gadamer's defense of truth, as well as the ontology of the transcendentals and Ideas that undergird our dialogical inquiries, rectifies that shortcoming. In my opinion, Gadamer shows that Heidegger was right to think that the question of Being was inseparable from the question of truth but shortsighted in not realizing that there is also an intimate connection between truth and dialogue as well. Just as important was Heidegger's failure to sustain reflection on the connection between the question of Being and the issues of the one, the beautiful, and the Good. Even though his early writings touch on the transcendentals a number of times (even as late as the *Basic Problems of Phenomenology*), Heidegger never made the transcendentals central to his ontology. Gadamer's work on Plato's ontology, particularly the ontology of the transcendentals, as well as his other reflections on the truth of art and the ever-present possibility of developing lines of agreement and solidarity between inquirers rectifies this one-sidedness of Heidegger's approach. We simply cannot raise the question of Being without also raising the issues of truth, goodness, and beauty, and we can raise none of these issues outside the dialogue in which they are found.

Heidegger's shortcoming was not to pursue these intimate connections, particularly the connection between Being and the Good.

But more importantly, I have stressed that the fact that Heidegger fails in this regard leads him to the profound mistake of thinking that he can conceive of Being as such as a "process," "movement," or "way" apart from its dialectical involvement in the one, the Good, the true, and the beautiful. On Gadamer's account, one cannot even raise the question of Being intelligibly without also implicitly raising these other issues. But if these concerns are inseparable, as Gadamer's account of them implies that they are, then the so-called Event of Being does not give us the standards of thinking and acting that govern any age in a way that leaves that age powerless to critique them. Rather, Gadamer should be taken to imply, in my opinion, that the ability to critique is always cogiven with the Event. The Event is itself not primary but is internally relativized by the copresence of the one, the Good, the true, and the beautiful. At base, reality is not an anarchy without principles, but a principled structure.[35] In my opinion, this is the profound meaning of the Gadamerian claim a larger portion of which I chose as the epigraph for this essay: "Reality is differentiated in itself; it itself is *logos*" (*HD*, 26). Reality is an internally differentiated whole that allows us the discern its own inherent order. Of course, this ability is seen by Gadamer as relative to the context of questioning. Inasmuch as there is always a plurality of questions to be asked there is always also a plurality of ways to conceive this order. But this plurality of interpretations is not vicious, because each interpretation presupposes a common involvement in the same reality. Thus it is always possible in principle to discern both the inherent connections and the relative shortcomings of any interpretation. In short, the life of reason, the life of the *logos* is always possible. We are neither consigned to a helpless nihilism nor promised the eventual knowledge of a god. Instead it is always possible for us in principle to discover the Good, the true, and the beautiful within the context of inquiry that we find ourselves in.

At the risk of redundancy I want to end my reflections by going back to what I take as the most important implication of our involvement in the transcendentals, namely, that ontological questions are always pursued in connection with ethical questions. The fundamental ethical question "What is the basis of our ability to act together?" drives ontological inquiry, because the first and foremost question for human beings is "How should we live?" We simply cannot escape this question. It is the issue that forms the horizon of all other human inquiry.[36] Plato saw this clearly. It was self-evident to him that Socrates's ethical questions, as well as the ethical quality of his life, lead to ontological reflection, and he saw that both the issue of how to live and the consequent ontological issues it raises cannot be escaped by anyone.

Gadamer accepts this connection, but Heidegger, it seems to me, resisted this insight, as the "Letter on Humanism" makes plain. In this work, Heidegger wants to defend the priority of ontology over ethics. According to Heidegger, we are not ready to think of the subject matter of ethics, i.e., what is of genuine worth, because our thinking is still too "metaphysical." We need to go back behind the metaphysics[37] that defines humanity as a rational animal or even as a political animal (and uses that definition as a basis for its decisions) in order to discover how it is that behind this definition thinking "comes from Being" and by "listening to Being."[38] This act of retrieval will hopefully open new possibilities for human life and human dignity. Such a life would aspire to be what Heidegger called "the Shepherd of Being," a life that "gains the essential poverty of the shepherd, whose dignity consists in being called by Being itself into the preservation of Being's truth."[39] Whether we can be such a "shepherd," however, depends, in my opinion, on having the resources to enter into a "critical partnership" with Being. If this is possible we must have the ability to discern what is best and not simply to learn "properly" to anticipate the Event of Being itself.

One can understand Heidegger's refusal to connect his ontological inquires with ethical concerns in the "Letter on Humanism" as a function of his critique of subjectivism in the West. Heidegger refuses to raise ethical questions in the context of his ontological inquiries because such a tendency is at one with the tendency to see Being as a human project, reflective of human concerns and susceptible to human control. In short, Heidegger thinks that such a tendency ignores the ontological difference between Being and beings, in this case human beings. Thus Heidegger insists on the radical difference between Being and all beings, especially the beings that call themselves human beings. His thought increasingly emphasizes Being's withdrawal into the near incomprehensible gift of meaning. The result is a growing insistence on the distance between human concerns and Being which manifests itself in a profound *Sprachnot.*

Gadamer's ontology has a different import, however. If we cannot raise issues of Being apart from other related issues like Being's relationship to the other transcendentals—including the Good—and these issues in turn involve us in questions about the relationships between transcendentals and Ideas, as well as Ideas and things, then we can longer insist on a strict and unequivocal ontological difference. This is perhaps the most profound implication of Gadamer's ontological insights. Gadamer's position implies a modern appropriation of the *analogia entis* and as such it emphasizes the analogical connections between all realities. Such ontological analogies or connections imply a challenge to any unbridgable gap or difference between Being and beings. If Heidegger's thought suffers from an increasing tendency to insist on this unbridgeable difference, Gadamer's thought relativizes the difference between Being and beings and draws them closer to each other without forgetting that there is also a difference to be preserved. The most important implication of this relativizing of the ontological difference is that questions about the Good can once again be seen as central to ontology. If Gadamer's thought implies nothing less than a softening or a relativization of the ontological difference, what it hopes to open up by bridging Heidegger's gap between Being and beings is a place for questions about the Good in our ontological inquiries. It is only because Gadamer insists on a common intelligibility inherent in all that is real—which is implicit in claims such as "subject and object belong together," or "word and thing participate in each other," or "Being and beings are intrinsically related"—that his thought must in the end point beyond Heidegger and beyond Heidegger's "Being." In doing so, Gadamer hopes to suggest that there is a real place for questions about the Good in our ontological inquiries.

In other words, it seems to me that Gadamer would agree with Heidegger's contention that traditional ethics needs to repeatedly reexamine its ontological roots, but he would not agree with Heidegger that ontology can be done "in isolation," as it were by invoking a concept of "thinking" which prescinds from questions of the Good and simply seeks the "preservation of Being's truth." If ontological considerations are inseparable from considerations about the Good, like they are in Plato, this implies a relativization of Heidegger's ontological difference between Being and beings. Gadamer would be quick to point out, however, that such thinking about the Good does not assume the unequivocal truth of any one historical ethical philosophy, but instead implies that the relevance of any moral philosophy must be made the subject of dialogue. Consequently, decisions should be similarly made in solidarity with those with whom we must act. What gives such a dialogue specific focus and such decisions particular force is the historical determinacy of the issues and historically mediated nature of the moral community which is posing real questions and seeking genuine answers. Not all ethical issues face every human being or human community and not all responses are possible in any given situation. What is to be done is a function of the ethical substance (or what Hegel called *Sittlichkeit*) of the community, which includes its customs, habits, its most important values and institutions, and in short, its entire way of life. As the individuals in the community seek to carry that "substance" into an unknown future, both in their individual and corporate decisions, new ethical issues come to the fore as new possibilities emerge or conflicts arise. How these situations are dealt with, for good or ill, is a function of moral discernment, of judgment or what Aristotle called "practical wisdom" (*phronesis*), which essentially involves the practice of "application" of the received judgments of the past into a potentially unique set of current circumstances. Such an ability implies a knowledge of the good but it "does not mean a universal knowledge of 'the good,' rather it means a knowledge of that to which one has to persuade people here and now and how one is to go about doing this and in respect to whom one is to do it" (*RAS*, 121).

Such "application" or discernment is prior to any theory we might appeal to in order to justify that application. This is so for the fundamental reason that the choice of any such theory would itself require judgment or practical wisdom. Such choices of theory presuppose knowledge of the Good. Such knowledge is not that of a single principle, like Kant's various versions of the categorical imperative which attempt to sum up the essence of all right behavior; neither is it a knowledge that cannot transcend the language of its own inception, such as we find in MacIntyre's attempt to articulate a version of Aristotelian ethics within a historicist epistemological framework. Rather, it is knowledge of the Good discerned in context of the need to make decisions in solidarity with each other. It is, in Gadamer's terms, an "application" of the Good. When the "application" is successful it is marked by the public defensibility of the decision, which is rooted in the inherent unity of a way of life. Where the Good is, there is an ability to defend one's decision in a rational way, to give a *logos* of it. In such situations, Gadamer reminds us that "only that individual knows who is capable of standing his ground right down to the final speech and response" (*RAS*, 121). Moreover, the ability to do this repeatedly and consistently leads to a unity that sustains and extends itself across time. A good life and a good society are marked by a kind of truth and consistency that maintains itself in changing circumstances, not by willfully suppressing its own problems and possible inconsistencies, but by subjecting them repeatedly to critical dialogue. If a person, institution, or society cannot do this because they lack the strength of character or their decisions are deeply at odds with themselves and others, then they lack the requisite integrity to be called "good." This kind of integrity is described by Gadamer as the "Doric harmony between *logos* and *ergon*,"[40] between word and act. It shows itself in the ability to give justification for one's acts and decisions, a justification that can withstand the critical scrutiny of a dialogue. Such unity or integrity is the mark of reason, of the *logos*, and in particular it is the height of human reason. Such integrity is modeled for us in an exemplary fashion in Plato's Socrates. It is to

Socrates that we might look to get a clearer picture of this idea and how it is that Gadamer thinks that "looking to the Good" is the inescapable task of any human thinking, even the thinking involved in the "thinking of Being."

It is well known that in many dialogues Socrates's inquiries into the nature of the various virtues and the virtuous life often ended in *aporia.* What was the purpose of reaching such impasses? Was it primarily to give his interlocutors a lesson in logic or did Socrates have something else in mind? Gadamer thinks that Socrates was not primarily concerned with logic or essential definitions but with real virtuous living. In this context, concerns of logic and definition are secondary, as is demonstrated by the fact that Socrates often used logically questionable arguments in his discussions with his various partners and never arrived at a definitive account of any of the virtues. This "deficiency" in reasoning was not due to any obvious lack in Socrates or Plato—although they could, of course, make mistakes—but it suggests that Socrates had other goals in mind. What he wanted more than mere consistency and clarity of reasoning was consistency and integrity of life.[41] Socrates often led his partners by whatever logical and rhetorical means available, even by means of sophistry sometimes, to an *aporia* in order to confront them with their own ignorance and lack of integrity regarding their claims to virtue. Socrates's use of *aporia* implies that he consciously used such impasses to create a moral crisis in this interlocutors. Socrates could even sometimes employ questionable logical means to make his point because the primary contradictions that moved him were not logical but practical. What Socrates is concerned about first and foremost is the consistency between what his interpreters say and do, or what Gadamer has called the "Doric harmony between *logos* and *ergon.*"

The fact, for example, that Euthyphro, in the dialogue of the same name, cannot justify his decision to prosecute his father, a decision which demanded that the conventional code of piety to honor one's father be overridden in light of his claim to a deeper, truer grasp of the nature of piety, tells us more about Euthyhro's life and his hollow claim to virtue than it tells us about logic and the nature of definition, although, to be sure, we can learn something in this dialogue of these matters. The *aporia* to which Socrates drives "poor Euthyphro" are meant to confront him with this lack of integral harmony in his own life and possibly in the reader's life as well. In other words, the point of the *aporia* is to force Euthyphro and us to "look to the Good." Socrates is not trying to make Euthyphro a "Platonist," i.e., someone who has supposedly timeless knowledge of the nature of holiness. If such were his goal, it might rightly be criticized as unreasonable. Who indeed could be expected to wait until they had such knowledge before acting? Such a demand would paralyze those who truly embraced it. Socrates's "sting" would be the end of the moral life rather than an advance within it. Rather, Socrates wants to challenge the shallow glibness of Euthyphro's self-knowledge. Euthyphro has not really availed himself of the rational resources that are within his reach. To do this, he must begin to think, i.e., to subject himself to the need "to give an account." He must be "turned around" and be forced to "look to the Good," which can only be begun to be discerned by "looking beyond" the conventions in which he has become all too comfortable. It is Gadamer's main point that we are always in this situation of Euthyphro of needing to "look to the Good," because who indeed either has definitive knowledge of the Good or can afford to ignore the demand to find the particular good that our situation offers us? To look properly we must learn neither to deny our need because we think we know what we do not know, nor pretend that the ability to make progress in our inquiry is simply impossible.

In this sense, the Socratic *aporia* are intended to be morally salutary in that they are meant to compel both interlocutors to genuinely search for the Good. Such a search involves nothing less than a dialogue with oneself and others, which questions what one thinks one knows and seeks a justification for a particular application of this knowledge to the specific circumstances that one finds oneself in. To find this justification is to demonstrate the unity of what one knows and what one proposes to do, a demonstration that can only really be given when the proposal is critically probed, i.e., "in dialogue." Gadamer's entire philosophical endeavor suggests that such an achievement of reason is the highest form of reason finite human beings can aspire to. What may emerge from such a critical dialogue is not always an *aporia* but neither is it a definitive knowledge of the Good. We never have such final knowledge because the Good withdraws or withholds itself as Socrates's *aporia* demonstrate. But the Good may also reveal itself. What may emerge from such a dialogue is a justification of a decision, like Socrates's decision to stay in prison, which recommends itself because it withstands critical scrutiny and evinces the inherent integrity of his life. In short, it shows itself as being genuinely "at one" with that life, a life that through its many possible variations and aberrations had found a way to give itself a lived unity, the kind of unity that is the mark of a good life. Such a life has a kind of "radiance," a kind of "beauty" that is evident to all. As Gadamer contends, this unity or beauty is the mark of the Good itself and it is the highest form of knowledge of the Good that we can achieve.

We find this unity or integrity through "dialectic," the very highest form of knowing that Plato reserves for the deliberative knowledge of the philosopher kings. It is this deliberative knowledge, which seeks the concrete good in unique circumstances by "looking to the Good," that Gadamer calls "dialogue" and Aristotle calls *phronesis,* "practical reason" or even "reasonableness." Such a knowledge looked like ignorance when compared with the knowledge of the craftsmen of Athens, and it looks like ignorance when compared with the logical necessity that is the mark of such learning as mathematics, or the empirical corroboration that the natural sciences often enjoy, but it is a true form of human knowing, and perhaps it is the highest form of knowing. It is in any case the most needed knowledge we can imagine. Our ability to have it presupposes that we know our own ignorance, i.e., that we recognize that we do not know the Good definitively, exhaustively, transparently, or timelessly. But such knowledge also presupposes that we can recognize a determinate form of the Good, i.e., that we can discern what is good for us in concrete circumstances by entering into a dialogue with ourselves and others.

Perhaps we can catch genuine glimpses of the Good, but never get a lasting look at it. Plato's myth in the *Phaedrus* of the journey of the soul above the heavens expresses this well. It is as if we can stick our heads above the clouds and briefly and partially view the true order of things only to be pulled down to the world of confusion, error, and distracting desires once again. Plato's myth suggests that it is not just the unruly horse of our passions that interferes with our vision but the very flow of time itself. This is a myth which expresses finitude, a finitude that warns us equally against claiming to know what we cannot know and of despairing of that knowledge which we can and must have.

Heidegger's question of Being hopes for too much—a new knowledge of Being prior to the question of the Good—and his talk of an ever-increasing *Seinsvergessenheit* despairs of too little. Gadamer himself is fond of quoting a line often used by Heidegger in his early lectures: "*Das Leben ist diesig—es nebelt sich immer wiederein*" ("Life is hazy—it always shrouds itself in fog again") (*HW,* 136). Such a saying anticipates Heidegger's more well-known claim that the showing of Being, the bringing of Being into light, always presupposes that Being withdraws into obscurity and shows itself in the light only against this prior darkness. If Heidegger increasingly emphasized this darkness, Gadamer's "corrective" intends to bring him back to his more original insight that the *movement* between light and darkness is always a *movement* back and forth between light and darkness, between knowledge and ignorance of the Good. If life always "shrouds itself in fog again," it is also sometimes bathed in light, a light that is clear enough to light our way or painfully remind us of our failures. It is in such light, the ever-changing but ever-giving light of the superabundant Good, that our real prospects for good and evil are to be found. On Gadamer's account, finite human beings should expect no more than a knowledge of the Good grasped through the process of dialogue which is always relative to a context of inquiry and which accordingly yields a knowledge that is limited to that context. But we should also expect no less. Our finitude does not leave us speechless when it comes to discovering how we should live. We have the *logoi* and through them we can learn to "look to the Good." For Gadamer, this is just good Platonism.

Notes

Introduction

1. Another key historical source for Gadamer's hermeneutics, which is often overlooked, is his reading of Hegel. Although I touch on Gadamer's debt to Hegel in the body of the text, its full scope is beyond the limits of this study.

2. Hans-Georg Gadamer, *Kleine Schriften,* vol. 3 (Tübingen: J.C.B. Mohr [Paul Siebeck], 1968), 118.

3. I refer the reader to the material cited in my list of abbreviated titles at the beginning of the book, as well as my discussion in Chapter 2, "Gadamer's Dialectical Platonism," for references to the places where Gadamer works out this interpretation of Plato.

4. See, e.g., Gadamer, "Mathematik und Dialektik bei Plato," in *GW* 7, 228–57; and "Plato's Unwritten Dialectic," in *Dialogue and Dialectic* (New Haven: Yale University Press, 1980), 124–55.

5. See, e.g., Jürgen Habermas, "Zu Gadamer's *Wahrheit und Methode,*" in *Hermeneutik und Ideologiekritik* (Frankfurt: Suhrkamp, 1971), 55.

6. See, e.g., John Caputo, "Gadamer's Closet Essentialism: A Derridean Critique," in *Dialogue and Deconstruction,* ed. Diane Michelfelder and Richard Palmer (Albany: SUNY Press, 1989), 263.

7. *TM,* xxxvii: "Hence the present investigations do not fulfill the demand for a reflexive self-grounding made from the viewpoint of the speculative transcendental philosophy of Fichte, Hegel, and Husserl. But is this dialogue with the whole of our philosophical tradition—a dialogue in which we stand and which as philosophers, we are—groundless? Does what has always supported us need to be grounded?"

8. *TM,* 482.

9. This remark was made in a letter to Leo Strauss reprinted in the *Independent Journal of Philosophy* 2 (1978), 8.

10. Gadamer's own remarks about the relationship between his own work on ancient philosophy and his debt to Heidegger both acknowledge the profundity of that debt and sound a note of fundamental criticism:

> The philosophical stimuli I received from Heidegger led me more and more into the realm of dialectic, Plato's as well as Hegel's. Decades of teaching were devoted to elaborating and testing what I have called here the Platonic-Aristotelian unitary effect. But in the background

was the continuous challenge posed for me by the path Heidegger's own thought took, and especially by his interpretation of Plato as the decisive step toward "metaphysical thought's" obliviousness to Being [*Sein*]. My elaboration and projection of a philosophical hermeneutics in *Wahrheit und Methode* bear witness to my efforts to withstand this challenge theoretically. (*IG*, 5)

11. Compare Heidegger's late remark in *Vier Seminare*, p. 184, that "*aletheia* has nothing to do with *Wahrheit.*"

12. *RAS*, 86.

Chapter 1

1. Hans-Georg Gadamer, *Wahrheit und Methode: Grundzüge einer philosophischen Hermeneutik*, 4th ed. (Tübingen: J.C.B. Mohr [Paul Siebeck]), 1976. Revised English translation: *Truth and Method*, trans. Joel Weinsheimer and Donald G. Marshall (New York: Crossroad, 1990).

2. Richard Rorty, *Philosophy and the Mirror of Nature* (Princeton: Princeton University Press, 1979), 315ff.

3. Ibid. It should be admitted that Rorty's use of the term "epistemology" is clearly polemical. Not all philosophers who think about the nature and conditions of human knowledge are haunted by the dream of refuting skepticism. Plato, for example, is not. Nevertheless, Rorty is generally correct, in my opinion, that this dream has driven a great deal of epistemology in the modern era.

4. Gadamer makes this point in "Was ist Wahrheit?" (1957), an essay that predates *Wahrheit und Methode* (1960). The fundamental point, however, remains essential to all his subsequent reflections on truth, although it often functions as an unspoken assumption in the later work. "Was ist Wahrheit?" originally appeared in Gadamer's *Klein Schiften*, vol. 1 (Tübingen: J.C.B. Mohr [Paul Siebeck], 1967), 46–58, *GW* 2, 44–56. An English translation of this essay by Brice R. Wachterhauser appears in *Hermeneutics and Truth*, ed. Brice R. Wachterhauser (Evanston: Northwestern University Press, 1994), 33–46 (hereafter *HT*).

5. Hans-Georg Gadamer, "The Phenomenological Movement," in *Philosophical Hermeneutics*, trans. and ed. David E. Linge (Berkeley: University of California Press, 1976), 130–81.

6. See *Phenomenology and Skepticism*, ed. Brice R. Wachterhauser (Evanston: Northwestern University Press, 1996), for a more detailed discussion of Husserl's relation to skepticism.

7. See *TM*, xxxvi: "It is true that my book is phenomenological in its method. . . . I have therefore retained the term "hermeneutics" . . . not in the sense of a methodology but as a theory of the real experience that thinking is." Gadamer's method is phenomenological in that it proceeds primarily by a descriptive showing or highlighting of certain phenomena and not by arguing from what purport to be self-evident first principles. In fact, Gadamer rejects the Husserlian project of seeking a foundation for knowledge in either self-evident first principles or in the transcendental ego. For more on the relationship between

phenomenology and hermeneutics, see Paul Ricoeur's "Phenomenology and Hermeneutics," in Ricoeur, *Hermeneutics and the Human Sciences,* trans. and ed. John B. Thompson (Cambridge: Cambridge University Press, 1981), 101–28.

8. Rorty sees himself and his pragmatism in this "Nietzschean" tradition: "I see Nietzsche as the figure who did the most to convince European intellectuals of the doctrines, which were purveyed to Americans by James and Dewey." Richard Rorty, from *Essays on Heidegger and Others* (Cambridge: Cambridge University Press, 1991), 2.

9. In *Philosophy and the Mirror of Nature* Richard Rorty gives a very "pragmatic" reading of Gadamer, the real upshot of which is Rorty's attempt to substitute "edifying discourses" for truth. This is a move which Gadamer would see as impossible to pull off. We cannot ignore the truth-claims of texts by reducing them to their "edifying" function. Even Rorty himself makes constant claims that depend for their meaning on the fact that they purport to be *true* and not merely "interesting" or "timely."

10. On Gadamer's realism, see Brice R. Wachterhauser, "Gadamer's Realism: The 'Belongingness' of Word and Reality," in *HT*, 148–71.

11. Gadamer's "holism" (a term he does not use) is evident in many of his writings, but it shows itself particularly in the essays in which he is most concerned with the "foundational" issues of human thinking. These essays are mostly to be found among his Greek studies, particularly the works on Plato's late ontology. See, e.g., the essays collected in *GW* 7.

12. On the nature of "prejudices" and their function in understanding, see *TM*, 265ff.

13. Despite these real differences between Gadamer and Hegel, Gadamer still owes a great deal to Hegel, particularly to Hegel's sensitivity to the way in which history contributes to our grasp of truth. Gadamer even acknowledges that it was Hegel's dialectic that first enabled him to better understand Plato's sense of dialectic. See Gadamer's "Hegel and the Dialectic of the Ancient Philosophers," in *Hegel's Dialectic* (New Haven: Yale University Press, 1976), 5–34 (hereafter *HD*). However, the full complexity of Gadamer's debt to Hegel is a subject for another study.

14. This Heideggerian concern is discussed in a very illuminating way in Theodore Kisiel, *The Genesis of "Being and Time"* (Berkeley: University of California Press, 1993), 15ff.

15. One important exception to this general rule is P. Christopher Smith's work. His efforts as a translator and commentator on Gadamer have helped to bring this side of Gadamer's thought more to the fore. See, e.g., his introductions and translator's notes to Gadamer's *The Idea of the Good in Platonic Aristotelian Philosophy* (New Haven: Yale University Press, 1986), and *Dialogue and Dialectic,* trans. P. Christopher Smith (New Haven: Yale University Press, 1980). Smith's work, however, does not attempt a more systematic study of how Gadamer's ontological concerns, which he works out largely in his work on Plato, informs his philosophical hermeneutics. The same can be said for Robert R. Sullivan's helpful work, *Political Hermeneutics: The Early Thinking of Hans-Georg Gadamer* (University

Park: Penn State University Press, 1989). Besides concentrating on the early work of Gadamer on Plato, which ignores most of the more important Plato essays, written roughly between 1970 and 1990, which deal with ontological concerns, Sullivan is not primarily interested in the ontological underpinnings of Gadamer's thought, but with its political consequences. I would argue that the "political" and the "ontological" are integrally related in Gadamer. Thus a deeper analysis of Gadamer requires a more sustained look at his ontology.

16. Hans-Georg Gadamer, *Kleine Schriften*, vol. 3 (Tübingen: J.C.B. Mohr [Paul Siebeck], 1968), 118.

17. See, e.g., E. D. Hirsch, *Validity in Interpretation* (New Haven: Yale University Press, 1979), 245–54.

18. Jürgen Habermas, "Zu Gadamer's *Wahrheit und Methode*," in *Hermeneutik und Ideologiekritik* (Frankfurt: Suhrkamp, 1971), 55.

19. For further elaboration, see Martin Heidegger, *Nietzsche*, vol. 1 (New York: Harper and Row, 1979), 151–220, and Martin Heidegger, *Plato's Lehre von der Wahrheit* (Bern: Francke, 1954).

20. For a more lengthy discussion, see Martin Heidegger, "The Question concerning Technology," in *Basic Writings*, ed. David Farell Krell (New York: Harper and Row, 1977), 283–317.

21. Hans-Georg Gadamer, *Heidegger's Ways* (Albany: SUNY Press, 1994), 25ff. (hereafter *HW*).

22. For example, see Hans-Georg Gadamer, "What Is Metaphysics?" in *HW*, 45–48; "Kant and the Hermeneutical Turn," in *HW*, 49–60; "The Language of Metaphysics," in *HW*, 69–80; "The Way in the Turn," in *HW*, 121–38, "The Greeks," in *HW*, 139–52; "Hegel and Heidegger," in *HD*, 100–116.

23. See Hans-Georg Gadamer, "Sokrates' Frömmigkeit des Nichtwissens," in *GW* 7, 83–117.

24. *HD*, 6.

25. Robert Bernasconi, "Seeing Double: *Destruktion* and Deconstruction," in *Dialogue and Deconstruction: The Gadamer-Derrida Encounter*, ed. Diane Michelfelder and Richard Palmer (Albany: SUNY Press, 1989), 245.

26. James Risser, "The Two Faces of Socrates: Gadamer Derrida," in *Dialogue and Deconstruction*, 184.

27. John Caputo, "Gadamer's Closet Essentialism: A Derridean Critique," in *Dialogue and Deconstruction*, 263.

28. Hans-Georg Gadamer, "Plato's Educational State," in *Dialogue and Dialectic*, 73–92.

29. For example, Joseph Margolis criticizes Gadamer for this supposed shortcoming. See his *Pragmatism Without Foundations* (Oxford: Basil Blackwell, 1986), 47.

30. Rorty, *Philosophy and the Mirror of Nature*, 266.

31. *TM*, xxxvii: "Hence the present investigations do not fulfill the demand for a reflexive self-grounding made from the viewpoint of the speculative transcendental philosophy of Fichte, Hegel, and Husserl. But is this dialogue with the whole of our philosophical tradition—a dialogue in which we stand and which

as philosophers, we are—groundless? Does what has always supported us need to be grounded?"

32. Bernard Williams, *Descartes: The Project of Pure Inquiry* (Harmondsworth: Penguin, 1978).

33. See Habermas's "Zu Gadamer's *Wahrheit und Methode*," 55.

34. See notes 27 and 29, above.

35. Hans-Georg Gadamer, *Reason in the Age of Science* (Cambridge: MIT Press, 1981), 75–82.

36. See Gadamer's "Zwischen Phänomenologie und Dialektik: Versuch einer Selbstkritik," in *GW* 2, 16.

37. *TM*, 296, 297.

38. *HD*, 7.

39. Cf., e.g., *TM*, 441.

Chapter 2

1. Hans-Georg Gadamer, *Hegel's Dialectic* (New Haven: Yale University Press, 1976), 7 (hereafter *HD*).

2. See, e.g., Kenneth M. Sayer, *Plato's Late Ontology* (Princeton: Princeton University Press, 1983).

3. Gadamer calls this the "Platonic-Aristotelian unity of effect" (*Wirkungseinheit*). This "unity of effect" is the subject of Gadamer's *The Idea of the Good in Platonic-Aristotelian Philosophy* (New Haven: Yale University Press, 1986) (hereafter *IG*), which, as the title suggests, appeals to Plato's concept of the Good to demonstrate that there is more in common between Plato and Aristotle than the latter was willing to recognize. Aristotle, of course, is well known for having been at times very selective in his representation of his predecessors. Gadamer contends that this tendency is nowhere more apparent than in his treatment of Plato.

4. Quoted in *Plato's Dialogues*, vol. 1, trans. and ed. R. E. Allen (New Haven: Yale University Press, 1984), 39.

5. Gadamer's first major work on Plato, albeit unpublished, was his doctoral dissertation of 1922 entitled "Platons Begriff der Lust," which he wrote under Paul Natorp, *the* preeminent neo-Kantian and Plato scholar. Gadamer's last published works on Plato, to date, appeared in *GW* 7, in 1991. A number of these essays were written as late as 1990.

6. Paul Natrop, *Platos Ideen Lehre* (Leipzig: Meiner, 1921).

7. Cf. *Sophist*, 260a.

8. The claim that there is an eidetic reality already implicit in language is a very important theme for Gadamer which we will turn to in the next chapter.

9. Cf. Hans-Georg Gadamer, "Plato's Unwritten Dialectic," in *Dialogue and Dialectic*, trans. P. Christopher Smith (New Haven: Yale University Press, 1980), 132, 133.

10. Ibid., 134.

11. For example, see *Studies in Plato's Metaphysics*, ed. R. E. Allen (London: Routledge and Kegan Paul, 1965), or *Plato I: Metaphysics and Epistemology*, ed. Gregory Vlastos (Notre Dame: University of Notre Dame Press, 1978).

12. For more elaboration, see *Dialogue and Dialectic*, 110ff.

13. Hans-Georg Gadamer, "Zur Vorgeschichte der Metaphysik," in *Um die Begriffswelt der Vorsokratiker* (Darmstadt, 1968), 377.

14. See *Dialogue and Dialectic*, 135ff. for a more extended discussion.

15. *IG*, 16–18.

16. *IG*, 18, 19.

17. *IG*, 16.

18. Cf. *Dialogue and Dialectic*, 133ff.

19. See, e.g., *Sophist*, 259ab:

> But with respect to the "what is not" that we have now asserted to exist, an opponent must either convince us that our account is wrong by refuting it, or so long as he proves unable to do that, he must accept our statements (a) that the kinds blend with one another; (b) that existence and difference pervade them all, and pervade one another, (c) that difference [or the different] by partaking of existence, *is* by virtue of that participation, but on the other hand *is not* that existence of which it partakes, but is different, and since it is different from existence [*or* an existent], quite clearly it must be possible that it should *be* a thing that *is not*, (d) and again, existence, having a part in difference, will be different from all the rest of the kinds, and because it is different from them all, it *is not* any one of them nor yet all the others put together, but is only itself, with the consequence, again indisputable, that existence *is not* myriads upon myriads of things, and that all the other kinds in the same way, whether taken severally or all together in many respects *are* and in many respects *are not*. (trans. F. M. Cornford)

20. The *Gorgias* is very persuasive in its use of this kind of negativity to characterize the sophist as a type. The dialogue the *Sophist* takes up the issue of "non-Being" in its more general, ontological function. The connection between these dialogues is not accidental in my opinion.

21. *IG*, 151.

22. *IG*, 152: "The universal-ontological sense of the one good would fit perfectly with Aristotle's doctrine of a god."

Chapter 3

1. Cf. *TM*, xxxi, 399.
2. *TM*, 412–14.
3. *TM*, 277ff.
4. Cf. *TM*, 416, 462ff.
5. Cf. *TM*, 475.

6. *TM*, 483.

7. I draw this inference on the basis of what Gadamer explicitly says about the parallel between the "symbolic" function of art and language. See *TM*, 31ff., 89ff.

8. Hans-Georg Gadamer, *Reason in the Age of Science* (Cambridge: MIT Press, 1981), 40 (hereafter, *RAS*).

9. The phenomenological priority of "experience" is attested to throughout Gadamer's work, particularly *Wahrheit und Methode*, but it is explicitly defended in the foreword to the second edition of the same work. See *TM*, xxxvi.

10. *TM*, 367–69.

11. *RAS*, 136.

12. See Charles Kahn, *The Art and Thought of Heraclitus* (Cambridge: Cambridge University Press, 1979), 19.

13. Ferdinand de Saussure, *Course in General Linguistics*, trans. Wade Baskin (London: Fontana, 1976).

14. *TM*, xxxvi, xxxvii: "I have recorded my acceptance of Kant's conclusions in the *Critique of Pure Reason:* I regard statements that proceed by wholly dialectical means from the finite to the infinite, from the temporal to the eternal, as doing no more than setting limits, and am convinced that philosophy can derive no actual knowledge from them. Nevertheless, the tradition of metaphysics and especially of its last great creation, Hegel's speculative dialectic, remains close to us. The task, the 'infinite relation' remains."

15. Ibid.

16. Hans-Georg Gadamer, "What Is Truth?" in *Hermeneutics and Truth*, ed. Brice R. Wachterhauser (Evanston: Northwestern University Press, 1994), 36.

17. Martin Heidegger, *Early Greek Thinking* (New York: Harper and Row, 1975), 70.

18. Cf. *RAS*, 90–92 and *Heidegger's Ways* (Albany: SUNY Press, 1994), 59.

19. "Practice is conducting oneself and acting in solidarity" (*RAS*, 87).

20. Cf. *RAS*, 90–93.

21. *TM*, 485.

22. Tanya Atwater to Allen Cox, quoted in John McPhee, *Basin and Range* (New York: Farrar, Straus, Giroux, 1981), 202–3.

23. For a more extended discussion of how Gadamer understands Aristotle's polemics against the Platonic notion of "the Good," see *The Idea of the Good in Platonic-Aristotelian Philosophy* (New Haven: Yale University Press, 1986), 152–59.

24. Cf. *TM*, 98, 99.

25. Rainer Maria Rilke, "Archaic Torso of Apollo," in *The Selected Poetry of Rainer Maria Rilke*, trans. Stephen Mitchell (New York: Random House, 1982), 61. Quoted in Hans-Georg Gadamer, *The Relevance of the Beautiful* (Cambridge: Cambridge University Press, 1986), 34.

26. Hans-Georg Gadamer, "Logos and Ergon in Plato's *Lysis*," in *Dialogue and Dialectic*, trans. P. Christopher Smith (New Haven: Yale University Press, 1980), 1.

Chapter 4

1. Gadamer's work on these dialogues is scattered in numerous works. In English, *Dialogue and Dialectic* gathers some relevant essays, some which are among Gadamer's earliest published work, but most of which are from the late sixties and early seventies. The German originals can now be found in *GW* 5–6. As evidence of his early interest in the later dialogues one should also consult Gadamer's *Habilitationsschrift, Platos dialektische Ethik,* which originally appeared in 1931. It can now be found in *GW* 5. This work focuses on the *Philebus* and shows Gadamer's early effort to wed his philological training to his philosophical motivations which stemmed primarily from Heidegger. An English translation by Robert Wallace is available as *Plato's Dialectical Ethics* (New Haven: Yale University Press, 1991). The most recent and in some ways the clearest essays demonstrating Gadamer's grasp of these later dialogues is found in *GW* 7 (*Griechische Philosophie III*: *Plato im Dialog*), which includes later essays from the eighties and nineties, as well as a reprint of Gadamer's *Die Idee des Guten zwischen Plato und Aristoteles.*

2. Gadamer, *Plato's Dialectical Ethics,* 103, 104.

3. *Philebus,* 21c.

4. *Philebus,* 22a.

5. *Philebus,* 21e.

6. Cf. *Philebus,* 27e–28a.

7. Cf. *TM,* 269–77.

8. *TM,* 300–7.

9. *TM,* 306–7.

10. *TM,* 307ff.

11. Hans-Georg Gadamer, "Zwischen Phanomenologie und Dialektik: Versuch einer Selbstkritik," in *GW* 2, 19–20. Cf. also *TM,* 148.

12. In what follows I am relying on Taylor's *Sources of the Self* (Cambridge: Harvard University Press, 1989), 368ff., as well as his work, *Hegel* (Cambridge: Cambridge University Press, 1975), 3ff.

13. Taylor, *Sources of the Self,* 174.

14. *TM,* 313ff.

15. Cf. *TM,* 320.

16. *TM,* 324ff.

17. *TM,* 293, 294.

18. *TM,* 184. See also "Plato as Porträtist," in *GW* 7, 228–57.

19. Cf. *TM,* 140, 423, 504.

20. *TM,* 141ff.

21. *TM,* 428.

22. Cf. *TM,* 418–19.

23. *TM,* 251.

24. Cf. *TM,* 101–10.

25. *TM,* 110–21.

26. Gadamer entitles the entire section of *Truth and Method* in which he discusses the concept of play as "Play as the clue to ontological explanation."

27. G.W.F. Hegel, *Lectures on the Philosophy of Religion* (1827), ed. Peter C. Hodgson (Berkeley: University of California Press, 1988), 102.

28. "It is possible to show that the introduction of a conventional system of signs can never complete itself in a closed system of these conventions, for every introduction of an artificial language already presupposes another language in which one speaks." Hans-Georg Gadamer, "What Is Truth?" in *Hermeneutics and Truth*, ed. Brice R. Wachterhauser (Evanston: Northwestern University Press, 1994), 39 (hereafter *HT*).

29. *TM*, 369ff.

30. See Jean Grondin, "Gadamer and Augustine: On the Origin of the Hermeneutical Claim to Universality," in *HT*, 137–47.

31. Hans-Georg Gadamer, "Errinerungen an Heidegger's Anfänge," *Dilthey-Jahrbuch* 4 (1986–87), 2.

Chapter 5

1. 1922 was the date of Gadamer's first encounter with Heidegger's written work, but the two men actually met for the first time in 1923, according to Gadamer. See *Heidegger's Ways* (Albany: SUNY Press, 1994), 17 (hereafter *HW*).

2. This manuscript was never published and had disappeared from private circulation, but it was recently found and printed as "Phänomenologische Interpretationen zu Aristoteles (Anzeige der hermeneutische Situation)," *Dilthey-Jahrbuch* (1989), 237–69. It is accompanied by an introduction by Gadamer entitled, "Heidegger's "theologische' Jugendschrift."

3. See *TM*, 265ff.

4. Martin Heidegger, "Letter on Humanism," in *Basic Writings*, ed. David Farrell Krell (New York: Harper and Row, 1977), 193.

5. It's not important to give a precise date of Heidegger's famous "turn" (*Kehre*) and I doubt that it is even possible. Nevertheless, Robert Dostal is certainly correct that there is strong evidence of it in the 1930–31 essay *Vom Wesen der Wahrheit.* See Robert Dostal, "Beyond Being: Heidegger's Plato," *Journal of the History of Philosophy* 23 (January 1985), 71–98. Stanley Rosen quotes an oral remark of Heidegger's which itself was quoted in the "Nachwort" by F. W. von Hermann to Heidegger's *Beiträge zur Philosophie, Gesamtausgabe*, vol. 65 (Frankfurt: Klostermann, 1989), 512, to the effect that the term "'E-vent' [*Er-eignis*] is," according to Heidegger, "since 1936 the leading word of my thinking." Quoted in Stanley Rosen, *The Question of Being* (New Haven: Yale University Press, 1993), xvi. I am indebted to both Dostal's and Rosen's work for my understanding of the relation between Heidegger and Plato. I should also mention that William J. Richardson's *Heidegger: Through Phenomenology to Thought* (The Hague: Martinus Nijhoff, 1963) was helpful as well.

6. Heidegger's "metaphysical" beginnings are well-documented in Theodore Kisiel, *The Genesis of Heidegger's "Being and Time"* (Berkeley: University of California Press, 1995). See also Rudiger Safranski, *Ein Meister aus Deutschland: Heidegger und seine Zeit* (Frankfurt: Klostermann, 1994).

7. *Gesamtausgabe*, vol. 26 (1978), 143, 237, 246, 284. This "metontology" was understood as an exploration of the key Platonic text which understand the Good as "beyond all Being" (*Republic* 509b). For Heidegger, the most significant issue becomes to explain the way in which Being (*Sein*), like Plato's *tou agathou*, is "beyond all Being." This is the task of "metontology." See Dostal, "Beyond Being: Heidegger's Plato," for more discussion.

8. See *Sein und Zeit* (Tübingen: Niemeyer, 1977), sec. 6, "Die Aufgabe einer Destruktion der Geschichte der Ontologie," 19ff.

9. Martin Heidegger, *Zür Sache des Denkens* (Tübingen: Niemeyer, 1969), 25.

10. "The Language of Metaphysics," in *HW*, 77ff.

11. "Martin Heidegger—75 Years," in *HW*, 25.

12. Reprinted in the *Independent Journal of Philosophy* 2 (1978), 8.

13. Heidegger claimed that "Durch die ganze Geschichte der Philosophie hindurch bleibt Platons Denken in abgewandelten Gestalten massgebend. Die Metaphsysik ist Platonismus." In *Zür Sache des Denkens*, 63. ("Through the entire history of philosophy Plato's thought in changing forms remains determinative. Metaphysics is Platonism.")

14. "Platons Lehre von der Wahrheit" is, of course, the principal text here, but the same position, in essence, is also given in the Nietzsche lectures from the forties.

15. "The essence of truth gives up the characteristic of unconcealment. . . . In *orthotes*, the correctness of the look, lies everything . . . truth becomes *orthotes*, the correctness of perception and expression. In this transformation of the essence of truth a change of the place of truth occurs at the same time. As unconcealment, truth is still a characteristic of the being itself. As correctness of the 'look,' however, truth becomes a characteristic of the human comportment toward being." "Platons Lehre von der Wahrheit," in *Wegmarken* (Frankfurt: Klostermann, 1967), 136–37 (hereafter PL).

16. PL, 137.

17. PL, 142.

18. PL, 133.

19. Martin Heidegger, *Nietzsche*, vol. 4 (Pfullingen: Neske), 141.

20. Richard Rorty, *Essays on Heidegger and Others* (Cambridge: Cambridge University Press, 1991), 2.

21. "It is indicative of a complete misunderstanding to attribute to Heidegger a position sympathetic to Nietzsche. Also, Derrida's endeavor to trap Heidegger by way of Nietzsche is in no way drawing out the true consequences of Heidegger's approach" (*HW*, 164).

22. Heidegger never backed away from his critique of Plato as the founder of "metaphysics," although in the later essay, "The End of Philosophy and the Task of Thinking" (1964), he does concede that "the assertion about the essential transformation of truth [in Plato] . . . from unconcealment to correctness is . . . untenable" (*Zür Sache des Denkens*, 78). Despite the concession, which was perhaps

precipitated by Friedländer's sharp critique (in his *Platon*, vol. 1, chap. 11) of Heidegger's analysis of *aletheia* in the early Greeks, he nevertheless continues to see Plato as the one ancient thinker who did the most to set the direction of metaphysics toward an inevitable nihilism. See the "Seminar at Thor" (1969) (reprinted in *Vier Seminare* [Frankfurt: Klostermann, 1977], 75) for the later Heidegger's claim that it was Plato who clearly sets fast (*festsetzen*) the tendency of metaphysics to see all Being as "presenting presence" (*anwesende Anwesenheit*). In this seminar Heidegger even says that this tendency was prefigured in the pre-Socratics.

23. Aristotle, *Nichomachean Ethics*, 1094, 13–14.

24. Hans-Georg Gadamer, *The Idea of the Good in Platonic-Aristotelian Philosophy* (New Haven: Yale University Press, 1986), 27, 28 (hereafter *IG*).

25. *IG*, 28.

26. See Robert Dostal, "The Experience of Truth for Gadamer and Heidegger: Taking Time and Sudden Lightening," in *Hermeneutics and Truth*, ed. Brice Wachterhauser (Evanston: Northwestern University Press, 1994), 47–67.

27. Heidegger, *Vier Seminare*, 82.

28. See Otto Pöggeler's remarks about Heidegger's move away from the question of truth as his main question and toward his growing concern with the "topology of Being" in "'Geschichtlichkeit' im Spätwerk Heideggers," *Heidegger und die hermeneutische Philosophie* (Freiburg: Alber, 1983), 160–61.

29. Heidegger, *Vier Seminare*, 134.

30. Heidegger, *Beiträge*, 3.

31. Ibid., 7.

32. I am indebted to Rosen's provocative critique of Heidegger for these points. It seems to me that Rosen's Heidegger critique clarifies very well the target at which Gadamer's Heidegger critique aims. Although Rosen does not cite Gadamer, it seems to me that they share similar worries about some of the tendencies in the later Heidegger's work.

33. See *IG*, 16.

34. Such an understanding of the Ideas as an "infinite task" would come much too close to the neo-Kantian interpretation of the Ideas as found in such philosophers as Paul Natorp, Gadamer's *Doktorvater*. Gadamer rejects the neo-Kantian claim that the Ideas are best understood in terms of a "static realm natural laws" (*ruhiges Reich von Gesetzen*), which we asymptotically approach. See Gadamer's *Philosophische Lehrjahre* (Frankfurt: Klostermann, 1977), 66. But Gadamer does see the Ideas as regulative in a certain sense. This suggests that Gadamer is not as far from his neo-Kantian roots on this point as some might think.

35. Reiner Schürmann makes a very detailed, compelling case for the "anarchist" reading of Heidegger. See his *Heidegger: On Being and Acting: From Principles to Anarchy* (Bloomington: Indiana University Press, 1990). Gadamer's reading shows, I think, that although this tendency toward "anarchy" exists in Heidegger, it is not inevitable.

36. Charles Taylor, *Sources of the Self* (Cambridge: Harvard University Press, 1989), is one work that makes it plain that the drive of modern philosophy toward "objective," "disinterested" inquiry carries with it an implicit ethic.

37. Heidegger, "Letter on Humanism," 202.

38. Ibid., 198.

39. Ibid., 221.

40. Hans-Georg Gadamer, "*Logos* and *Ergon* in Plato's *Lysis*," in *Dialogue and Dialectic*, trans. P. Christopher Smith (New Haven: Yale University Press, 1980), 1.

41. See Hans-Georg Gadamer, "Sokrates Frömmigkeit des Nichtwissens," in *GW* 7, 83–117.

Index